SCIENCE
COMICS

PLAGUES
The Microscopic Battlefield

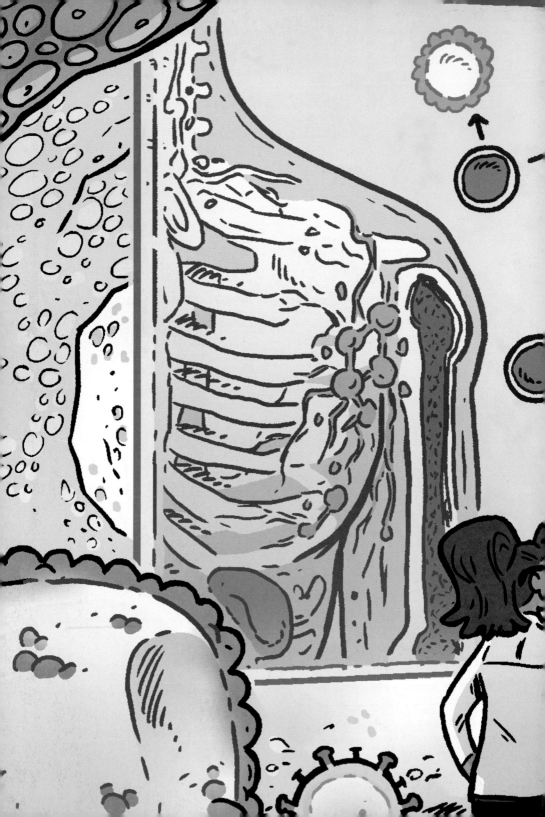

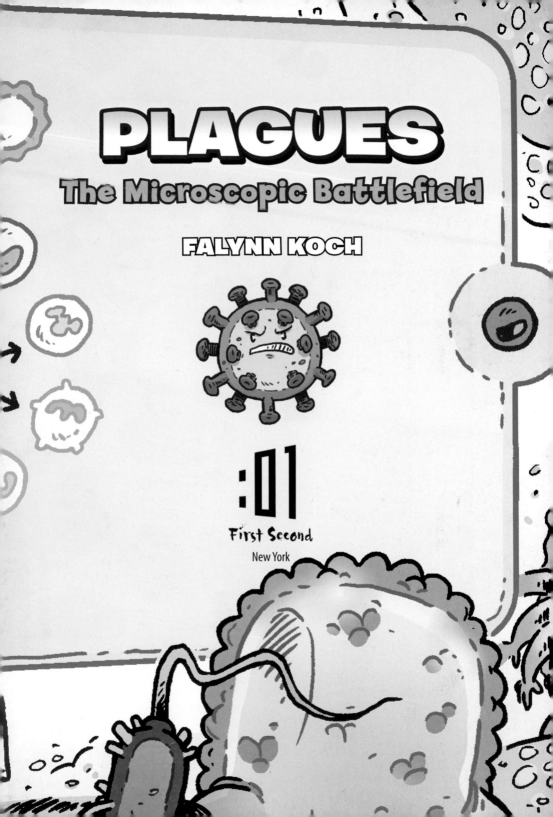

PLAGUES

The Microscopic Battlefield

FALYNN KOCH

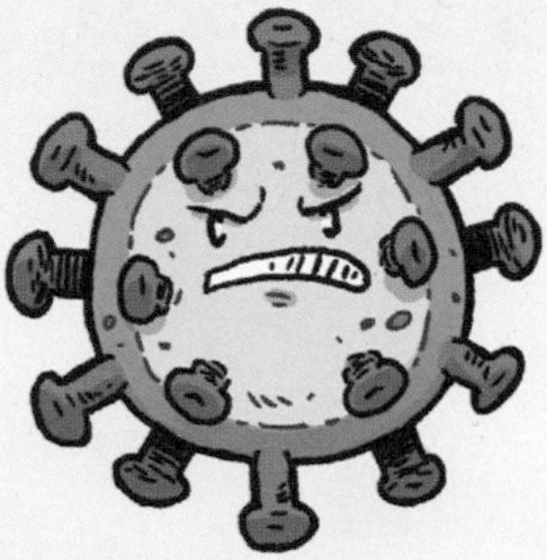

:01 First Second
New York

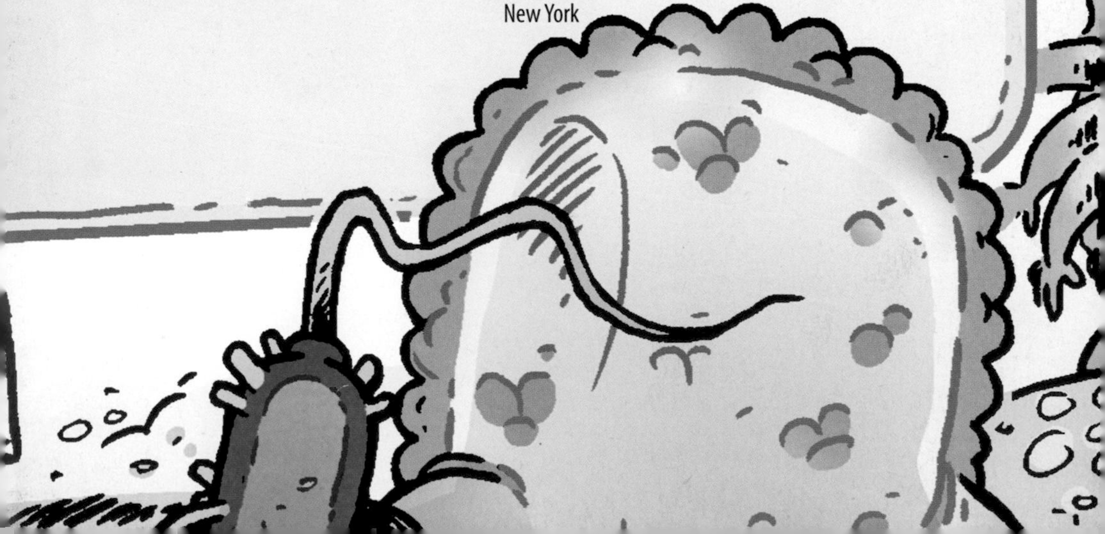

First Second

Penciled with a light blue Staedtler Triplus Fineliner and Manga Studio.
Inked with a Maru-style digital nib and colored digitally in Photoshop.
Lettered with the Comicrazy font from Comicraft.

Published by First Second
First Second is an imprint of Roaring Brook Press,
a division of Holtzbrinck Publishing Holdings Limited Partnership
175 Fifth Avenue, New York, New York 10010

Library of Congress Control Number: 2016945566

Paperback ISBN 978-1-62672-752-6
Hardcover ISBN 978-1-62672-753-3

Our books may be purchased in bulk for promotional, educational, or business use. Please
contact your local bookseller or the Macmillan Corporate and Premium Sales Department
at (800) 221-7945 ext. 5442 or by e-mail at MacmillanSpecialMarkets@macmillan.com.

First edition 2017
Series editor: Dave Roman
Plagues consultant: Dorothy H. Crawford
Book design by John Green

Printed in China by Toppan Leefung Printing Ltd., Dongguan City, Guangdong Province
Paperback: 10 9 8 7 6 5 4 3 2 1
Hardcover: 10 9 8 7 6 5 4 3 2 1

"A plague o' both your houses!"

—William Shakespeare, *Romeo and Juliet*

We live in a world teeming with microorganisms, creatures that go back to the very beginnings of our world, if not before. Long after we have vanished as a species and all evidence of our civilization has turned to dust, bacteria and viruses will still be here.

For over a decade, the Canadian poet and self-taught geneticist Christian Bök has been trying to weave a poem into the genome of *Deinococcus radiodurans*, a bacterium so tough it can survive the vacuum of outer space and the intense radiation of a nuclear reactor without mutating. If successful, Bök's poem, *The Xenotext*, will become an integral part of *Deinococcus radiodurans*'s genetic code. Millions of years from now, some advanced species may crack that code, read Bök's poem, and know that once upon a time we were here. It's even possible, as astrophysicist Paul Davies has suggested, that some now-extinct civilization in a solar system far, far away may have already tried this form of interstellar texting. If only we had the right app, some of the viruses and bacteria with whom we share our world—perhaps even some that make us sick, like yellow fever or the bubonic plague—may turn out to have arrived here long ago with a mission to endlessly replicate an eternal message: we exist, we exist, we exist.

I had the good luck to be born in Southern California after the invention of the polio vaccine, only a few years before the eradication of smallpox. The US Public Health Service ensured I was vaccinated against those diseases as well as measles, diphtheria, whooping cough, and other historical scourges of childhood. I had access to antibiotics in an era before there was much antibiotic resistance. When I got sick, science helped me get well. So in junior high, when I read *A Distant Mirror: The Calamitous 14th Century*, Barbara Tuchman's riveting account of the late Middle Ages, her chapter on the Black Death blew my mind. The idea of an epidemic that could kill tens of millions of people in a span of years seemed like science fiction, a zombie apocalypse that actually happened. Tuchman's book sparked my lifelong fascination with science and history. When I chose illustration for a career, I gravitated toward clients like *National Geographic*, *Scientific American*, and NASA. When I finally started writing and illustrating my own books for kids, I focused on disasters, epidemics, climate change, and the West's deep debt to the scientific culture of the medieval Muslim world. The opening chapter of my own book about plagues, *Outbreak*, focuses on the Black Death.

Before Louis Pasteur proved the germ theory of disease, we blamed plagues not on bacteria and viruses but on God, Satan, evil spirits, and bad smells. We especially blamed the powerless: hated ethnic groups, outsiders, uppity women, and people who looked different, talked different, or believed different than we did. We ostracized them, murdered them, then stole their property. Eventually the plague would burn itself out. Killing everyone it could kill, the disease would die out until new susceptible victims were born. Then it would return. Locals would say, "People wearing red hats moved into our village, and then smallpox came to our village. We killed all the red hat people and smallpox stopped. Therefore, the red hat people caused smallpox." This is the classic logical error of *post hoc ergo proctor hoc*. Because this event follows that event, this event must have been *caused* by that event.

When it comes to infectious disease, human beings are still susceptible to this kind of false logic. Homosexuals were blamed and persecuted during the early years of the AIDS epidemic as the cause of the disease; public health workers were attacked for the same reasons during the Ebola crisis; terrified conspiracy theorists blamed the Zika virus on corporate pesticides: "They sprayed pesticides and Zika showed up. Therefore, the pesticides caused Zika." Lacking knowledge, we succumb to fear, make stuff up, find connections where there are none, and hope it's the truth. We want to believe that we have some power over the chaos of our lives.

So Falynn Koch's *Plagues: The Microscopic Battlefield* is just what the doctor ordered. With clarity, humor, and insight, her accessible investigation into the cause and history of plagues provides real power over infectious disease: the power of science. None of this understanding came easily. Plagues killed billions of people before we learned why and how to make them stop. We're still learning. You owe it to yourself and to those died before you to get this invaluable education.

Read. Learn. And wash your hands.

—Bryn Barnard
Author of *Outbreak! Plagues That Changed History*

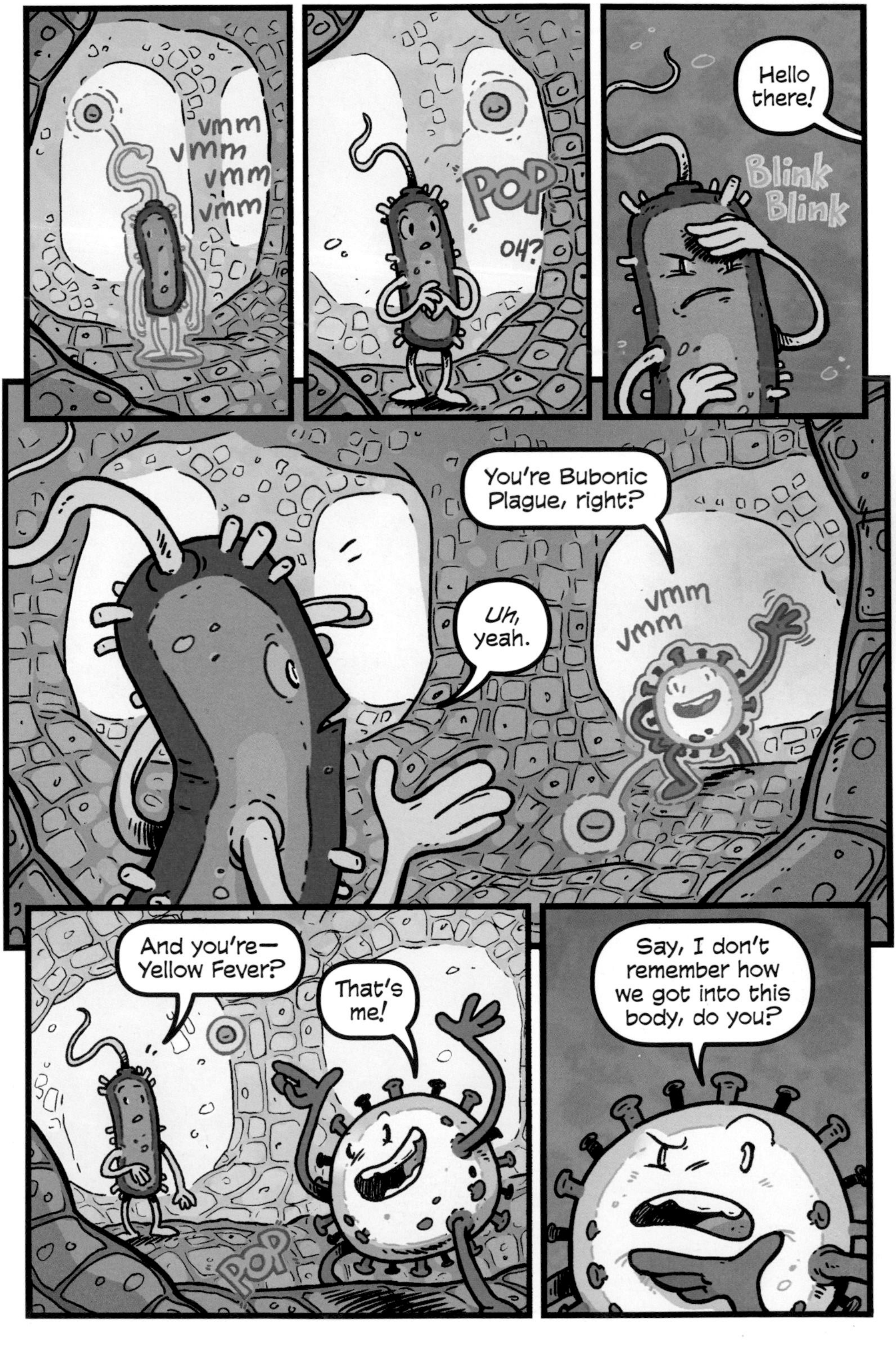
vmm
vmm
vmm
vmm
POP
OH?
Hello there!
Blink
Blink
You're Bubonic Plague, right?
Uh, yeah.
vmm
vmm
And you're— Yellow Fever?
That's me!
POP
Say, I don't remember how we got into this body, do you?

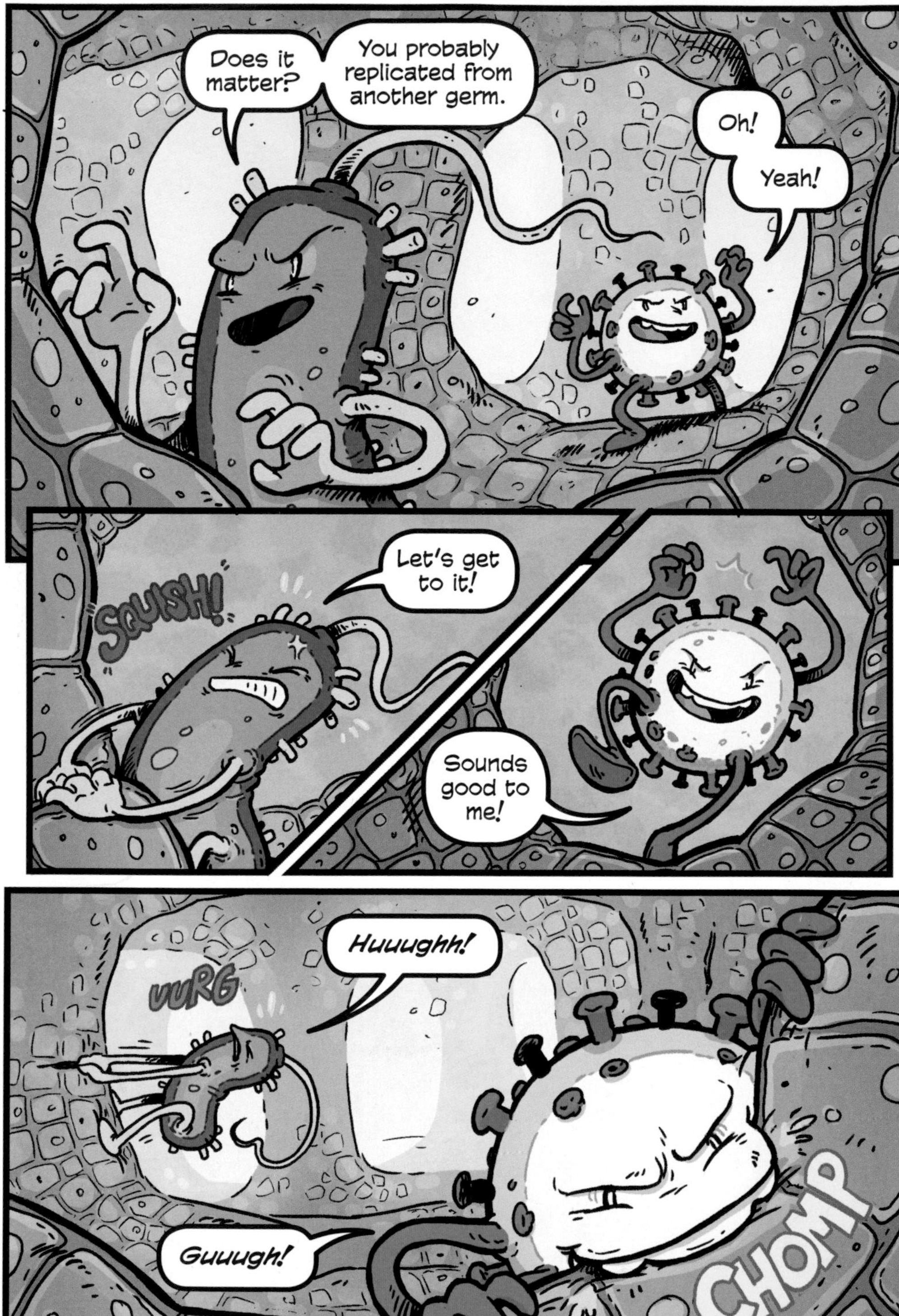
Does it matter?
You probably replicated from another germ.
Oh!
Yeah!
SQUISH!
Let's get to it!
Sounds good to me!
Huuughh!
VURG
Guuugh!
CHOMP

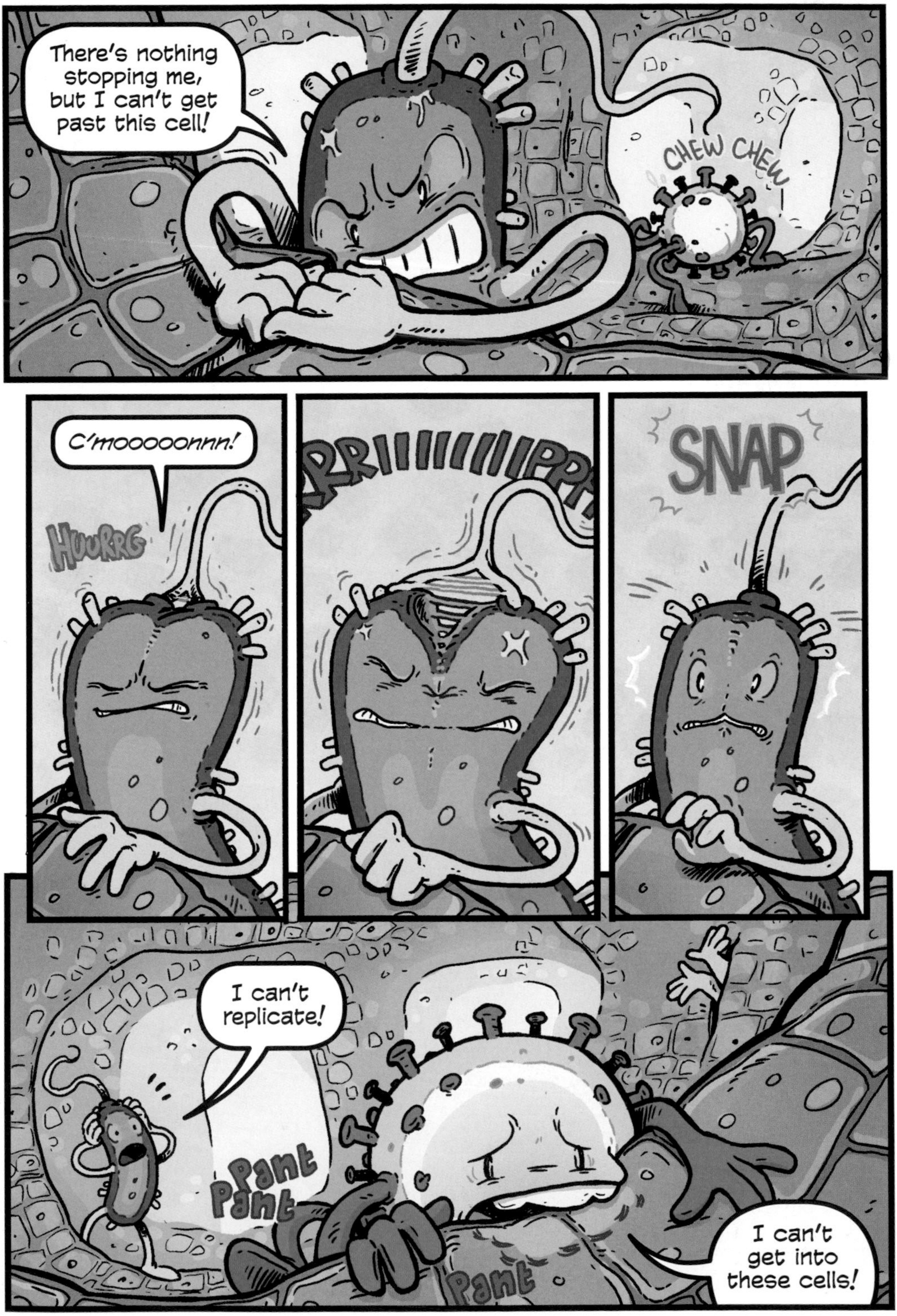
There's nothing stopping me, but I can't get past this cell!
CHEW CHEW
C'moooooonnn!
HUURRG
SNAP
I can't replicate!
Pant
Pant
I can't get into these cells!
Pant

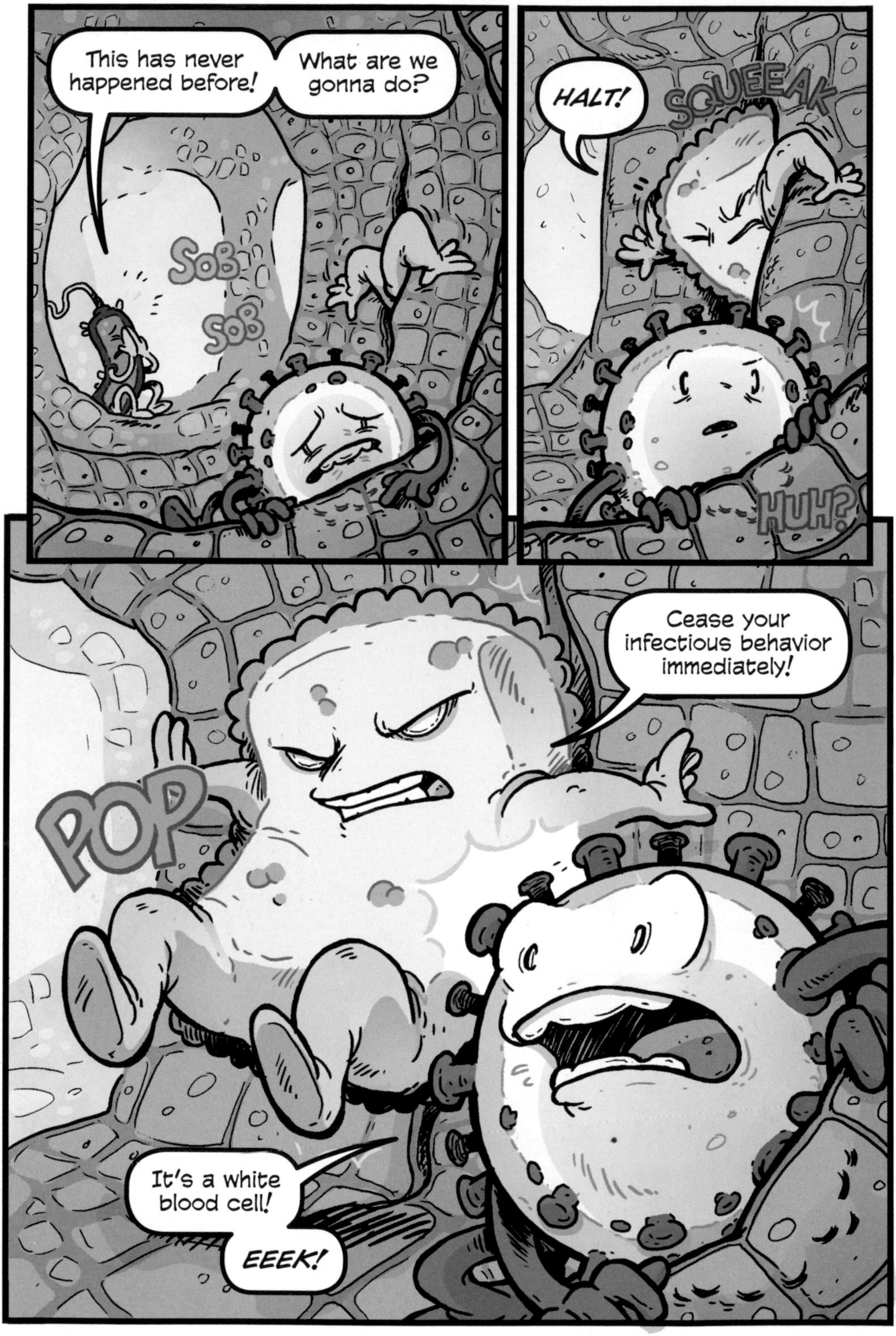
This has never happened before!
What are we gonna do?
SOB
SOB
HALT!
SQUEEEAK
HUH?
Cease your infectious behavior immediately!
POP
It's a white blood cell!
EEEK!

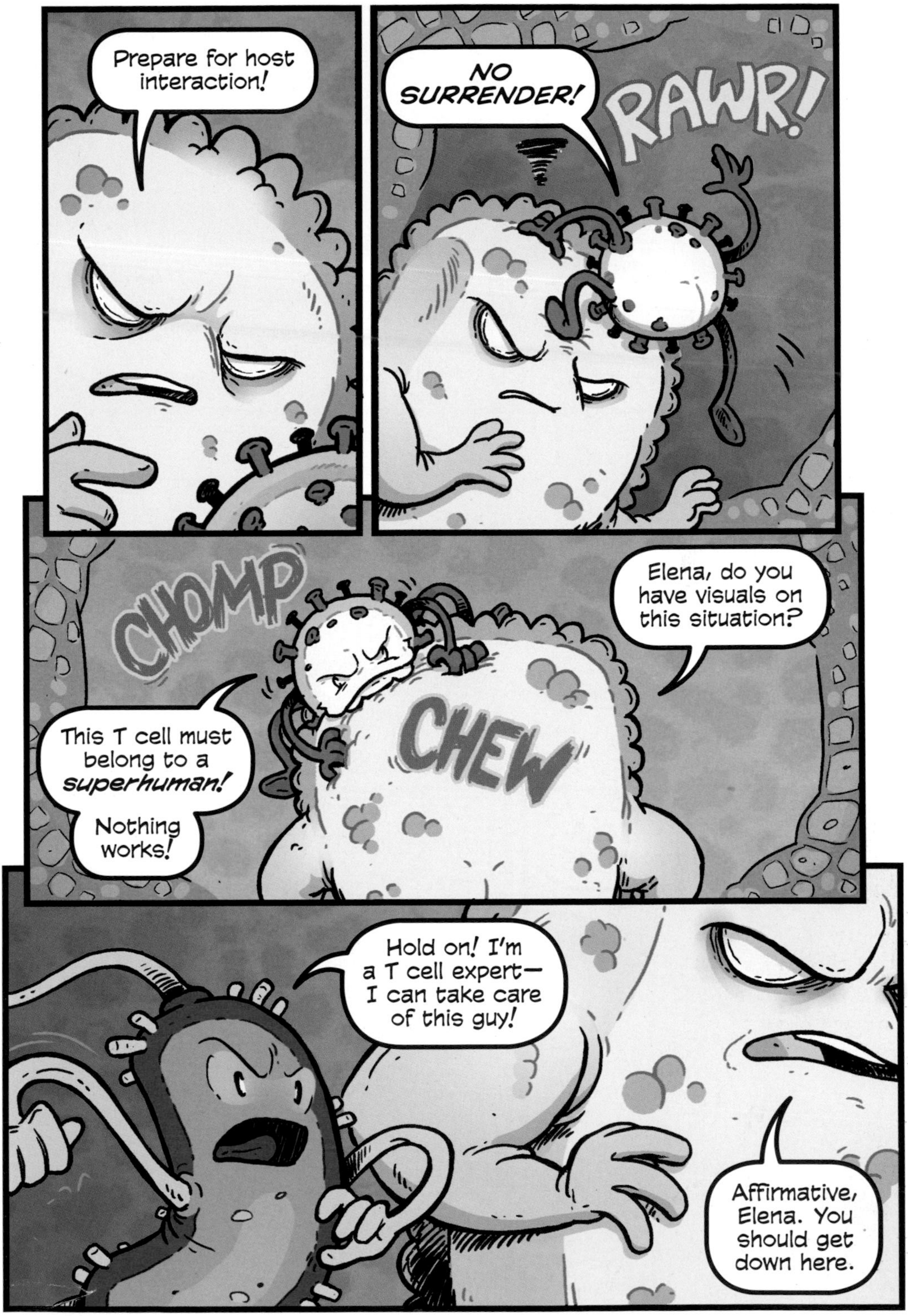
Prepare for host interaction!
NO SURRENDER!
RAWR!
CHOMP
CHEW
Elena, do you have visuals on this situation?
This T cell must belong to a *superhuman!*
Nothing works!
Hold on! I'm a T cell expert—I can take care of this guy!
Affirmative, Elena. You should get down here.

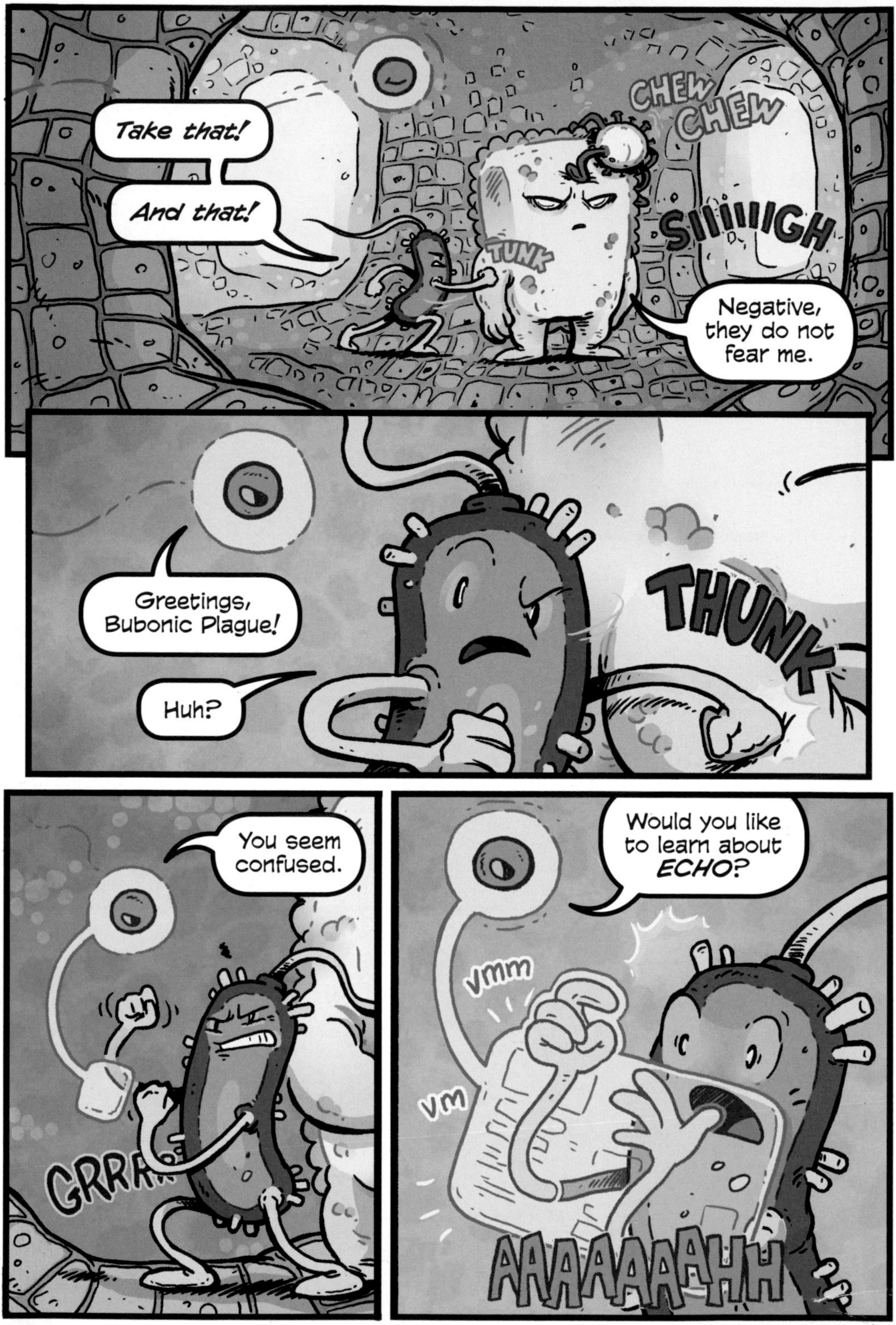
Take that!
And that!
CHEW CHEW
TUNK
SIIIIIGH
Negative, they do not fear me.
Greetings, Bubonic Plague!
Huh?
THUNK
You seem confused.
GRRR
Would you like to learn about *ECHO*?
VMM
VM
AAAAAAAHH

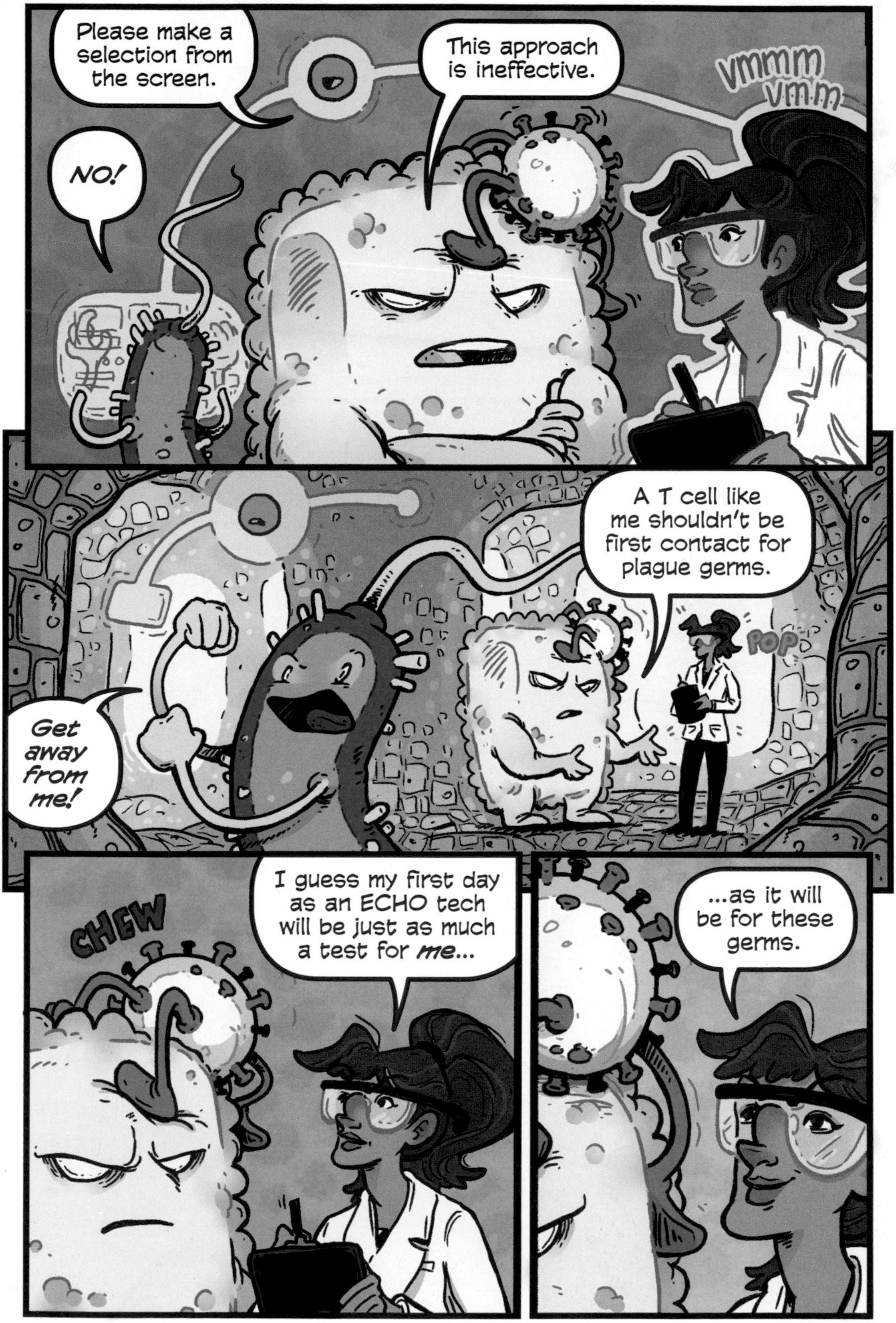
Please make a selection from the screen.
This approach is ineffective.
VMMM VMM
NO!
A T cell like me shouldn't be first contact for plague germs.
POP
Get away from me!
CHEW
I guess my first day as an ECHO tech will be just as much a test for *me*...
...as it will be for these germs.

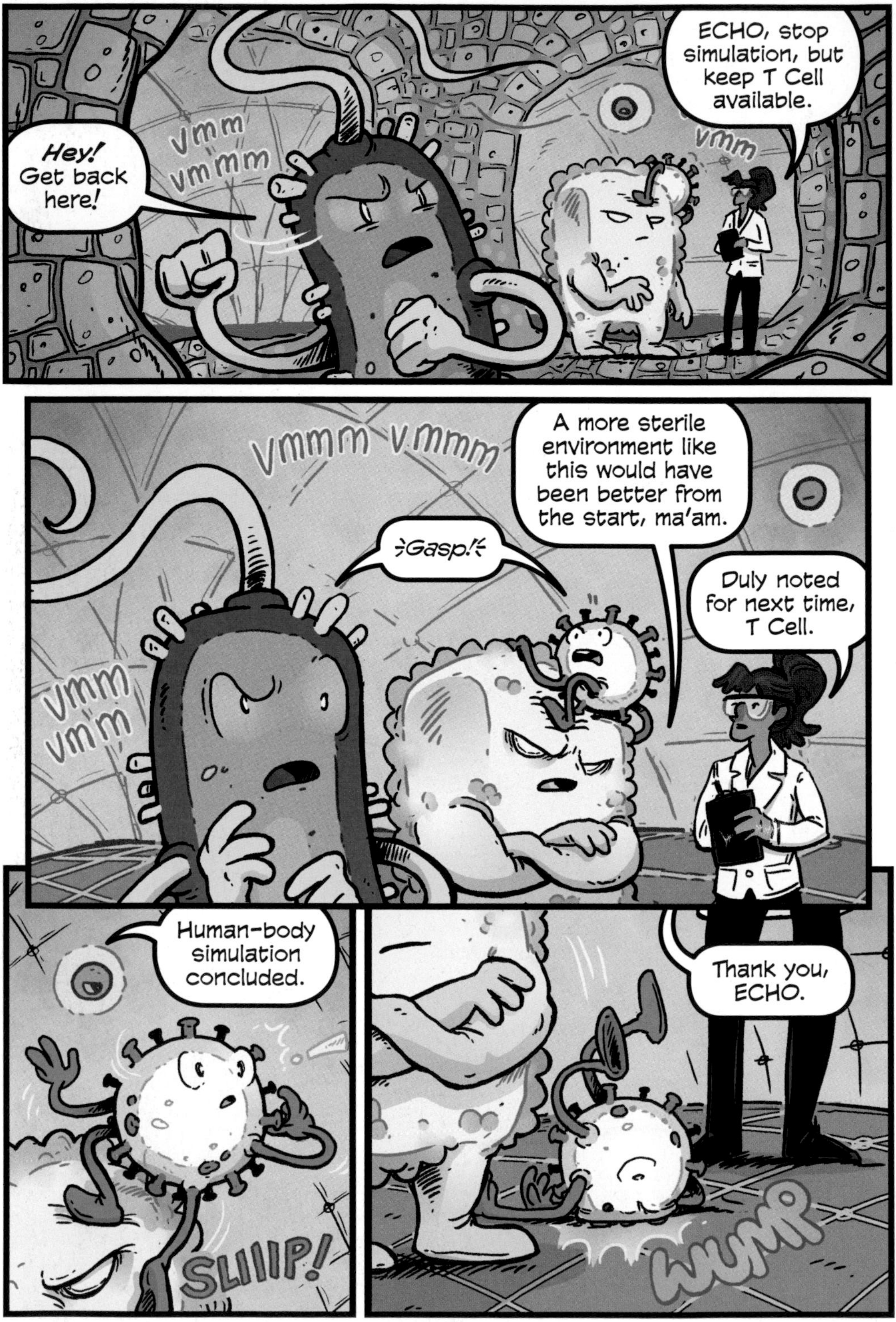
ECHO, stop simulation, but keep T Cell available.
Hey! Get back here!
vmm vmmm
vmm
vmmm vmmm
A more sterile environment like this would have been better from the start, ma'am.
Gasp!
Duly noted for next time, T Cell.
vmm vmm
Human-body simulation concluded.
SLIIIP!
Thank you, ECHO.
WUMP

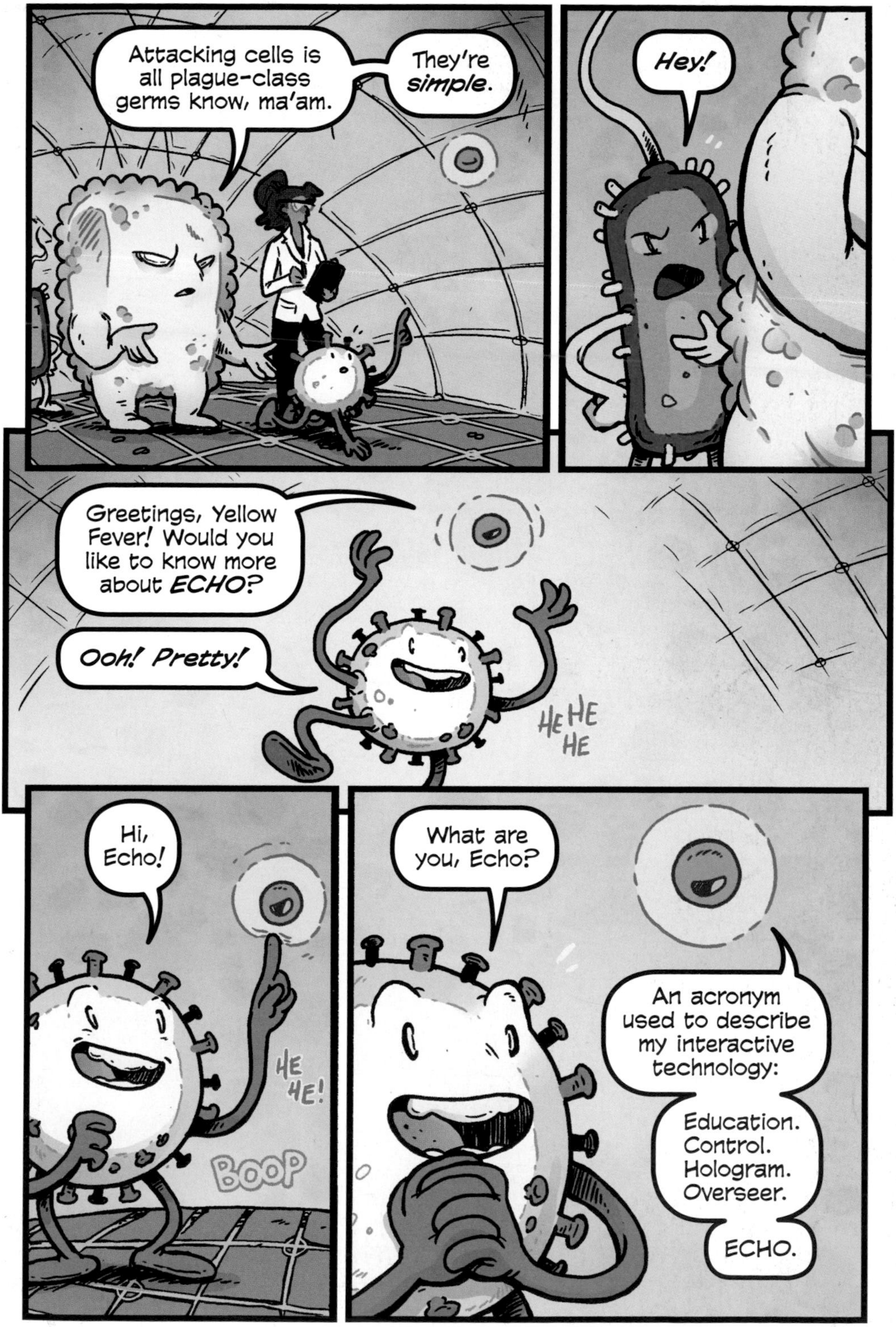
Attacking cells is all plague-class germs know, ma'am.
They're *simple*.
Hey!
Greetings, Yellow Fever! Would you like to know more about *ECHO*?
Ooh! Pretty!
HE HE HE
Hi, Echo!
HE HE!
BOOP
What are you, Echo?
An acronym used to describe my interactive technology:
Education. Control. Hologram. Overseer.
ECHO.

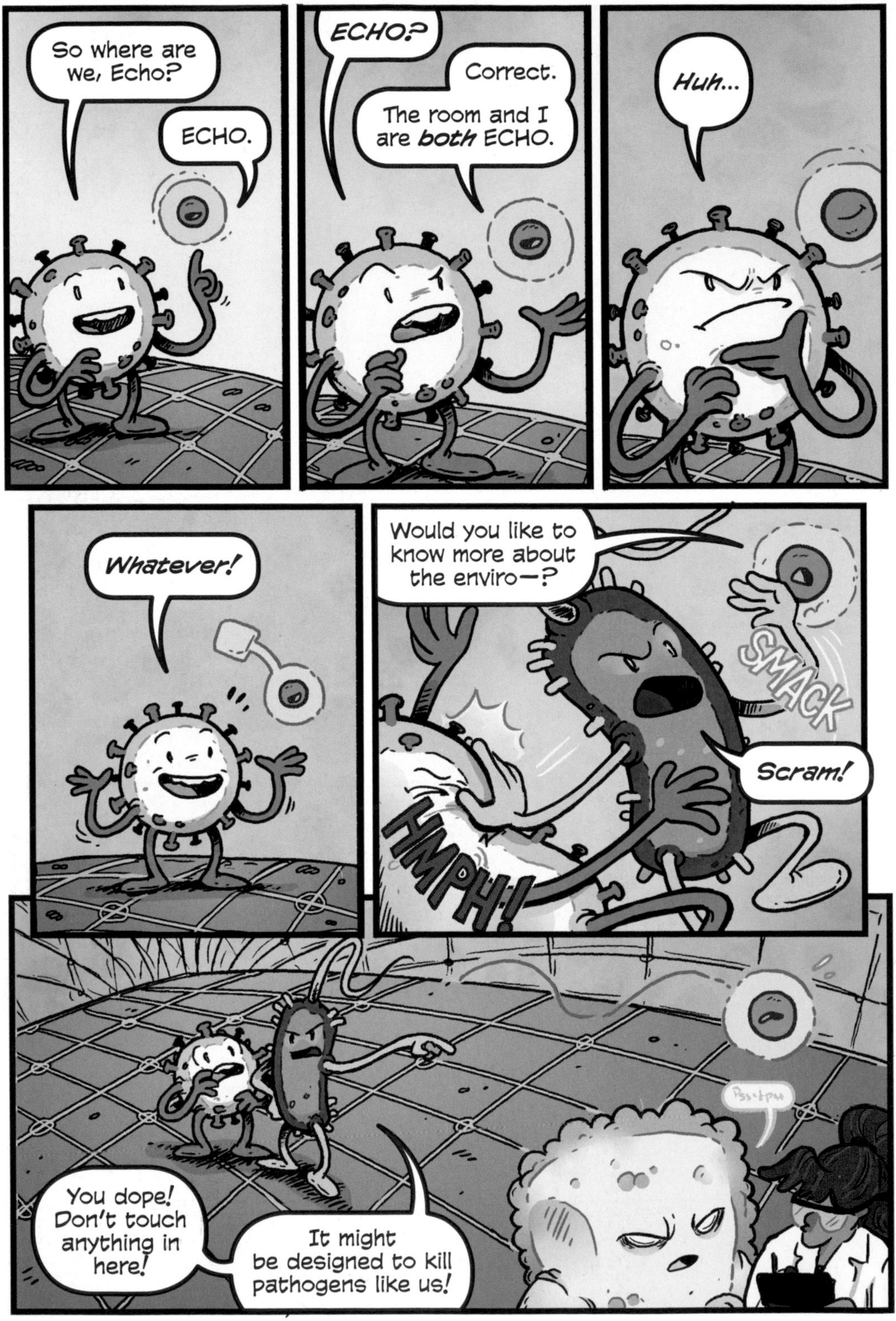
So where are we, Echo?
ECHO.
ECHO?
Correct.
The room and I are *both* ECHO.
Huh...
Whatever!
Would you like to know more about the enviro—?
SMACK
HMPH!
Scram!
You dope! Don't touch anything in here!
It might be designed to kill pathogens like us!

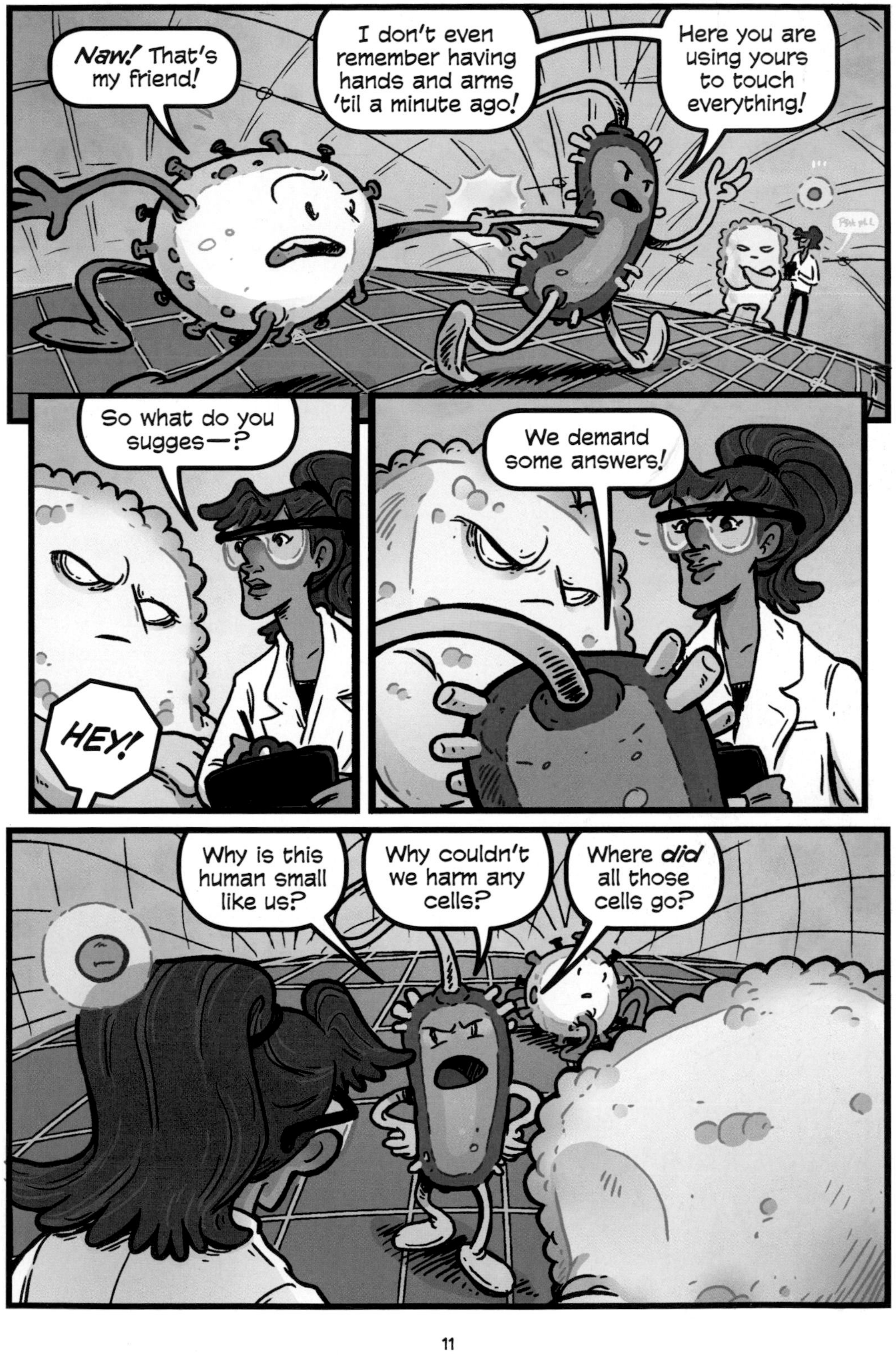
Naw! That's my friend!
I don't even remember having hands and arms 'til a minute ago!
Here you are using yours to touch everything!
So what do you sugges—?
HEY!
We demand some answers!
Why is this human small like us?
Why couldn't we harm any cells?
Where *did* all those cells go?

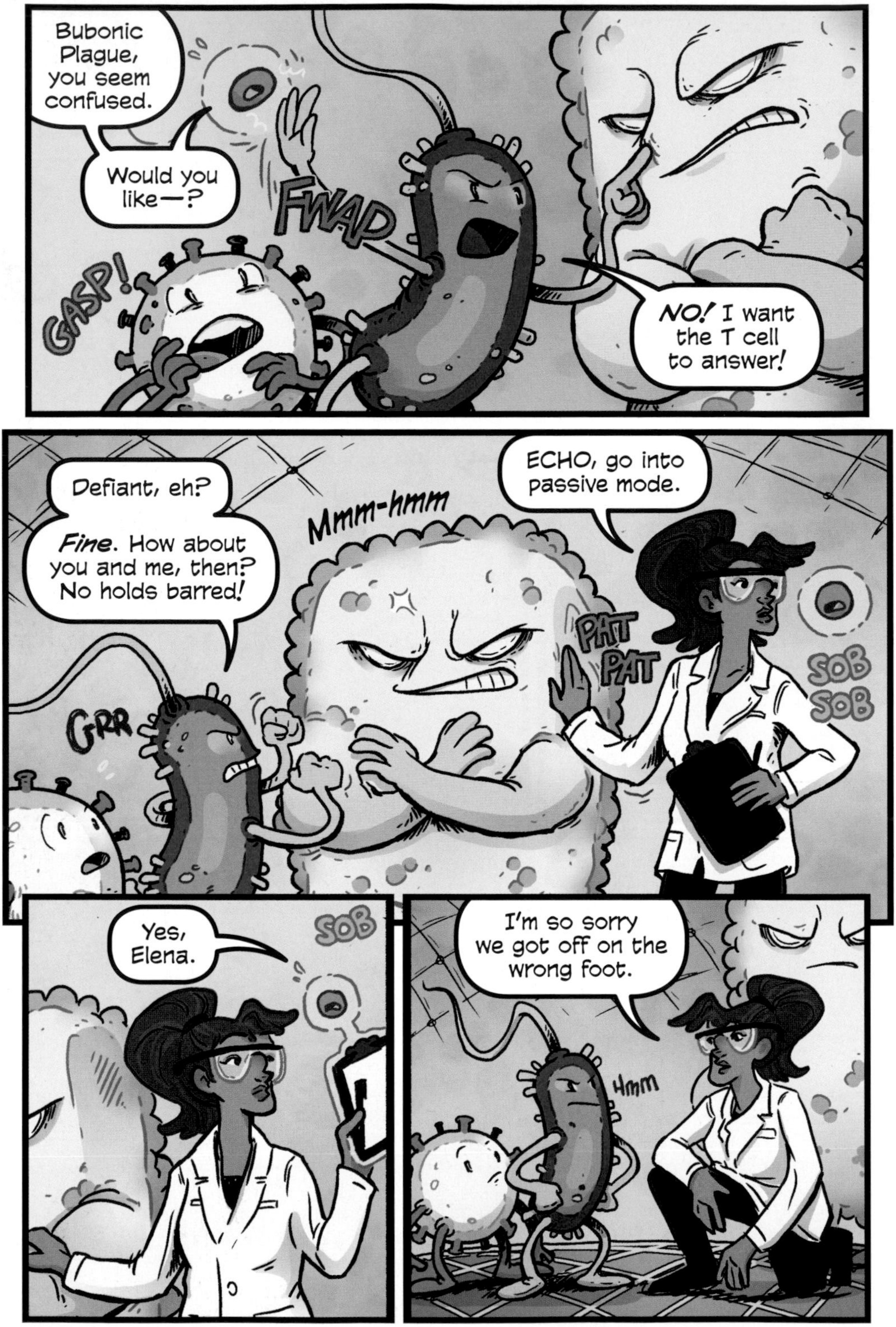
Bubonic Plague, you seem confused.
Would you like—?
FWAP
GASP!
NO! I want the T cell to answer!
Defiant, eh?
Fine. How about you and me, then? No holds barred!
Mmm-hmm
ECHO, go into passive mode.
PAT PAT
SOB SOB
GRR
Yes, Elena.
SOB
I'm so sorry we got off on the wrong foot.
Hmm

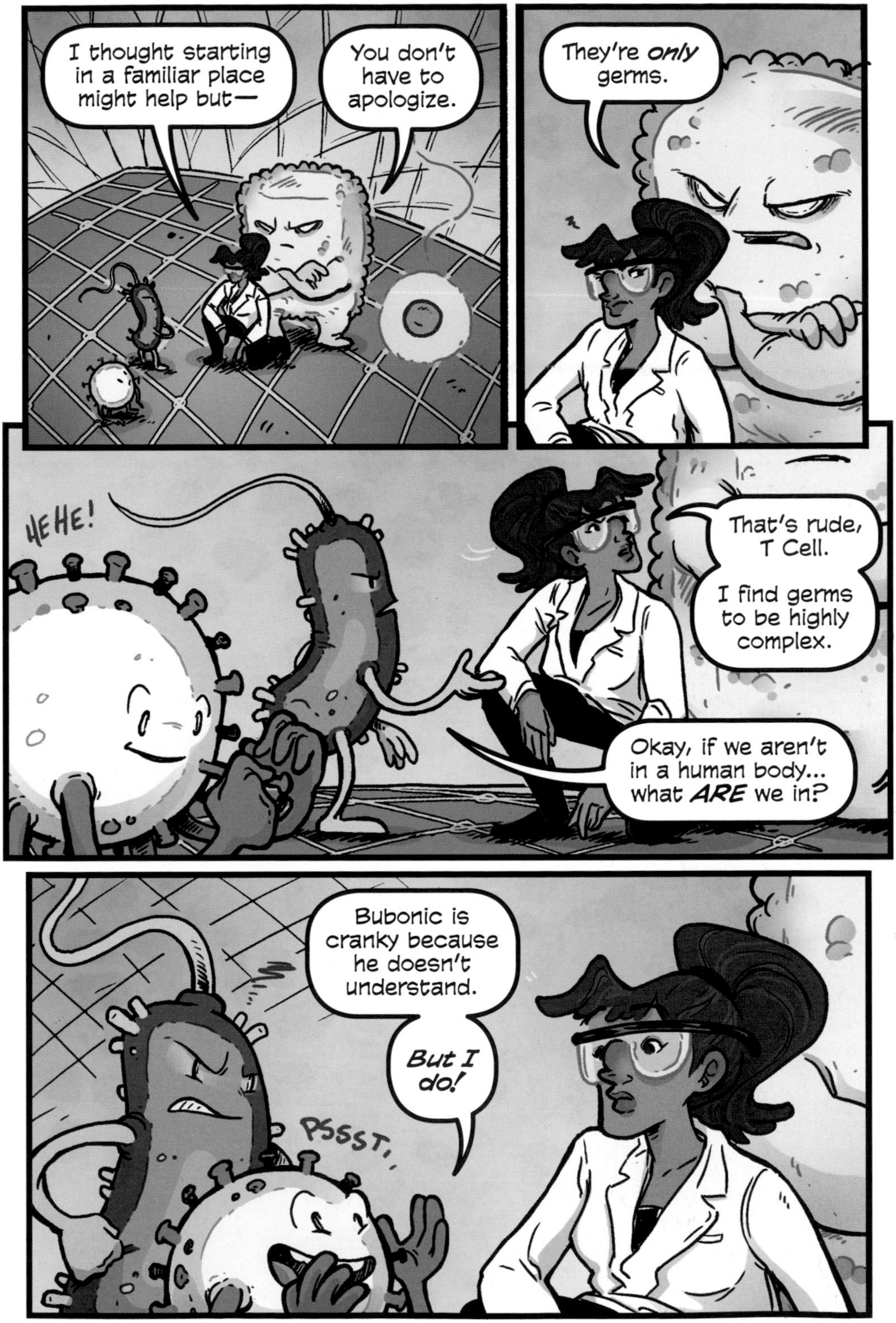
I thought starting in a familiar place might help but—
You don't have to apologize.
They're *only* germs.
HEHE!
That's rude, T Cell.
I find germs to be highly complex.
Okay, if we aren't in a human body... what *ARE* we in?
Bubonic is cranky because he doesn't understand.
But I do!
PSSST.

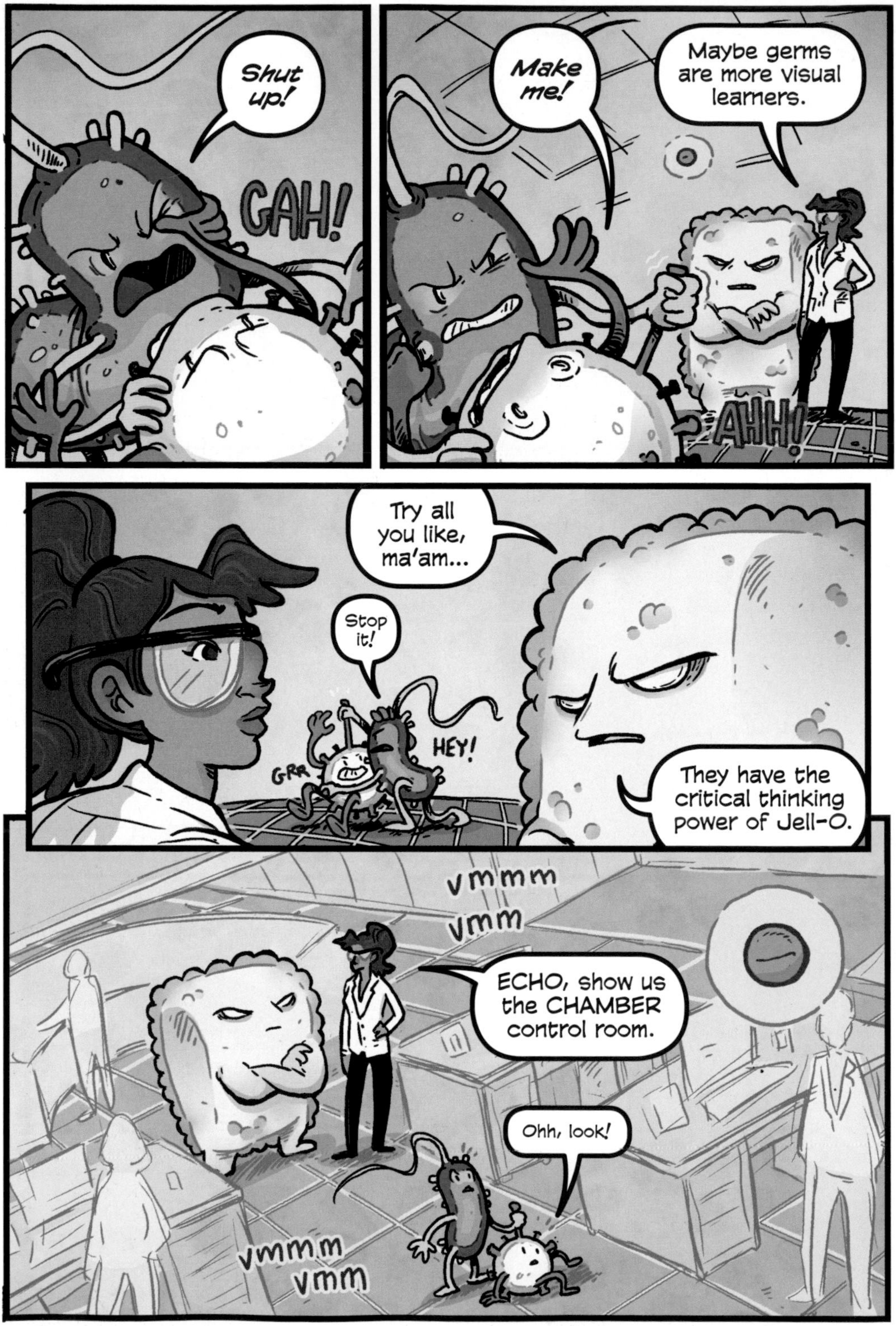
Shut up!
GAH!
Make me!
Maybe germs are more visual learners.
AHH!
Try all you like, ma'am...
Stop it!
HEY!
GRR
They have the critical thinking power of Jell-O.
vmmm
vmm
ECHO, show us the CHAMBER control room.
Ohh, look!
vmmm
vmm

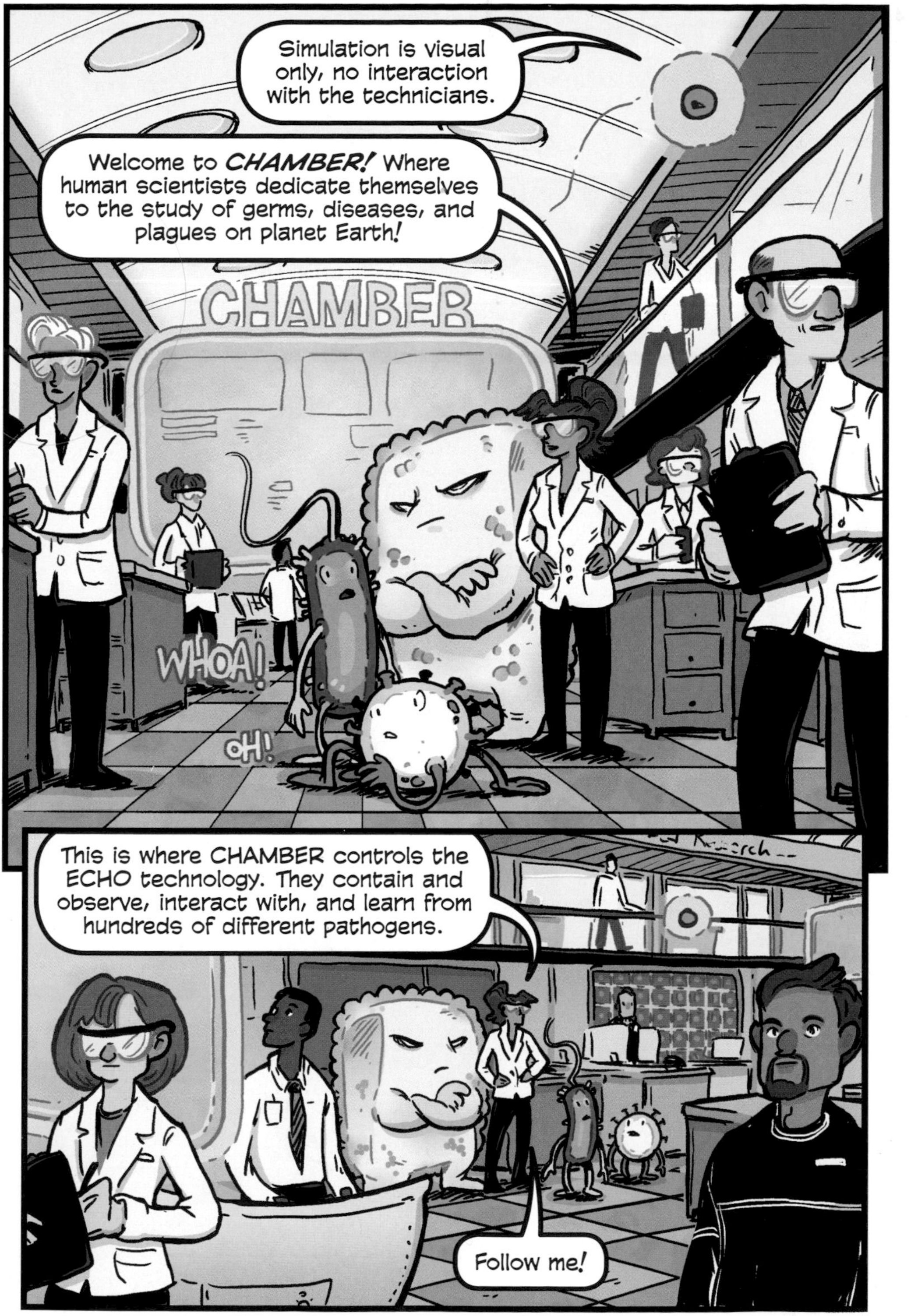
Simulation is visual only, no interaction with the technicians.
Welcome to *CHAMBER!* Where human scientists dedicate themselves to the study of germs, diseases, and plagues on planet Earth!
CHAMBER
WHOA!
OH!
This is where CHAMBER controls the ECHO technology. They contain and observe, interact with, and learn from hundreds of different pathogens.
Follow me!

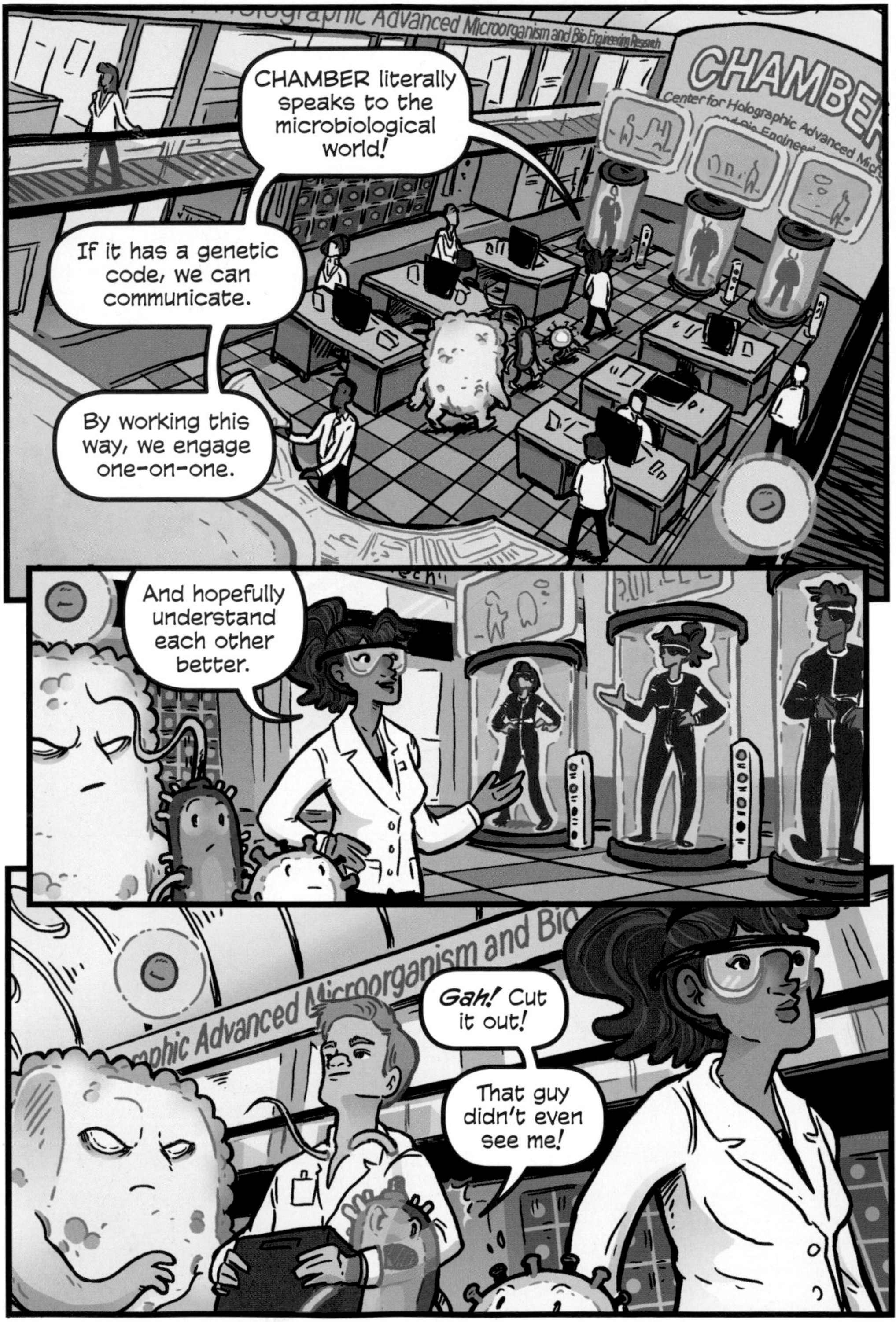
CHAMBER
CHAMBER literally speaks to the microbiological world!
If it has a genetic code, we can communicate.
By working this way, we engage one-on-one.
And hopefully understand each other better.
Gah! Cut it out!
That guy didn't even see me!

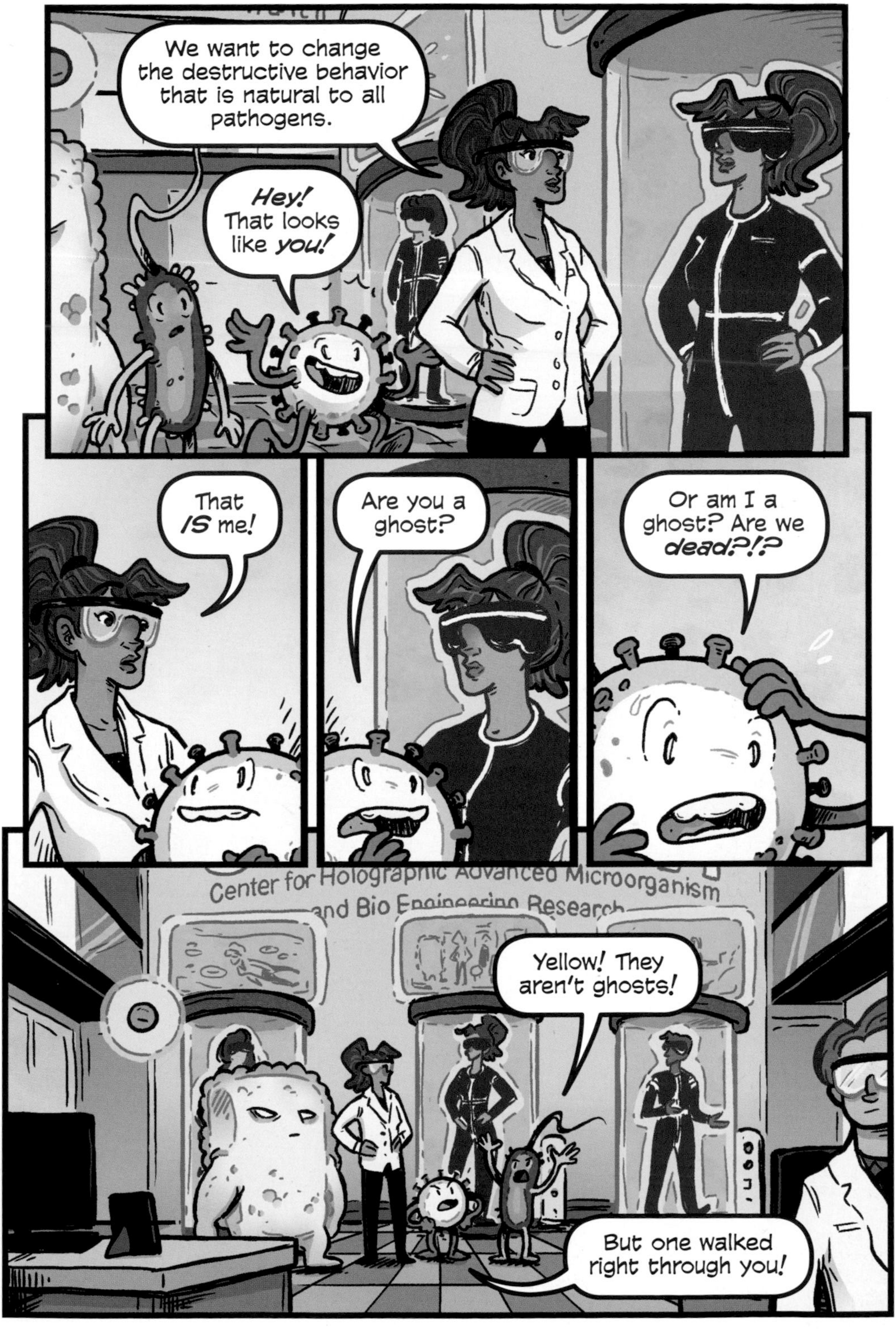

We want to change the destructive behavior that is natural to all pathogens.
Hey! That looks like you!
That IS me!
Are you a ghost?
Or am I a ghost? Are we dead?!?
Center for Holographic Advanced Microorganism and Bio Engineering Research
Yellow! They aren't ghosts!
But one walked right through you!

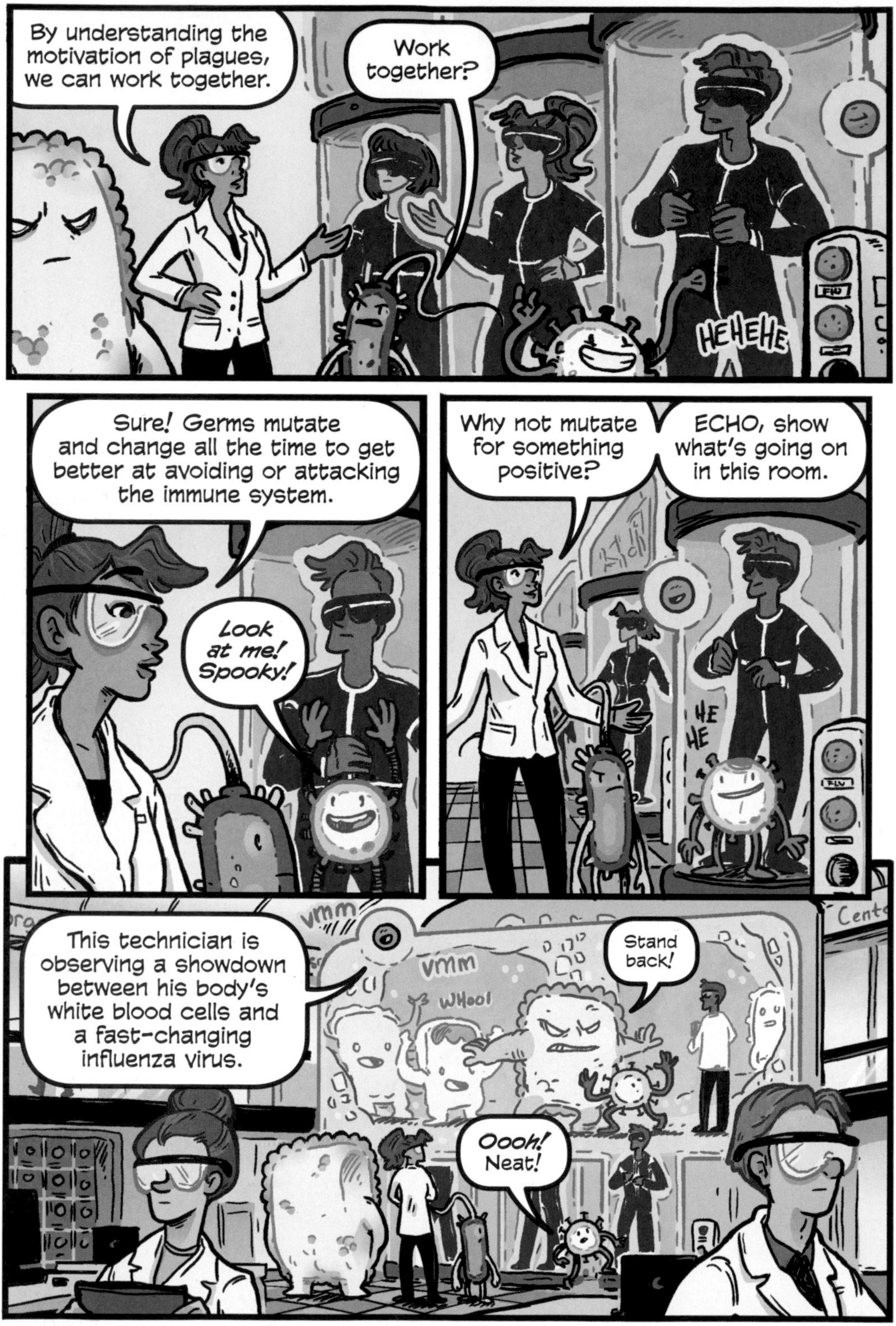

By understanding the motivation of plagues, we can work together.
Work together?
HEHEHE
FLU
Sure! Germs mutate and change all the time to get better at avoiding or attacking the immune system.
Look at me! Spooky!
Why not mutate for something positive?
ECHO, show what's going on in this room.
HE HE
FLU
This technician is observing a showdown between his body's white blood cells and a fast-changing influenza virus.
vmm
vmm
WHoo!
Stand back!
Oooh! Neat!

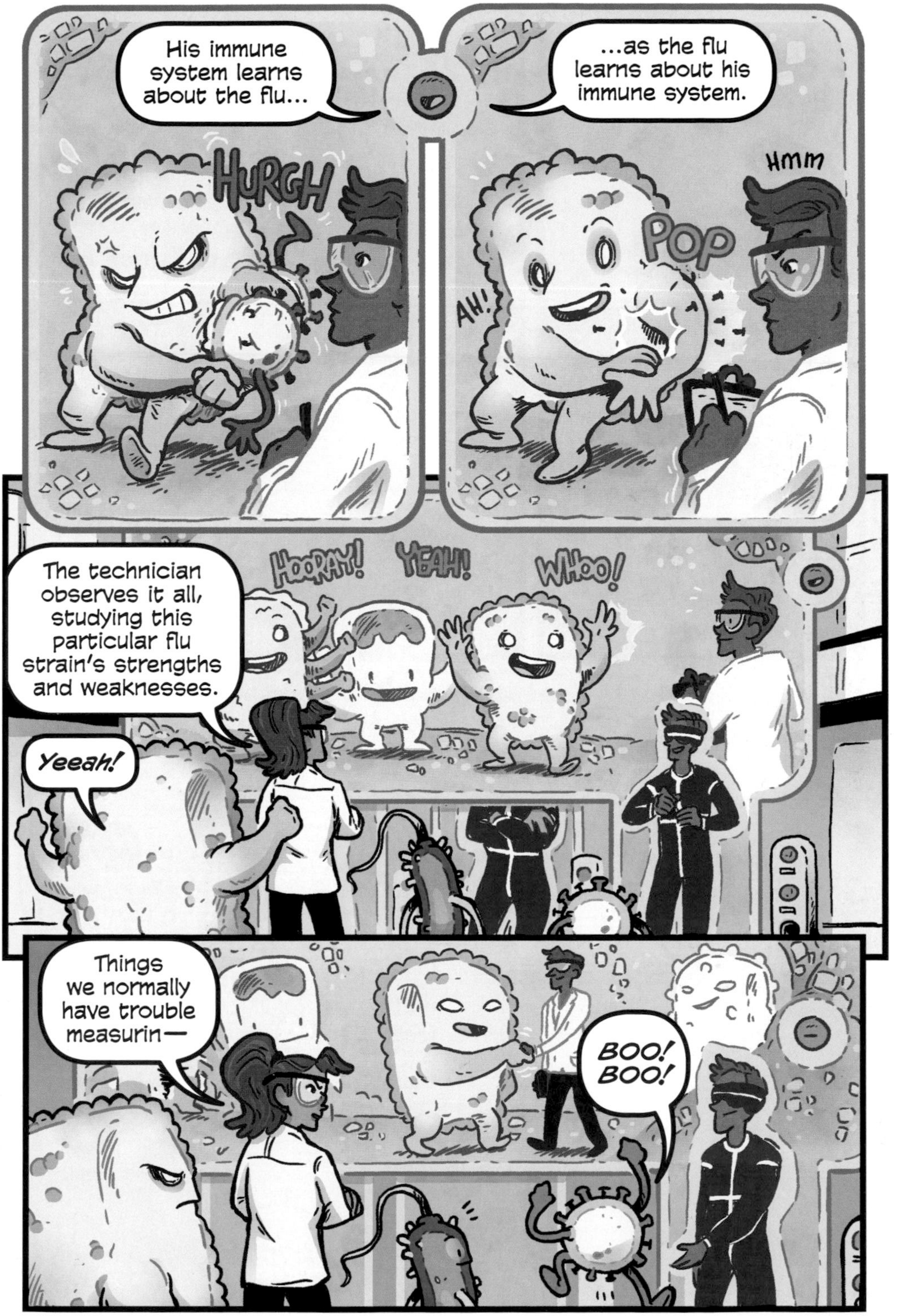
His immune system learns about the flu...
HURGH
...as the flu learns about his immune system.
HMM
POP
AH!
The technician observes it all, studying this particular flu strain's strengths and weaknesses.
HOORAY!
YEAH!
WHOO!
Yeeah!
Things we normally have trouble measurin—
BOO! BOO!

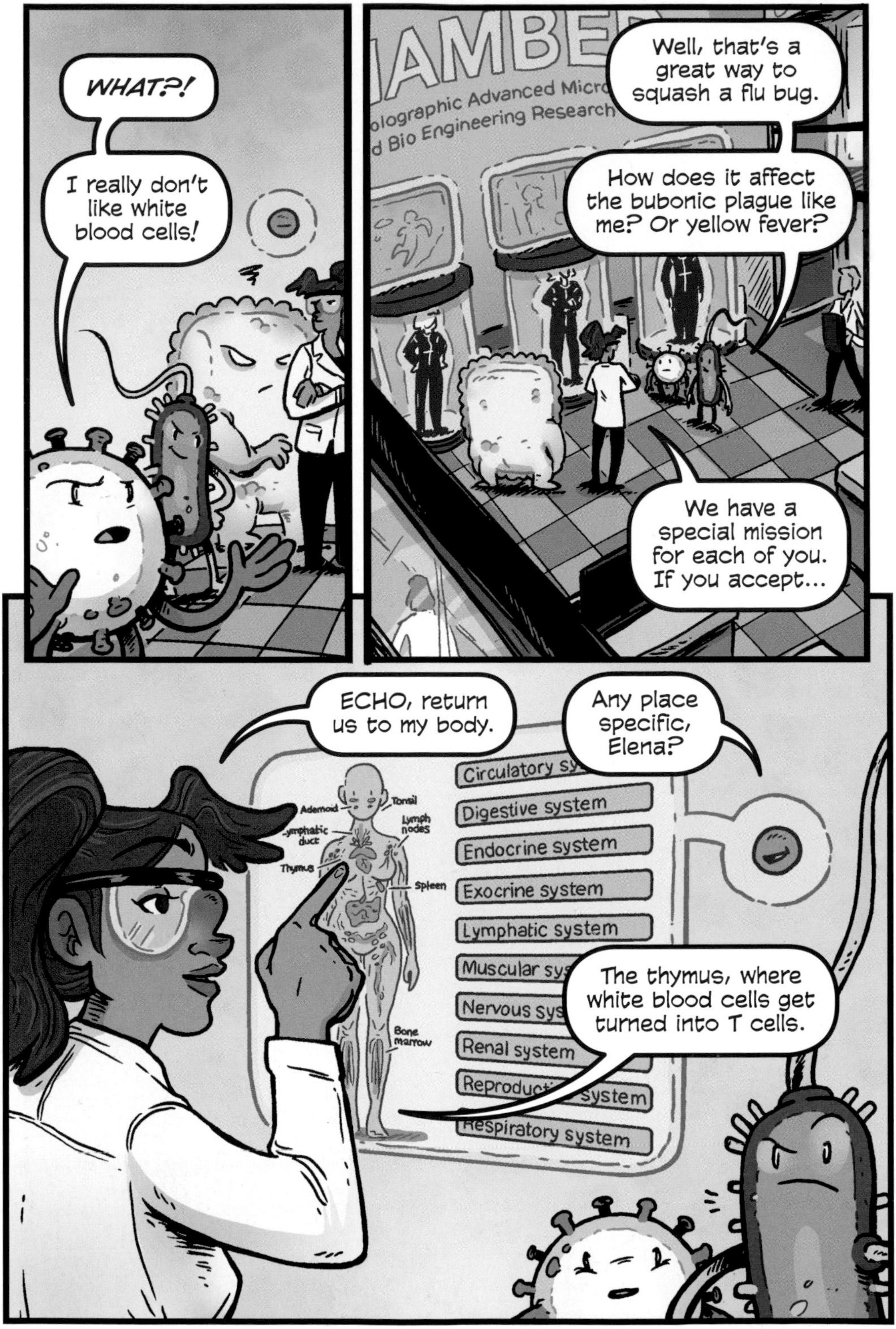
WHAT?!
I really don't like white blood cells!
olographic Advanced Micro
d Bio Engineering Research
Well, that's a great way to squash a flu bug.
How does it affect the bubonic plague like me? Or yellow fever?
We have a special mission for each of you. If you accept...
ECHO, return us to my body.
Any place specific, Elena?
Adenoid
Tonsil
Lymph nodes
Thymus
Spleen
Bone marrow
Circulatory sy
Digestive system
Endocrine system
Exocrine system
Lymphatic system
Muscular sys
Nervous sys
Renal system
Reproduct system
Respiratory system
The thymus, where white blood cells get turned into T cells.

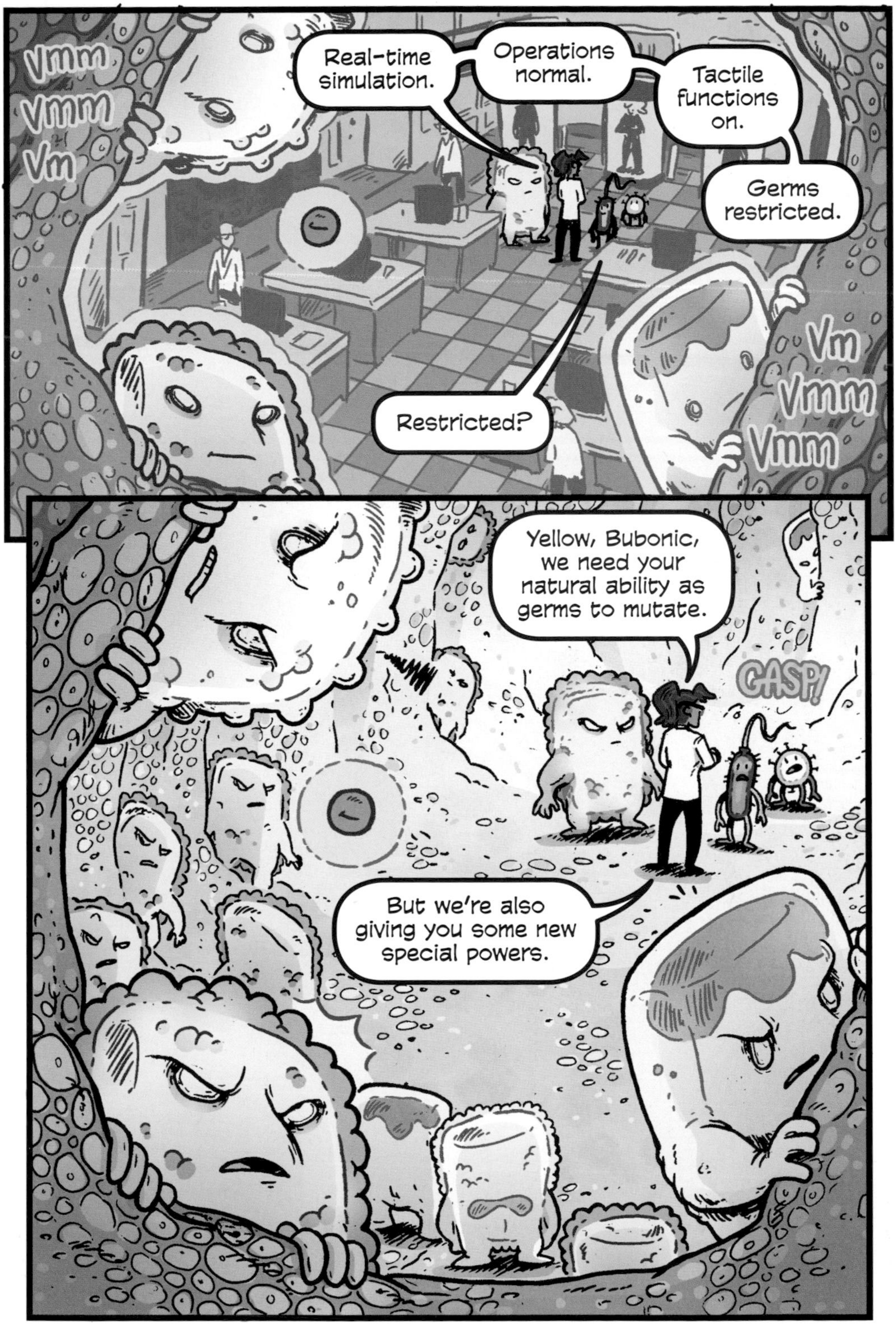
Vmm
Vmm
Vm
Real-time simulation.
Operations normal.
Tactile functions on.
Germs restricted.
Vm
Vmm
Vmm
Restricted?
Yellow, Bubonic, we need your natural ability as germs to mutate.
GASP!
But we're also giving you some new special powers.

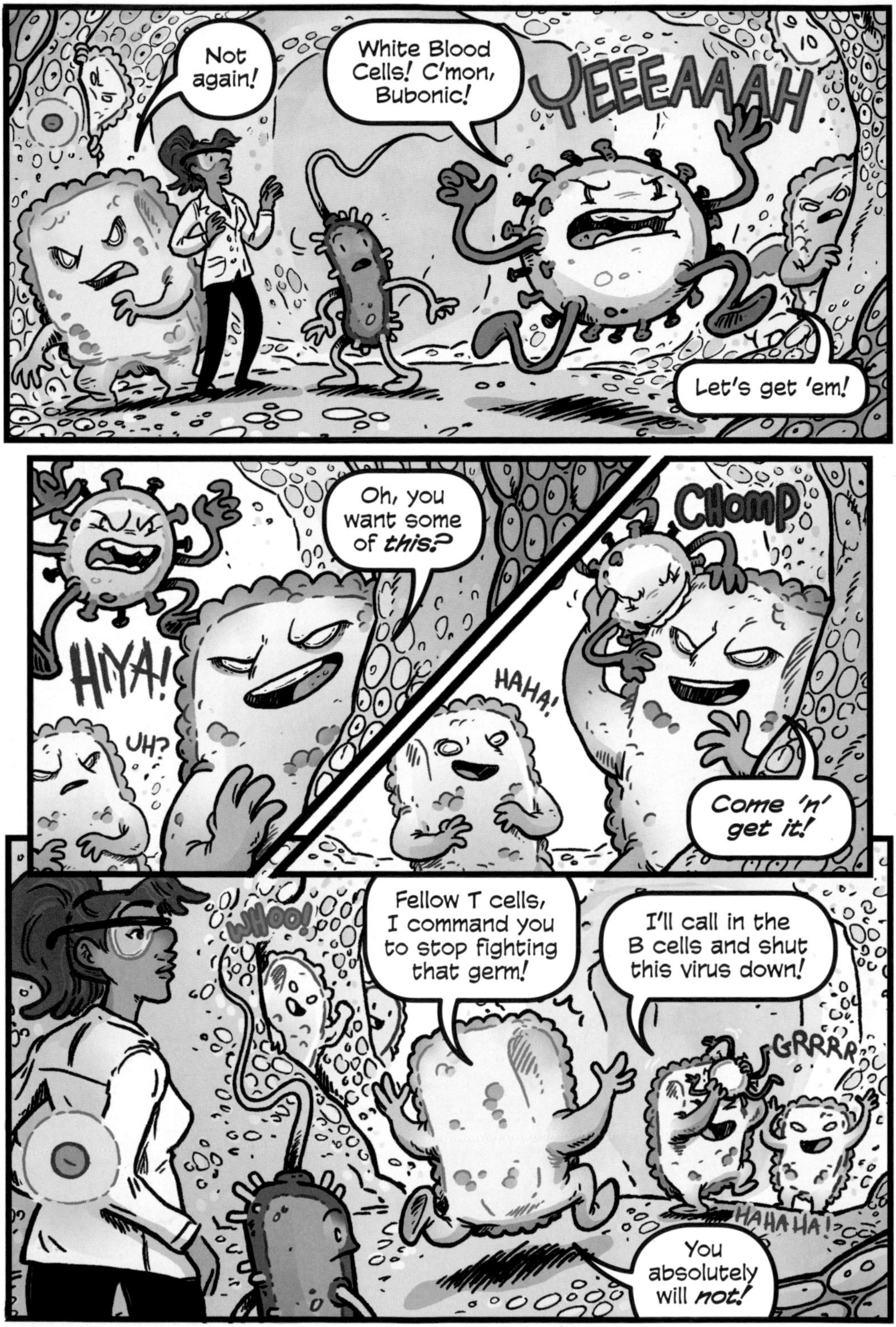

Not again!
White Blood Cells! C'mon, Bubonic!
YEEEAAAH
Let's get 'em!
Oh, you want some of *this?*
HIYA!
UH?
CHOMP
HAHA!
Come 'n' get it!
WHOO!
Fellow T cells, I command you to stop fighting that germ!
I'll call in the B cells and shut this virus down!
GRRRR
HAHAHA!
You absolutely will *not!*

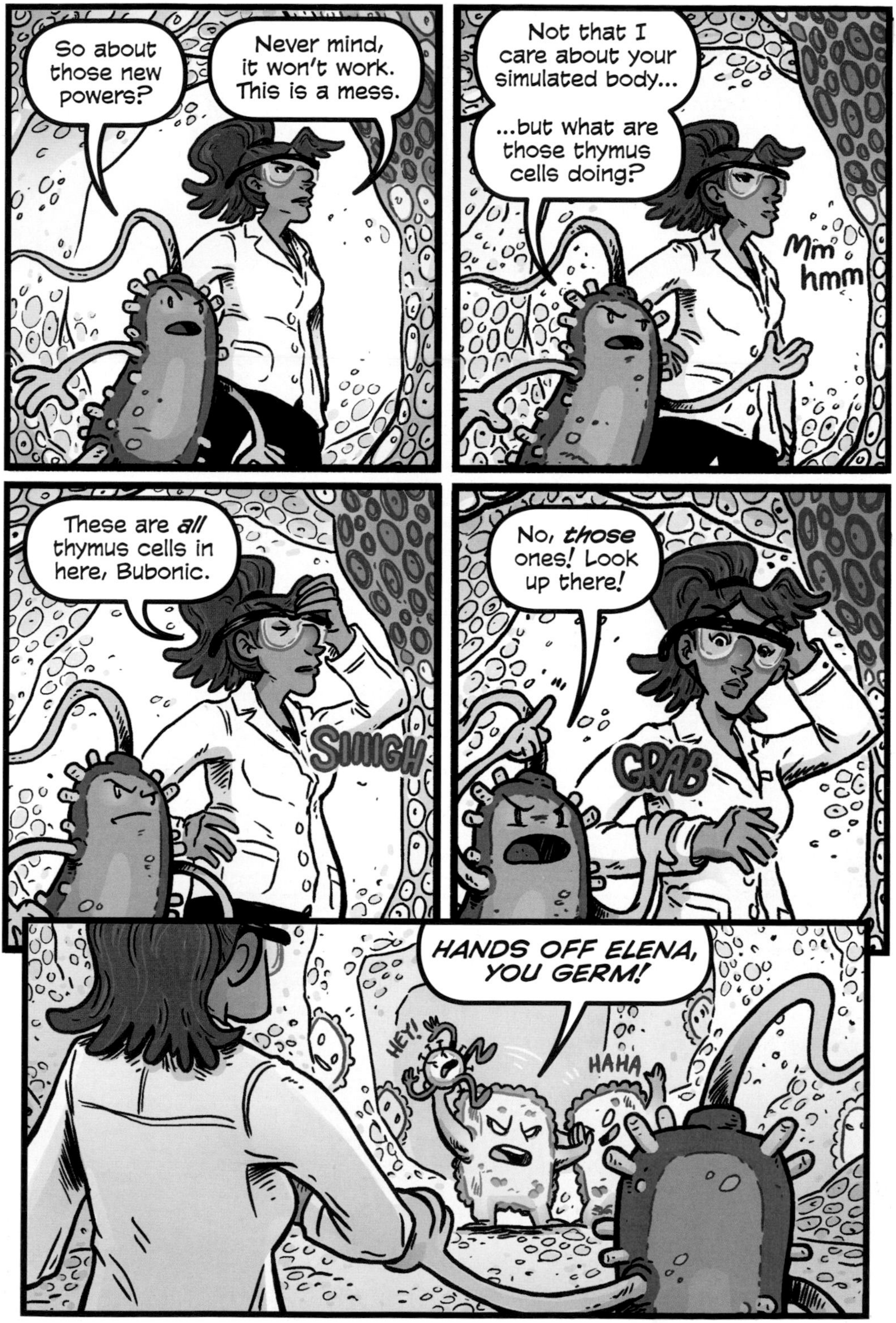
So about those new powers?
Never mind, it won't work. This is a mess.
Not that I care about your simulated body...
...but what are those thymus cells doing?
Mm hmm
These are *all* thymus cells in here, Bubonic.
SIIIGH
No, *those* ones! Look up there!
GRAB
HANDS OFF ELENA, YOU GERM!
HEY!
HAHA

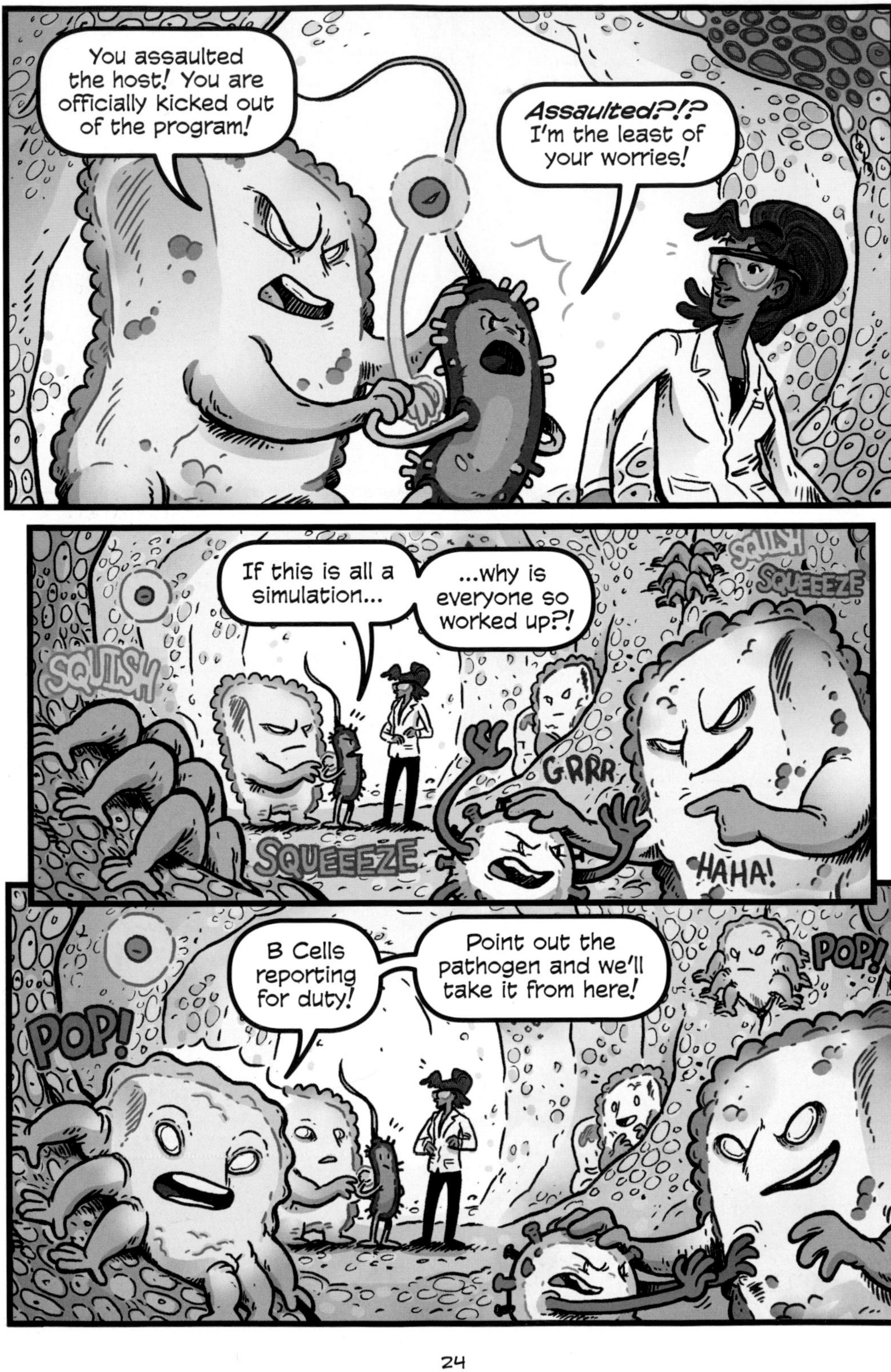
You assaulted the host! You are officially kicked out of the program!
Assaulted?!? I'm the least of your worries!
If this is all a simulation...
...why is everyone so worked up?!
SQUISH
SQUEEEZE
SQUISH
SQUEEEZE
GRRR
HAHA!
B Cells reporting for duty!
Point out the pathogen and we'll take it from here!
POP!
POP!

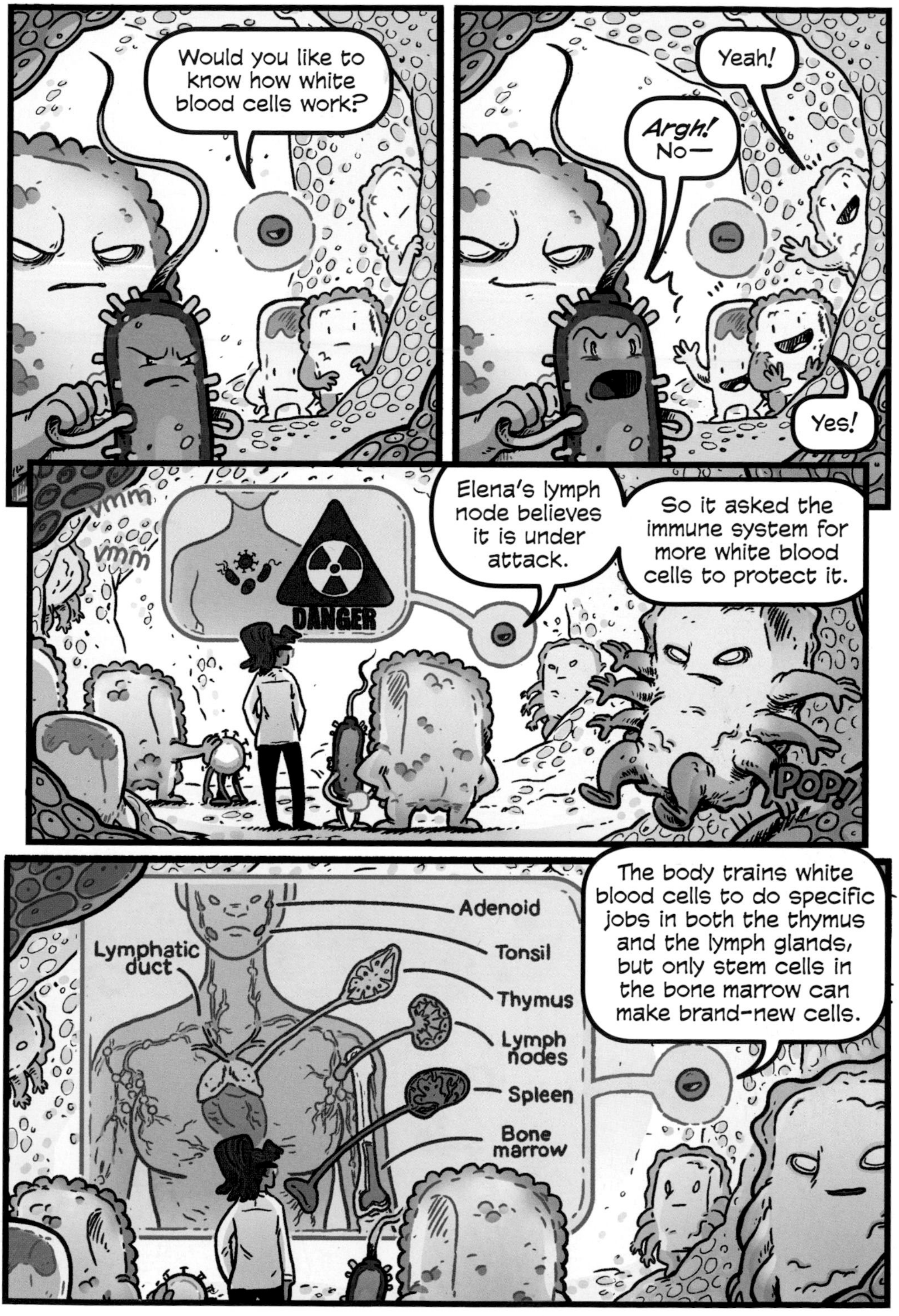

Would you like to know how white blood cells work?
Yeah!
Argh! No—
Yes!
vmm vmm
DANGER
Elena's lymph node believes it is under attack.
So it asked the immune system for more white blood cells to protect it.
POP!
Adenoid
Tonsil
Lymphatic duct
Thymus
Lymph nodes
Spleen
Bone marrow
The body trains white blood cells to do specific jobs in both the thymus and the lymph glands, but only stem cells in the bone marrow can make brand-new cells.

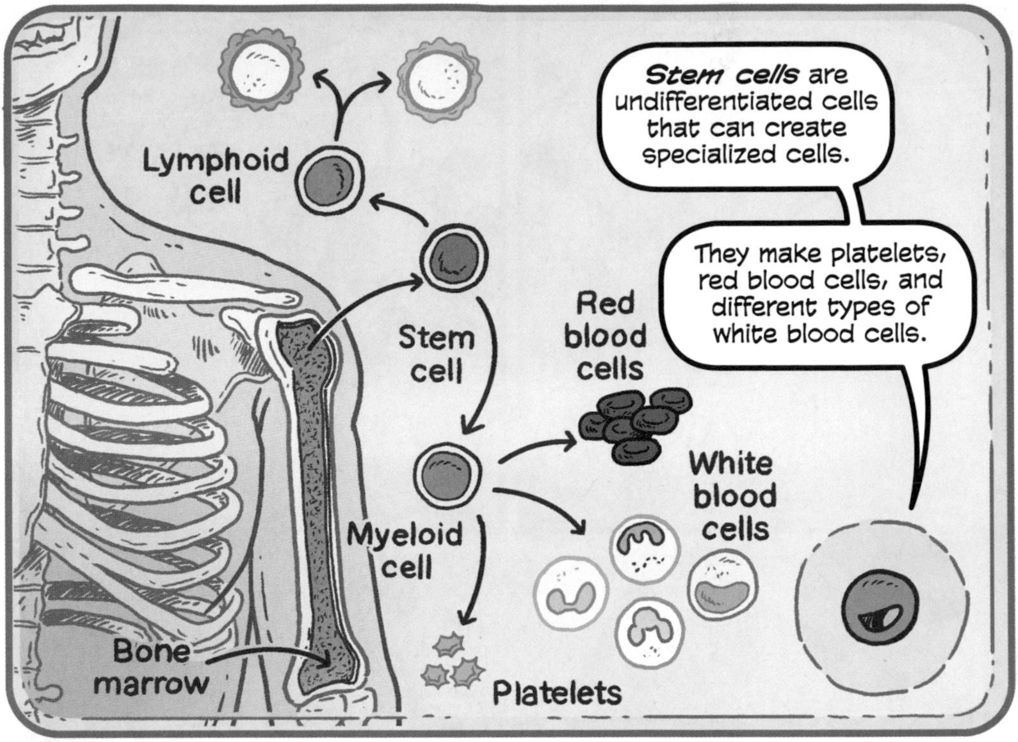
Stem cells are undifferentiated cells that can create specialized cells.
They make platelets, red blood cells, and different types of white blood cells.
Lymphoid cell
Stem cell
Red blood cells
White blood cells
Myeloid cell
Bone marrow
Platelets

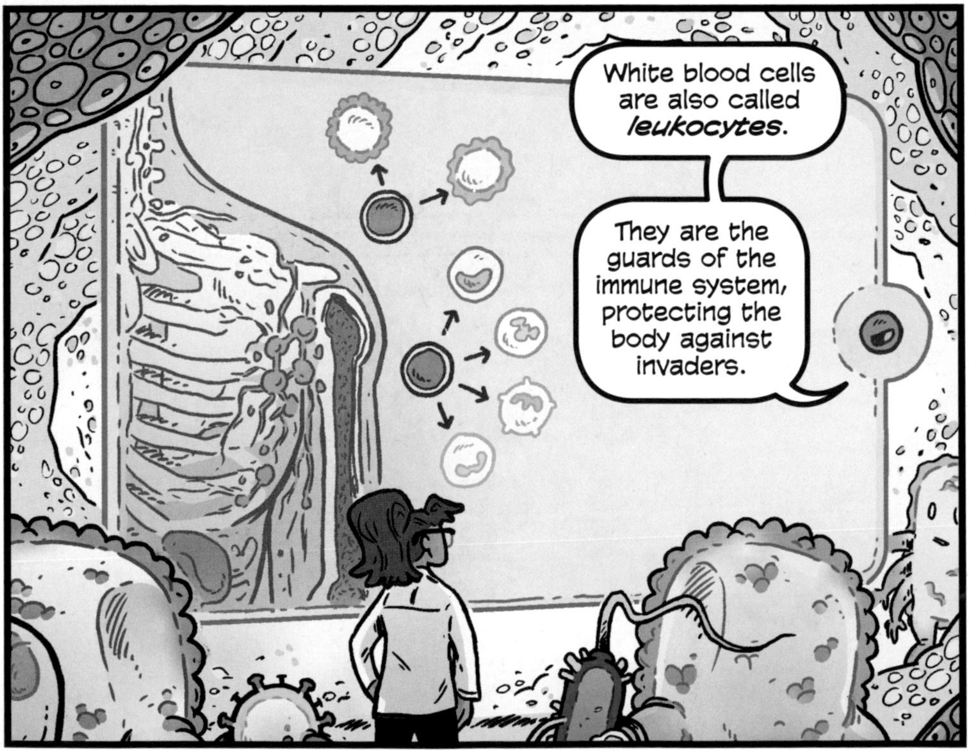
White blood cells are also called *leukocytes*.
They are the guards of the immune system, protecting the body against invaders.

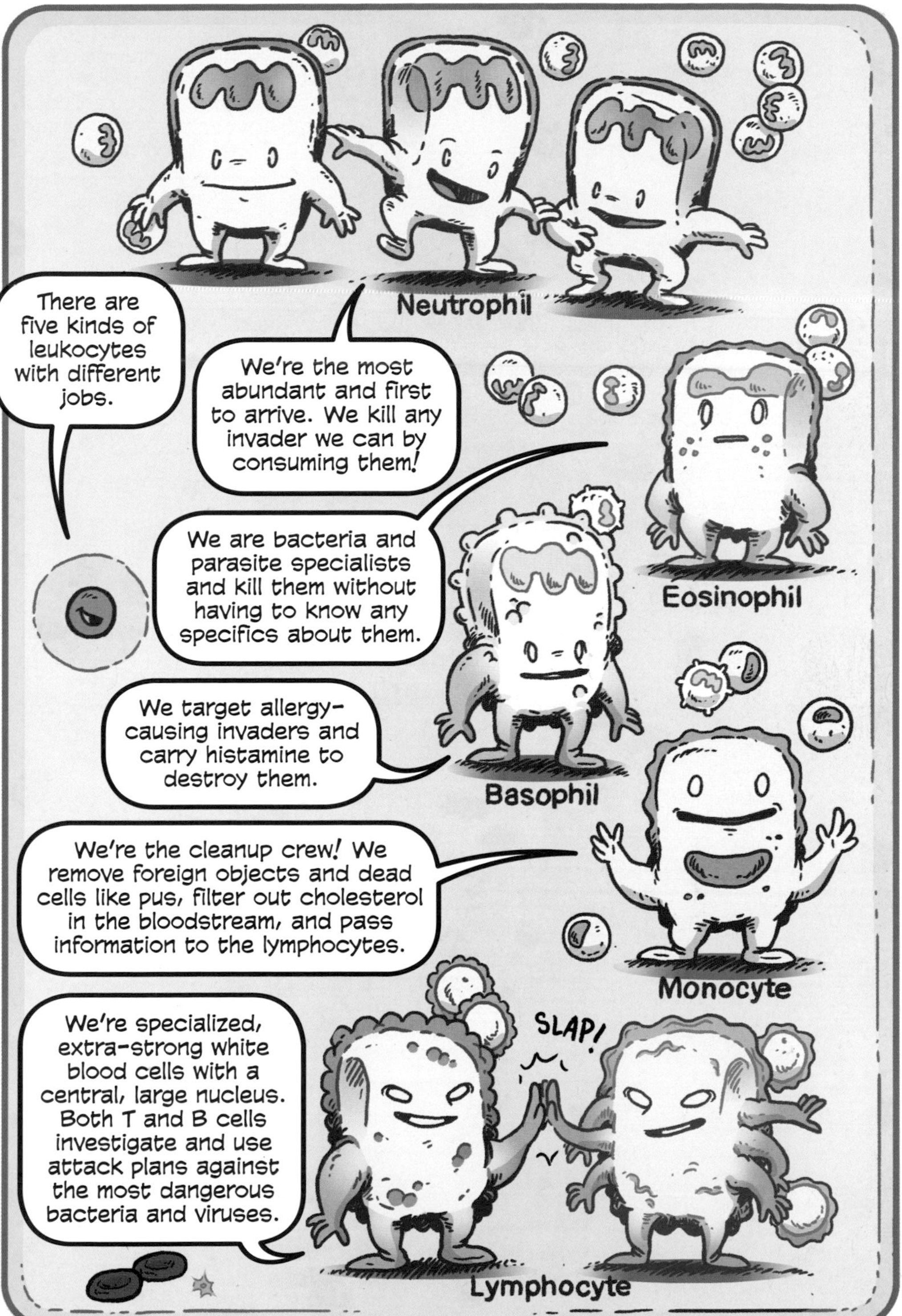
Neutrophil
There are five kinds of leukocytes with different jobs.
We're the most abundant and first to arrive. We kill any invader we can by consuming them!
Eosinophil
We are bacteria and parasite specialists and kill them without having to know any specifics about them.
We target allergy-causing invaders and carry histamine to destroy them.
Basophil
We're the cleanup crew! We remove foreign objects and dead cells like pus, filter out cholesterol in the bloodstream, and pass information to the lymphocytes.
Monocyte
We're specialized, extra-strong white blood cells with a central, large nucleus. Both T and B cells investigate and use attack plans against the most dangerous bacteria and viruses.
SLAP!
Lymphocyte

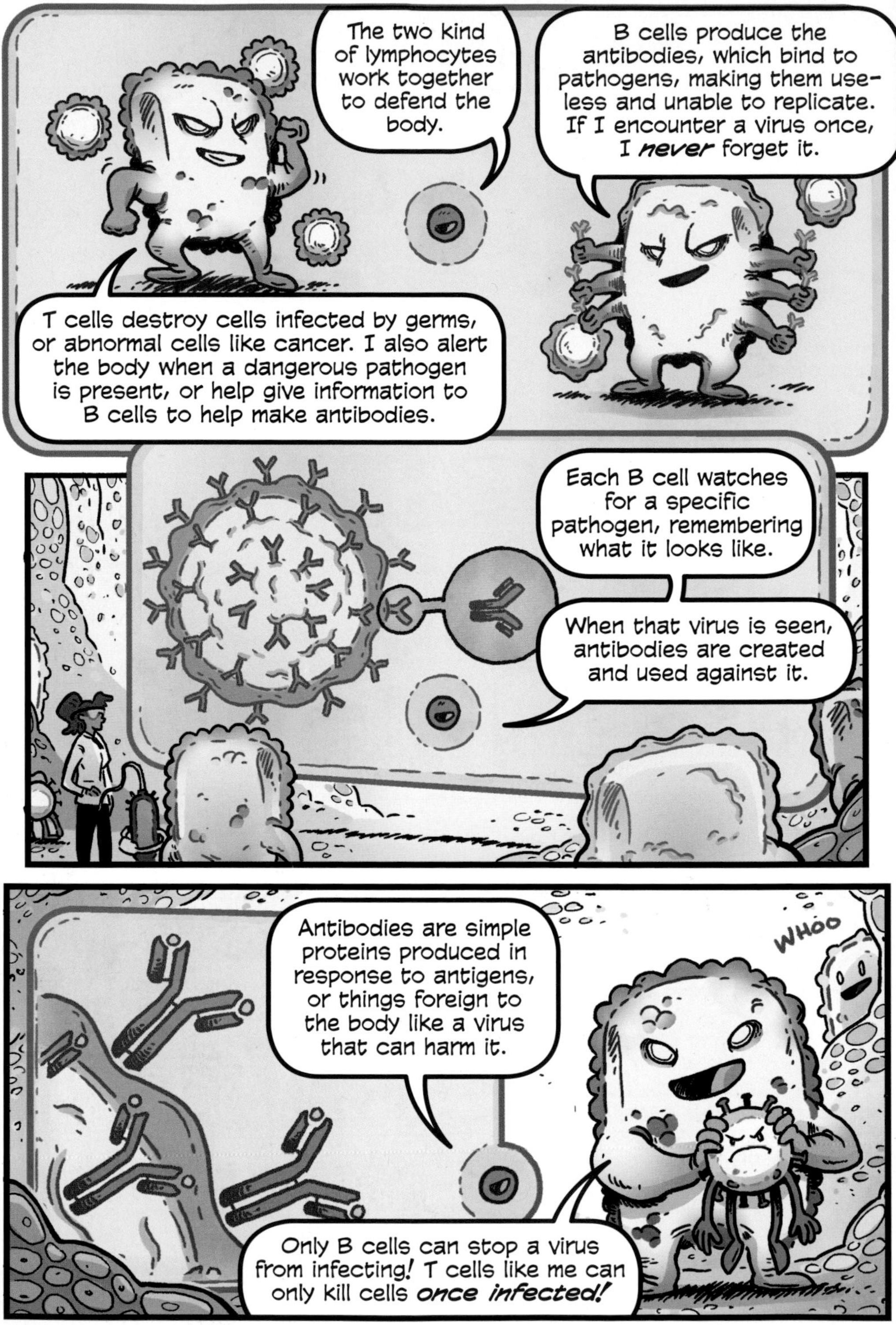
The two kind of lymphocytes work together to defend the body.
B cells produce the antibodies, which bind to pathogens, making them useless and unable to replicate. If I encounter a virus once, I *never* forget it.
T cells destroy cells infected by germs, or abnormal cells like cancer. I also alert the body when a dangerous pathogen is present, or help give information to B cells to help make antibodies.
Each B cell watches for a specific pathogen, remembering what it looks like.
When that virus is seen, antibodies are created and used against it.
Antibodies are simple proteins produced in response to antigens, or things foreign to the body like a virus that can harm it.
WHOO
Only B cells can stop a virus from infecting! T cells like me can only kill cells *once infected!*

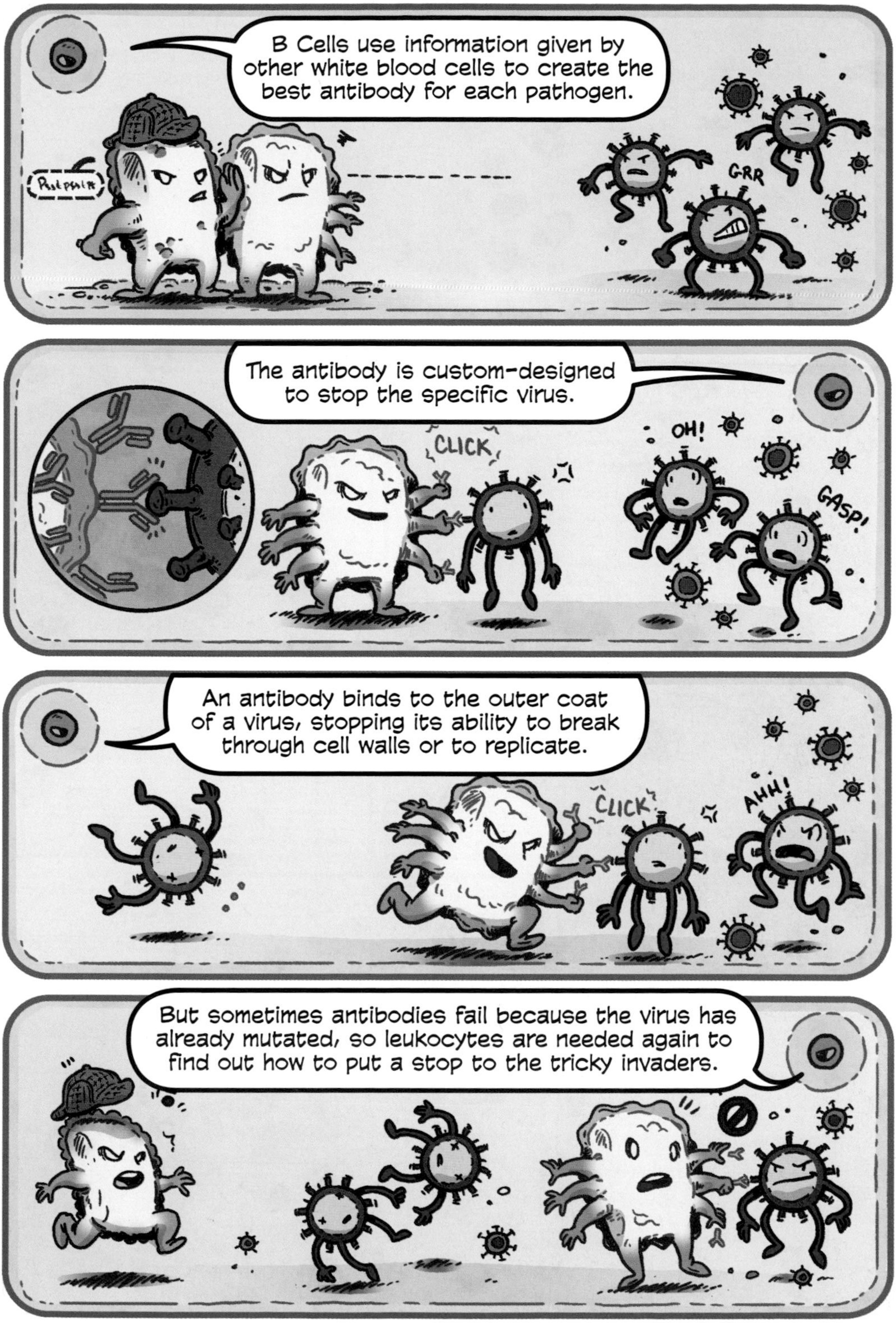
B Cells use information given by other white blood cells to create the best antibody for each pathogen.
GRR
The antibody is custom-designed to stop the specific virus.
CLICK
OH!
GASP!
An antibody binds to the outer coat of a virus, stopping its ability to break through cell walls or to replicate.
CLICK
AHH!
But sometimes antibodies fail because the virus has already mutated, so leukocytes are needed again to find out how to put a stop to the tricky invaders.

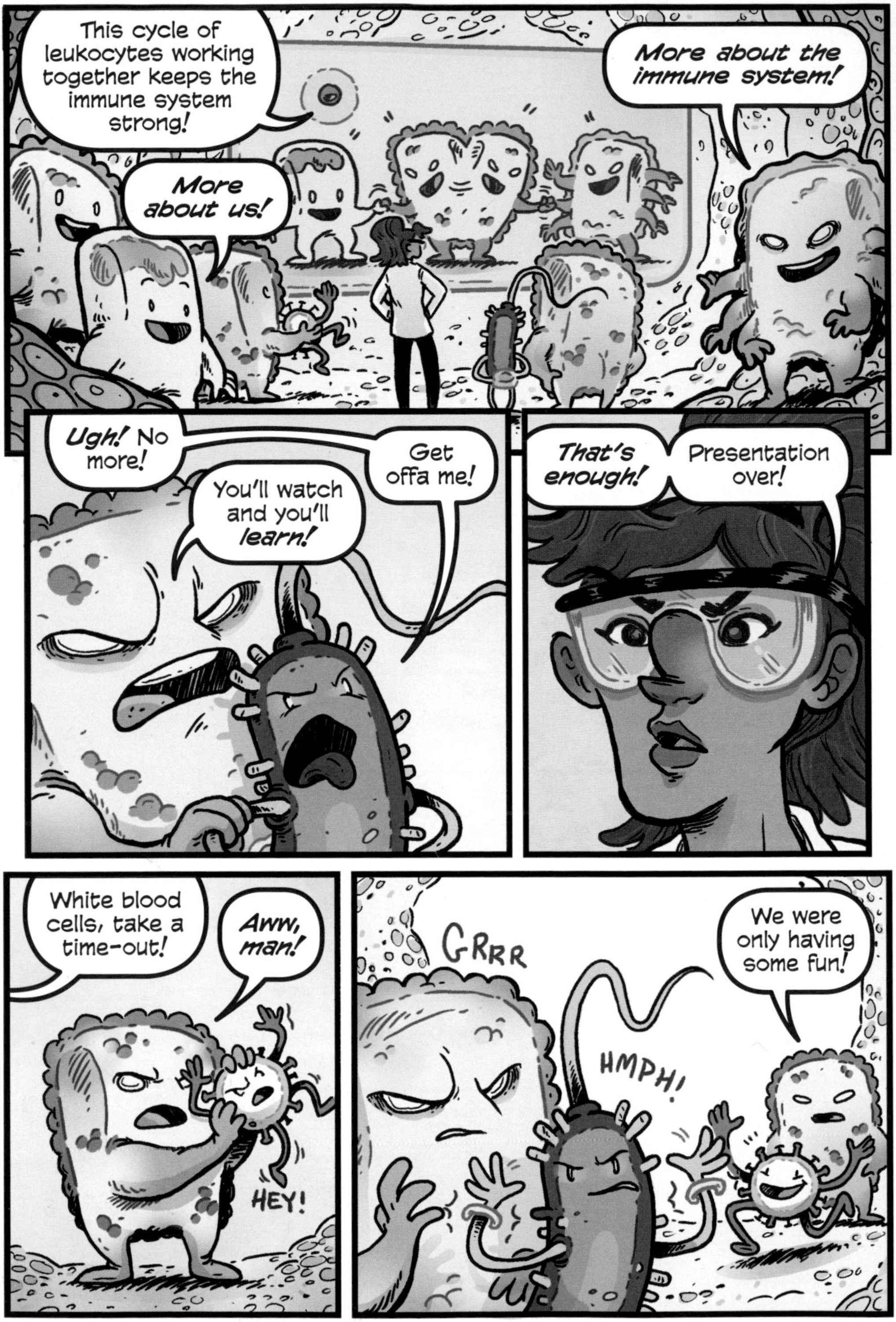
This cycle of leukocytes working together keeps the immune system strong!
More about the immune system!
More about us!
Ugh! No more!
Get offa me!
You'll watch and you'll learn!
That's enough!
Presentation over!
White blood cells, take a time-out!
Aww, man!
HEY!
GRRR
HMPH!
We were only having some fun!

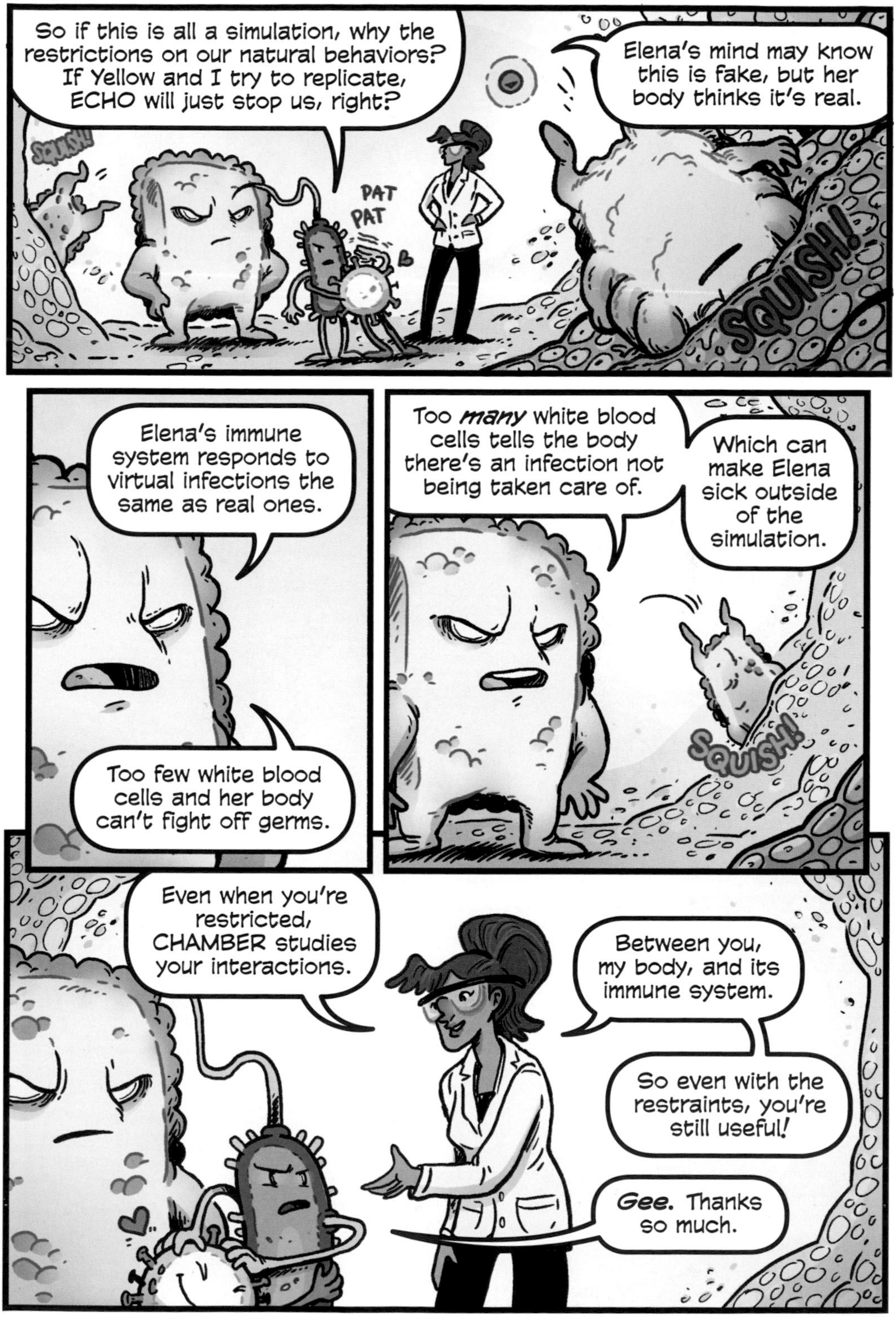

So if this is all a simulation, why the restrictions on our natural behaviors? If Yellow and I try to replicate, ECHO will just stop us, right?
SQUISH!
PAT PAT
Elena's mind may know this is fake, but her body thinks it's real.
SQUISH!
Elena's immune system responds to virtual infections the same as real ones.
Too few white blood cells and her body can't fight off germs.
Too *many* white blood cells tells the body there's an infection not being taken care of.
Which can make Elena sick outside of the simulation.
SQUISH!
Even when you're restricted, CHAMBER studies your interactions.
Between you, my body, and its immune system.
So even with the restraints, you're still useful!
Gee. Thanks so much.

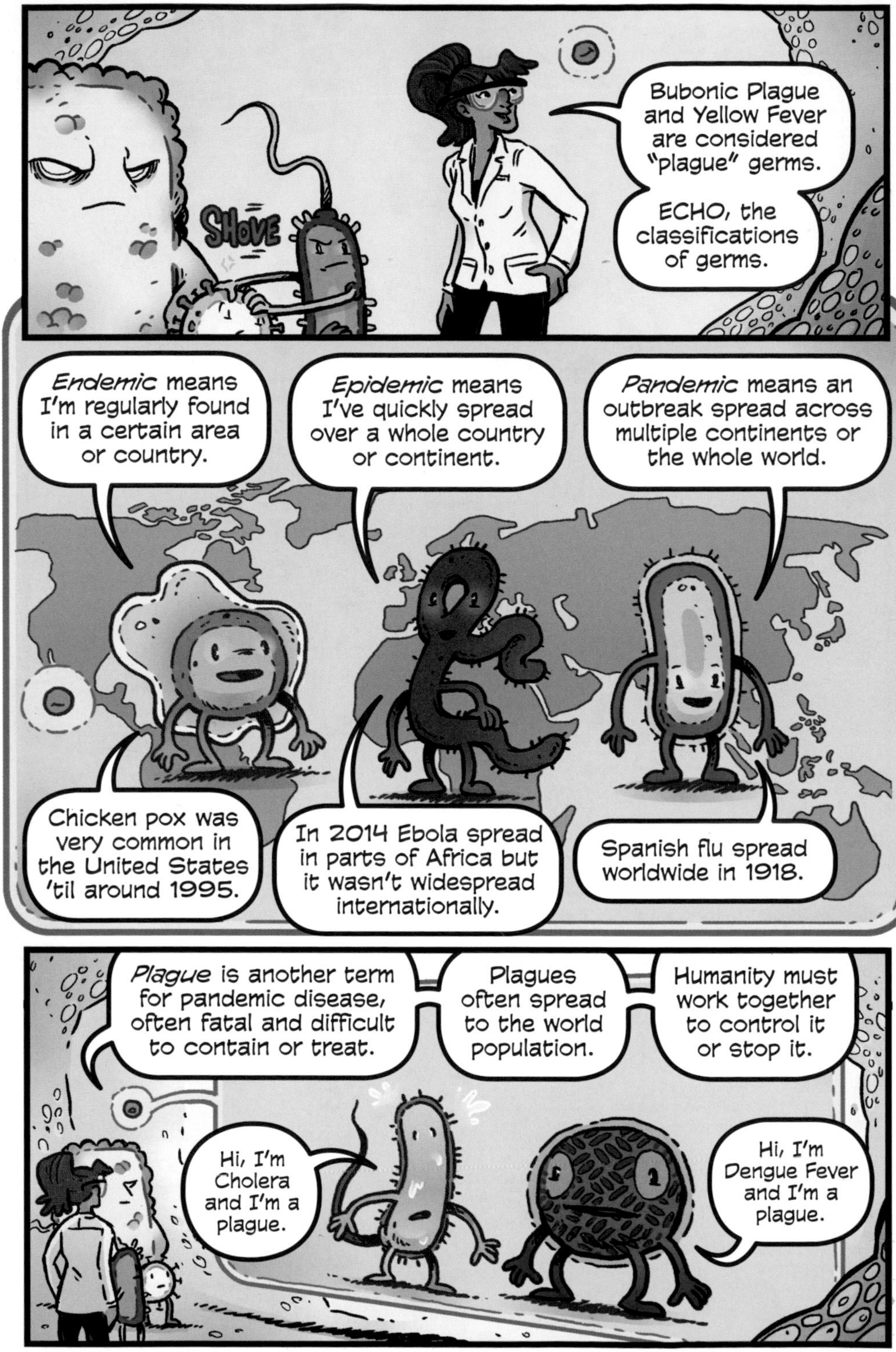
Bubonic Plague and Yellow Fever are considered "plague" germs.
ECHO, the classifications of germs.
SHOVE
Endemic means I'm regularly found in a certain area or country.
Chicken pox was very common in the United States 'til around 1995.
Epidemic means I've quickly spread over a whole country or continent.
In 2014 Ebola spread in parts of Africa but it wasn't widespread internationally.
Pandemic means an outbreak spread across multiple continents or the whole world.
Spanish flu spread worldwide in 1918.
Plague is another term for pandemic disease, often fatal and difficult to contain or treat.
Plagues often spread to the world population.
Humanity must work together to control it or stop it.
Hi, I'm Cholera and I'm a plague.
Hi, I'm Dengue Fever and I'm a plague.

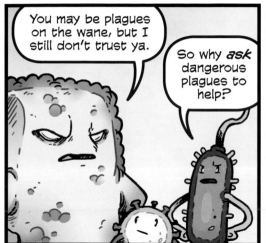

You may be plagues on the wane, but I still don't trust ya.

So why *ask* dangerous plagues to help?

I need a bacterium and a virus, like each of you, for missions.

You both attack cells in unique ways.

You could mutate, with our help, to target the negative things inside humans and be our undercover agents.

But if we're mutated through science...

...will we still be *germs?*

No, you wouldn't.

Germ is a word used to describe any microorganism that makes us sick.

ECHO, please explain.

33

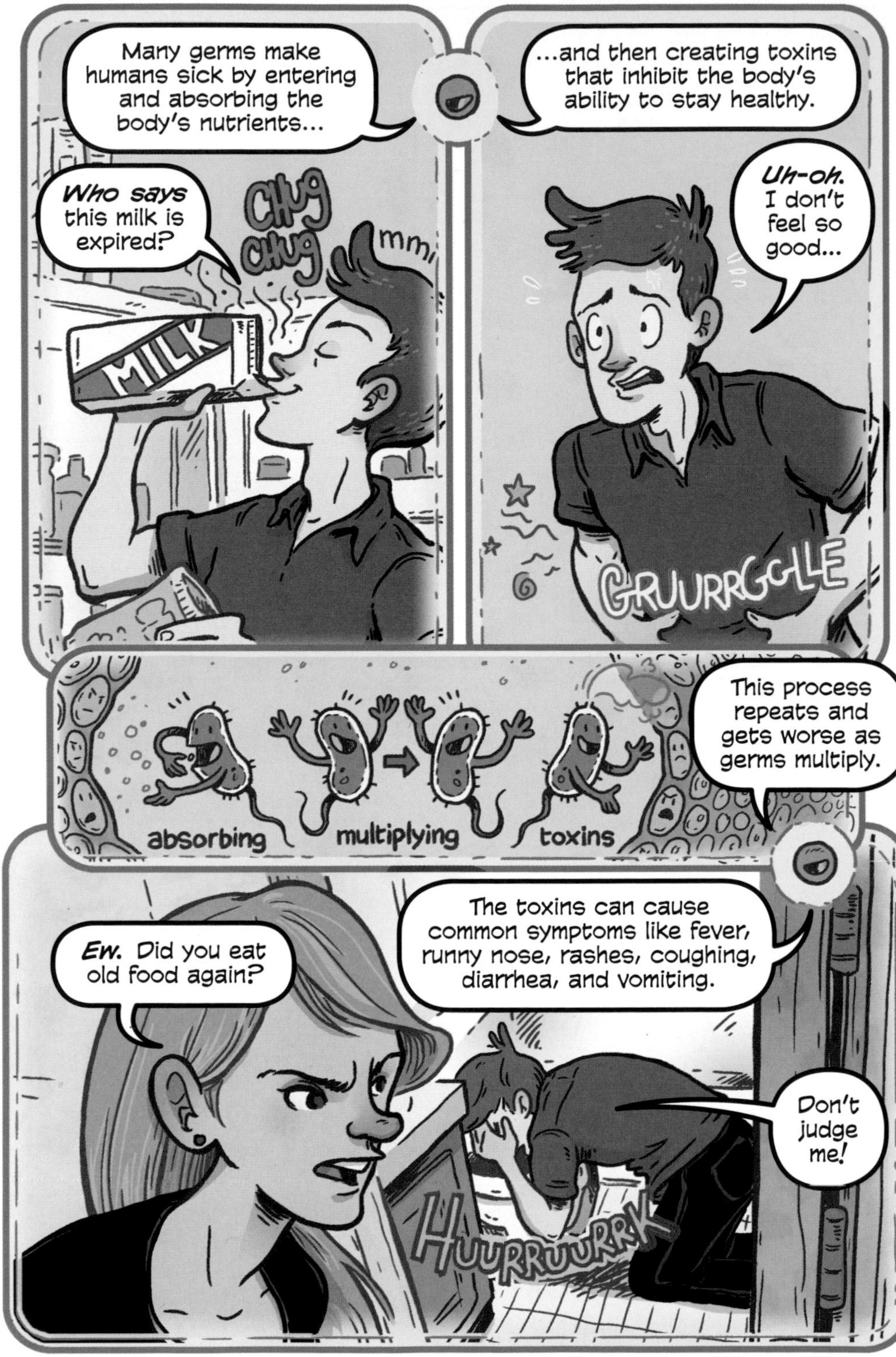
Many germs make humans sick by entering and absorbing the body's nutrients...
Who says this milk is expired?
CHUG CHUG
mm
MILK
...and then creating toxins that inhibit the body's ability to stay healthy.
Uh-oh. I don't feel so good...
GRUURRGGLLE
This process repeats and gets worse as germs multiply.
absorbing
multiplying
toxins
Ew. Did you eat old food again?
The toxins can cause common symptoms like fever, runny nose, rashes, coughing, diarrhea, and vomiting.
Don't judge me!
HUURRUURRK

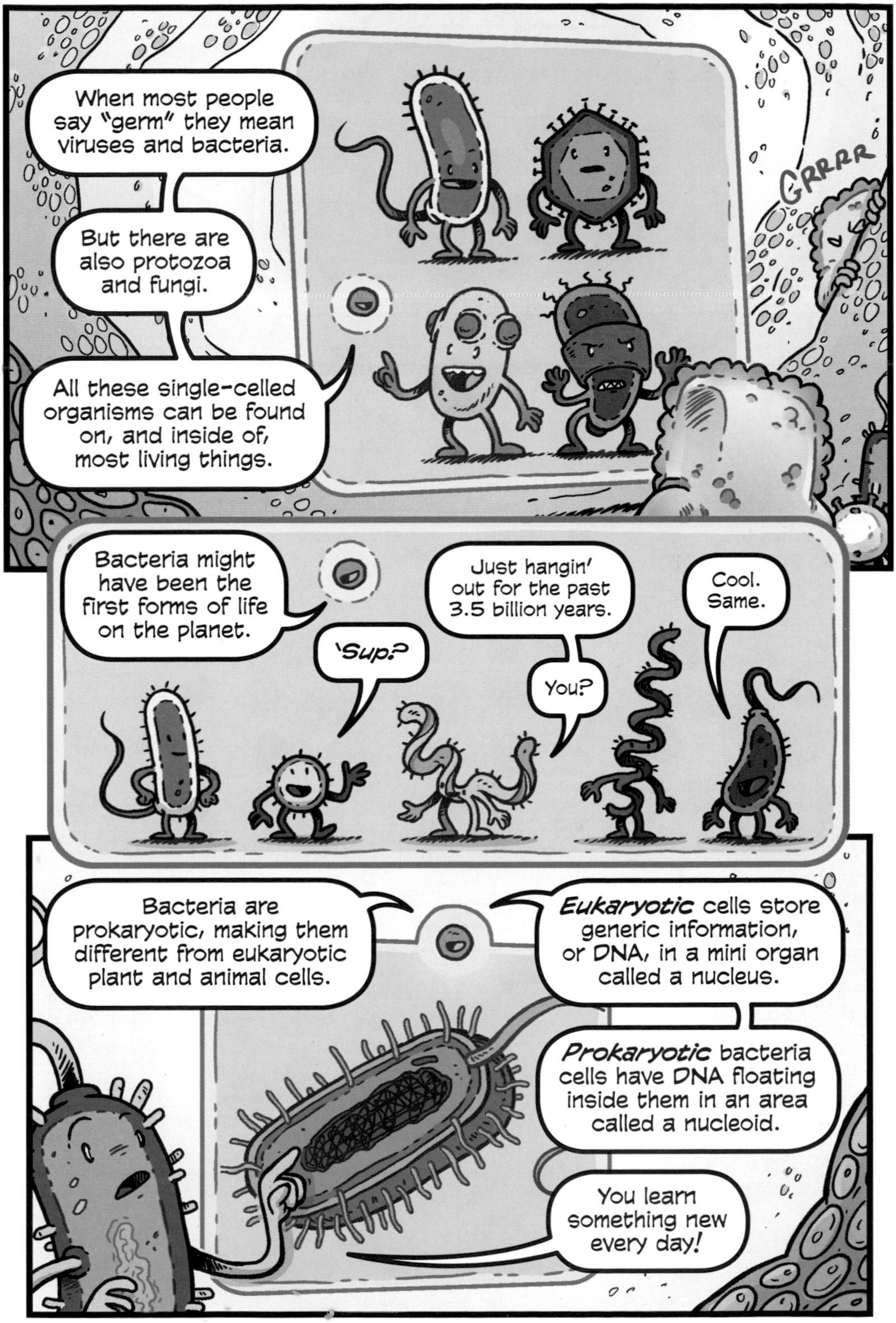

When most people say "germ" they mean viruses and bacteria.
But there are also protozoa and fungi.
All these single-celled organisms can be found on, and inside of, most living things.
GRRRR
Bacteria might have been the first forms of life on the planet.
'Sup?
Just hangin' out for the past 3.5 billion years.
You?
Cool. Same.
Bacteria are prokaryotic, making them different from eukaryotic plant and animal cells.
Eukaryotic cells store generic information, or DNA, in a mini organ called a nucleus.
Prokaryotic bacteria cells have DNA floating inside them in an area called a nucleoid.
You learn something new every day!

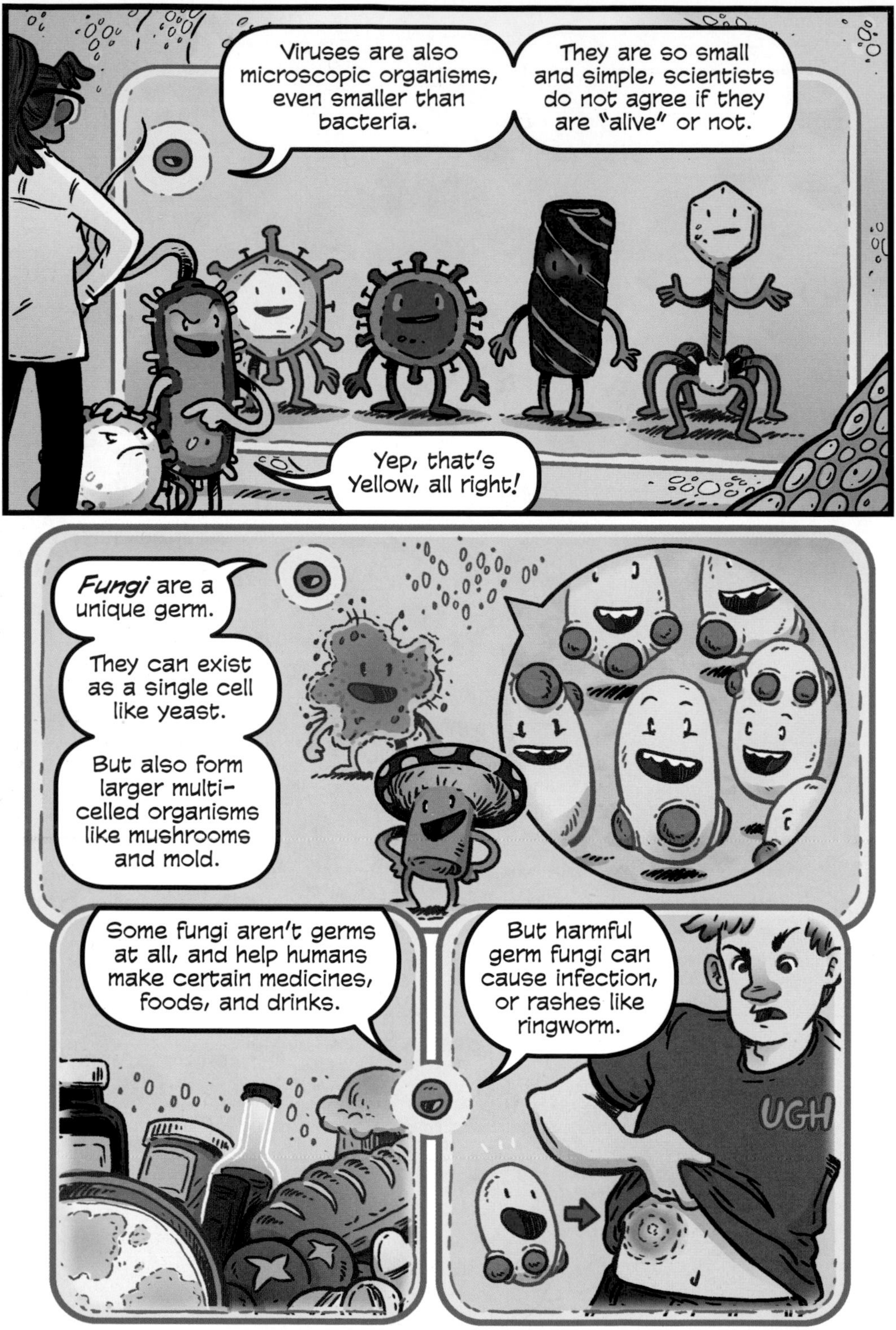
Viruses are also microscopic organisms, even smaller than bacteria.
They are so small and simple, scientists do not agree if they are "alive" or not.
Yep, that's Yellow, all right!
Fungi are a unique germ.
They can exist as a single cell like yeast.
But also form larger multi-celled organisms like mushrooms and mold.
Some fungi aren't germs at all, and help humans make certain medicines, foods, and drinks.
But harmful germ fungi can cause infection, or rashes like ringworm.
UGH

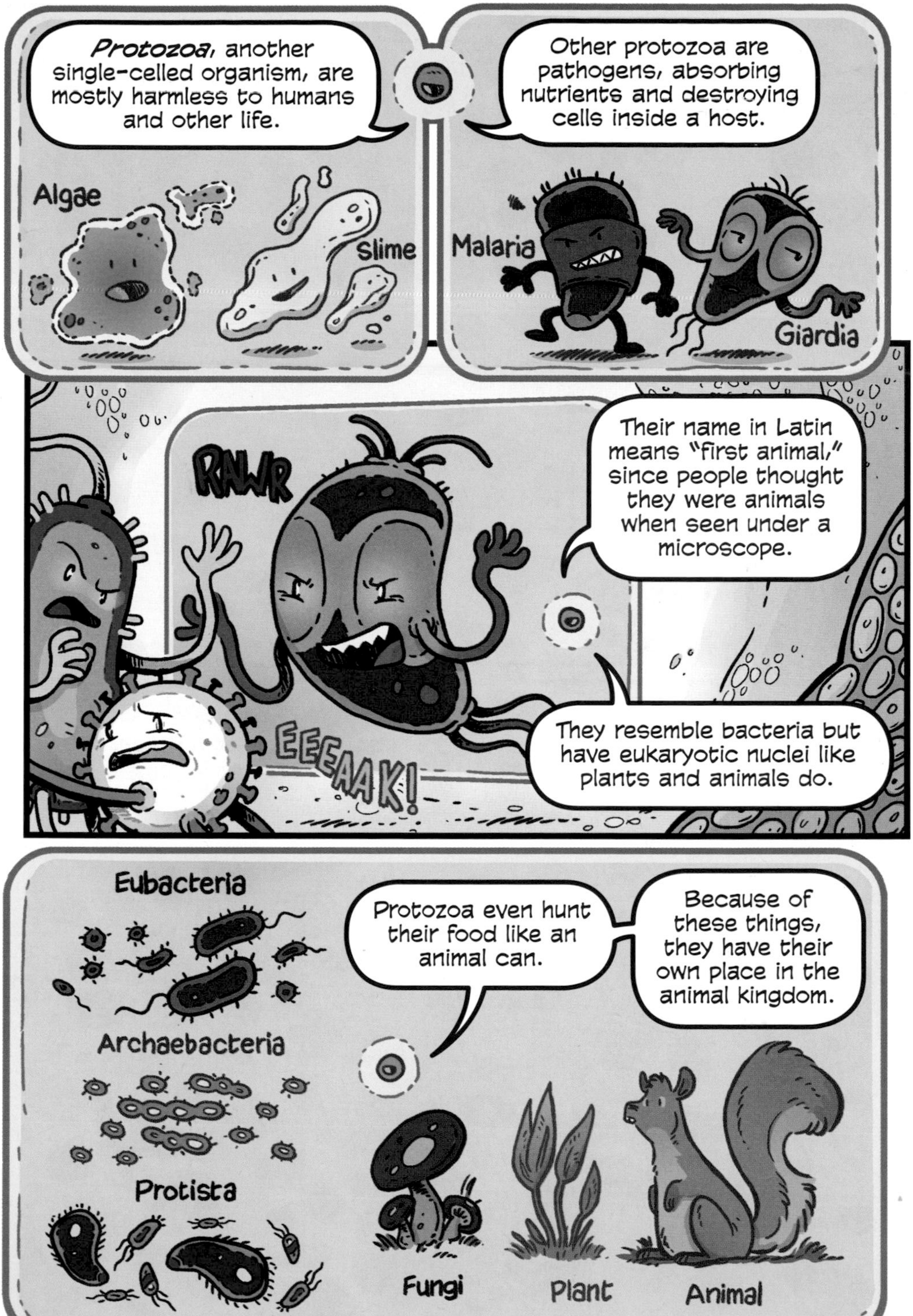
Protozoa, another single-celled organism, are mostly harmless to humans and other life.
Algae
Slime
Other protozoa are pathogens, absorbing nutrients and destroying cells inside a host.
Malaria
Giardia
RAWR
Their name in Latin means "first animal," since people thought they were animals when seen under a microscope.
EEEAAK!
They resemble bacteria but have eukaryotic nuclei like plants and animals do.
Eubacteria
Archaebacteria
Protista
Protozoa even hunt their food like an animal can.
Because of these things, they have their own place in the animal kingdom.
Fungi
Plant
Animal

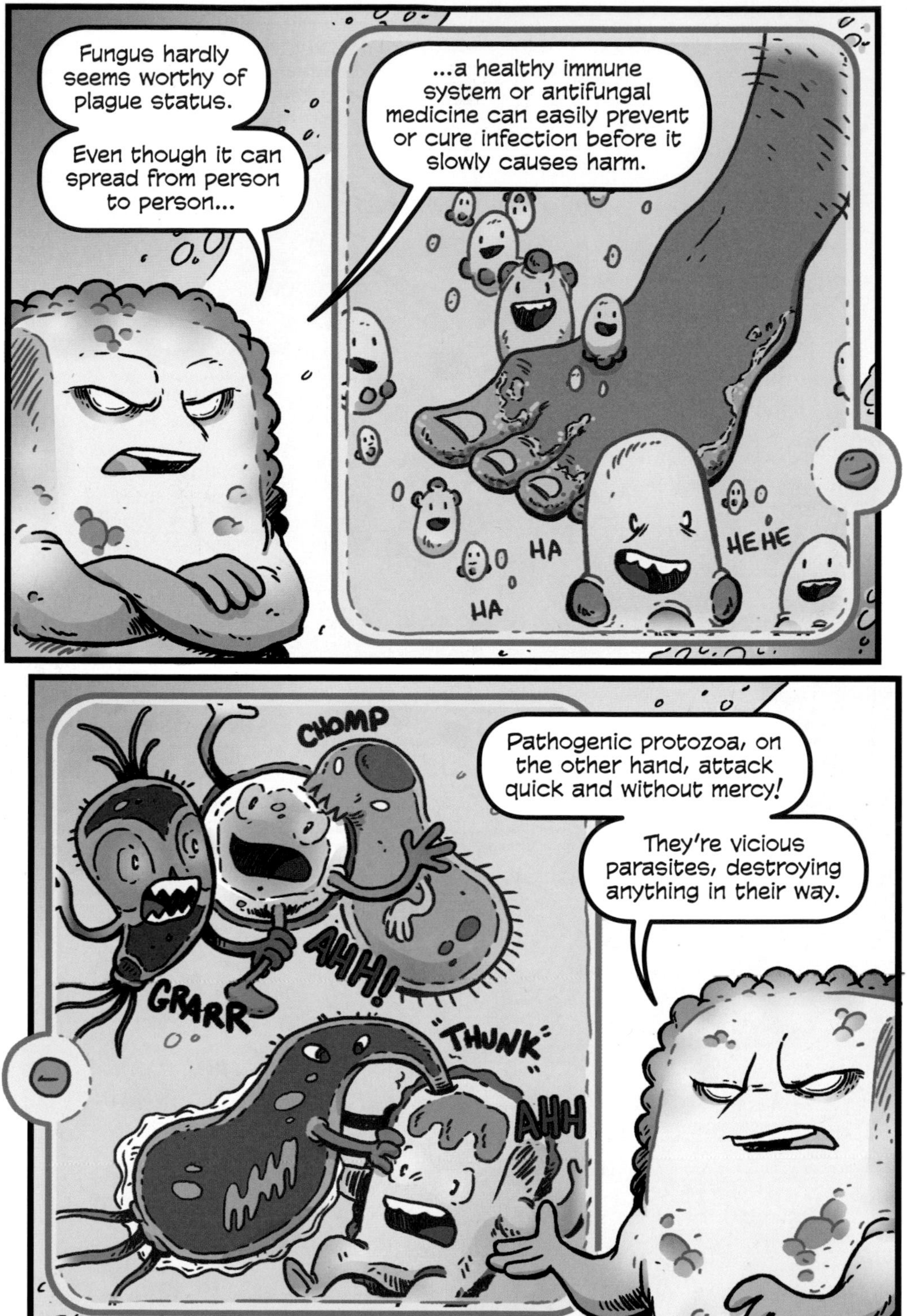

Fungus hardly seems worthy of plague status.
Even though it can spread from person to person...
...a healthy immune system or antifungal medicine can easily prevent or cure infection before it slowly causes harm.
HA
HA
HEHE
CHOMP
AHH!
GRARR
"THUNK"
AHH
Pathogenic protozoa, on the other hand, attack quick and without mercy!
They're vicious parasites, destroying anything in their way.

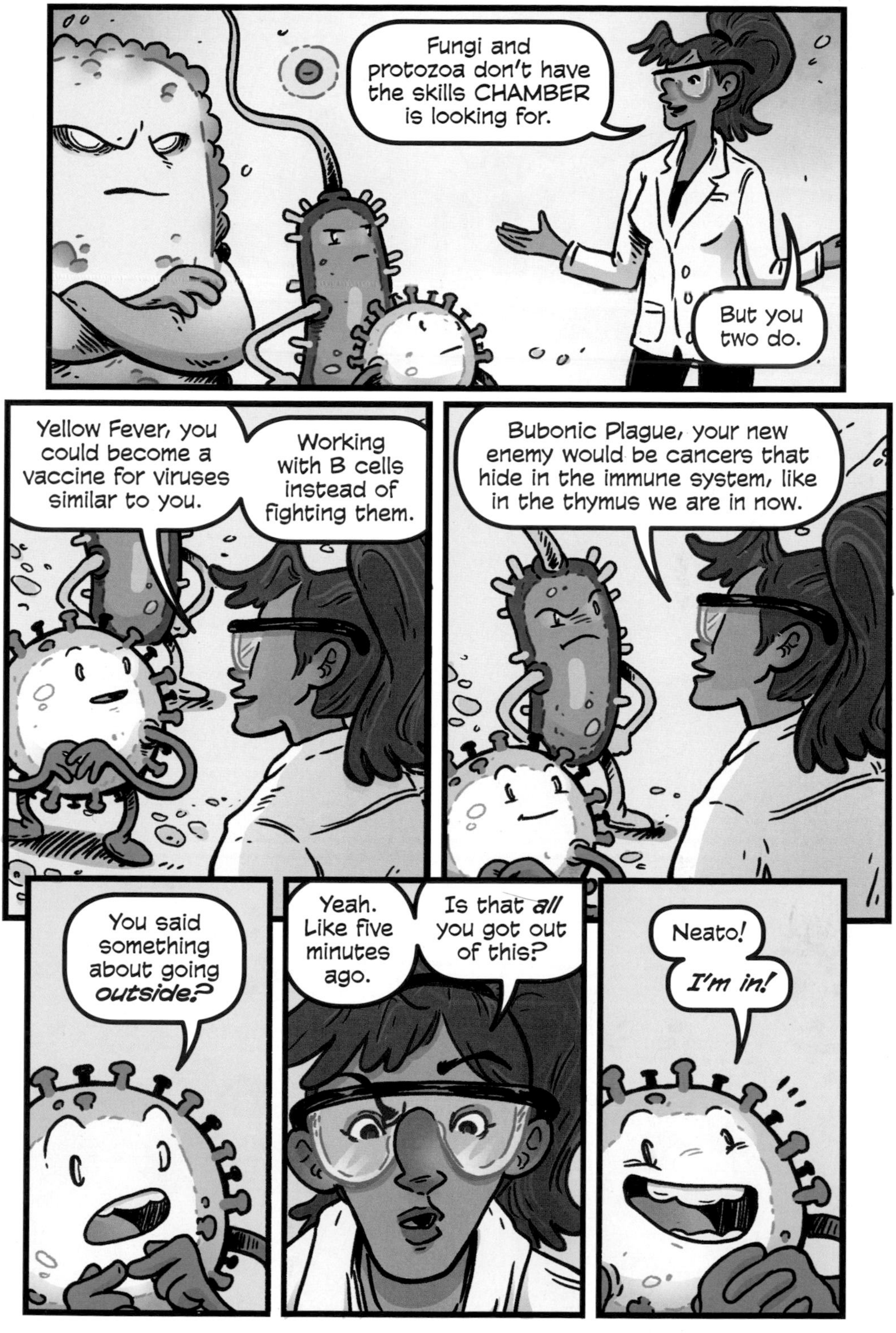

Fungi and protozoa don't have the skills CHAMBER is looking for.
But you two do.
Yellow Fever, you could become a vaccine for viruses similar to you.
Working with B cells instead of fighting them.
Bubonic Plague, your new enemy would be cancers that hide in the immune system, like in the thymus we are in now.
You said something about going *outside?*
Yeah. Like five minutes ago.
Is that *all* you got out of this?
Neato!
I'm in!

Are you kidding, Yellow? They'll turn you into a *pet!*

I just want to go outside!

Touch *real* stuff again!

They can't hold us in this hologram prison forever!

We ruled the planet for millions of years before they even showed up!

You can work with them, get your DNA all changed around, but not me!

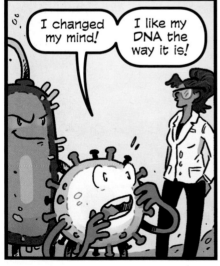

I changed my mind! I like my DNA the way it is!

So much for progress.

Can we move on to Plan B, now?

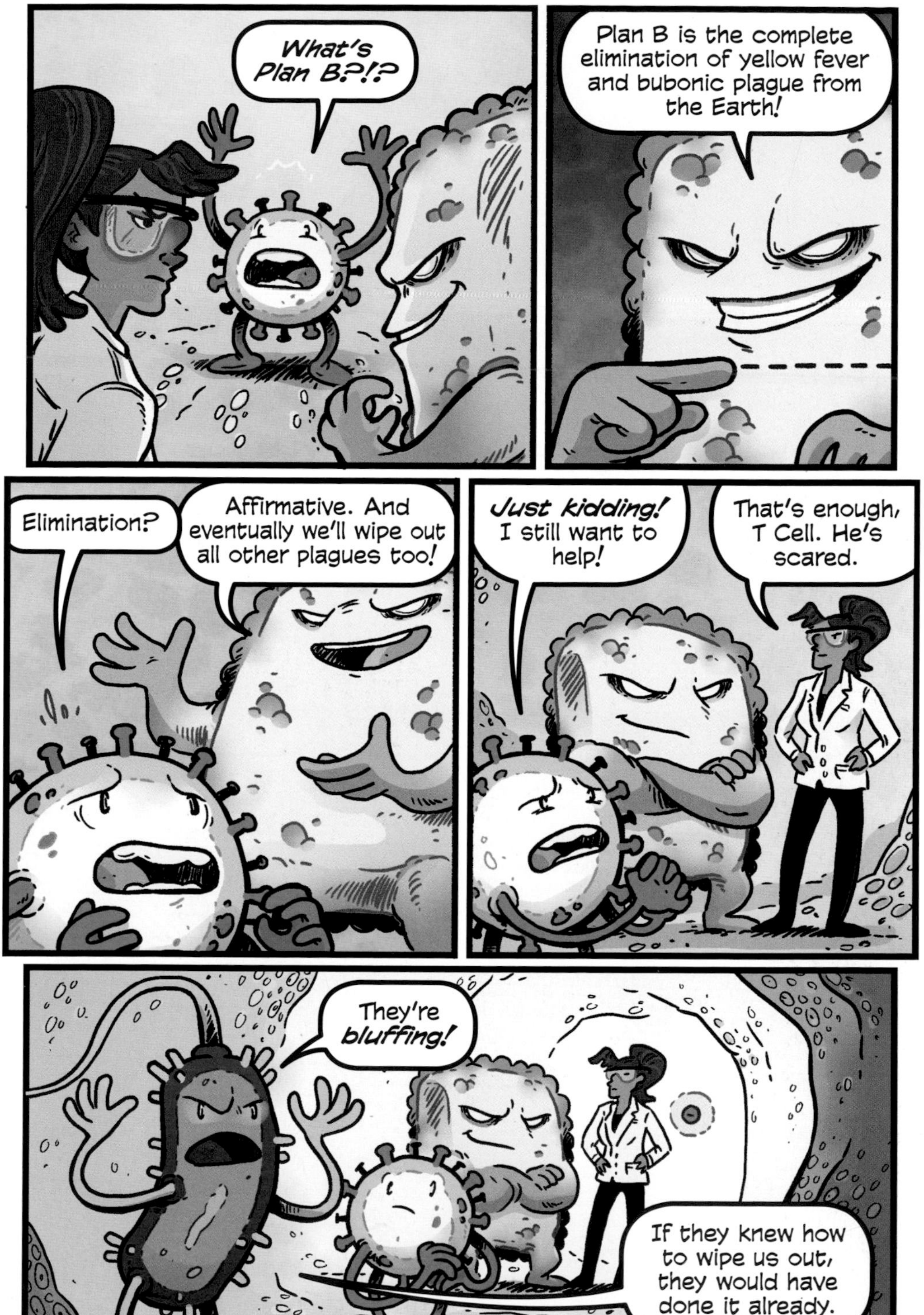
What's Plan B?!?
Plan B is the complete elimination of yellow fever and bubonic plague from the Earth!
Elimination?
Affirmative. And eventually we'll wipe out all other plagues too!
Just kidding! I still want to help!
That's enough, T Cell. He's scared.
They're bluffing!
If they knew how to wipe us out, they would have done it already.

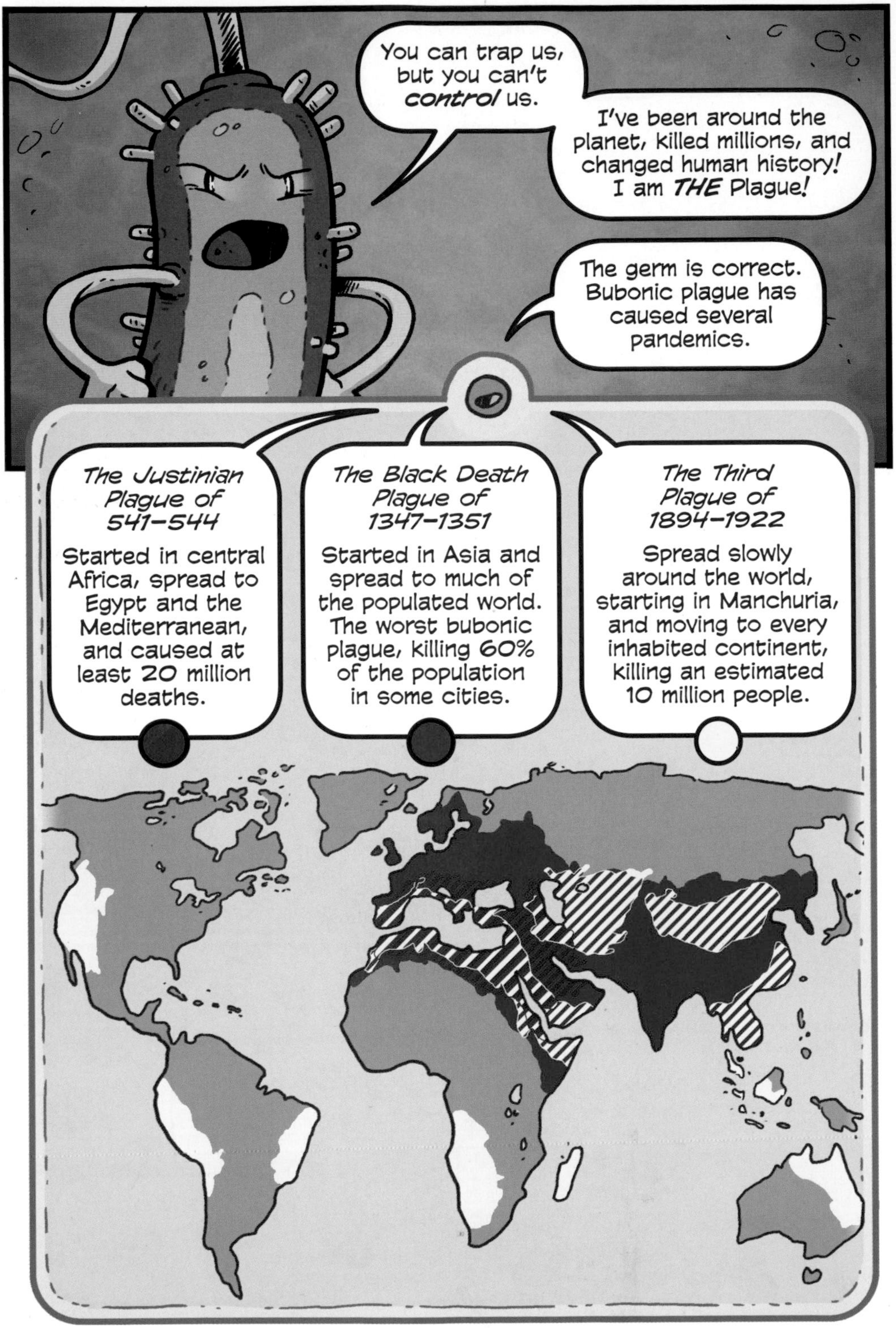

You can trap us, but you can't *control* us.
I've been around the planet, killed millions, and changed human history! I am *THE* Plague!
The germ is correct. Bubonic plague has caused several pandemics.
The Justinian Plague of 541–544
Started in central Africa, spread to Egypt and the Mediterranean, and caused at least 20 million deaths.
The Black Death Plague of 1347–1351
Started in Asia and spread to much of the populated world. The worst bubonic plague, killing 60% of the population in some cities.
The Third Plague of 1894–1922
Spread slowly around the world, starting in Manchuria, and moving to every inhabited continent, killing an estimated 10 million people.

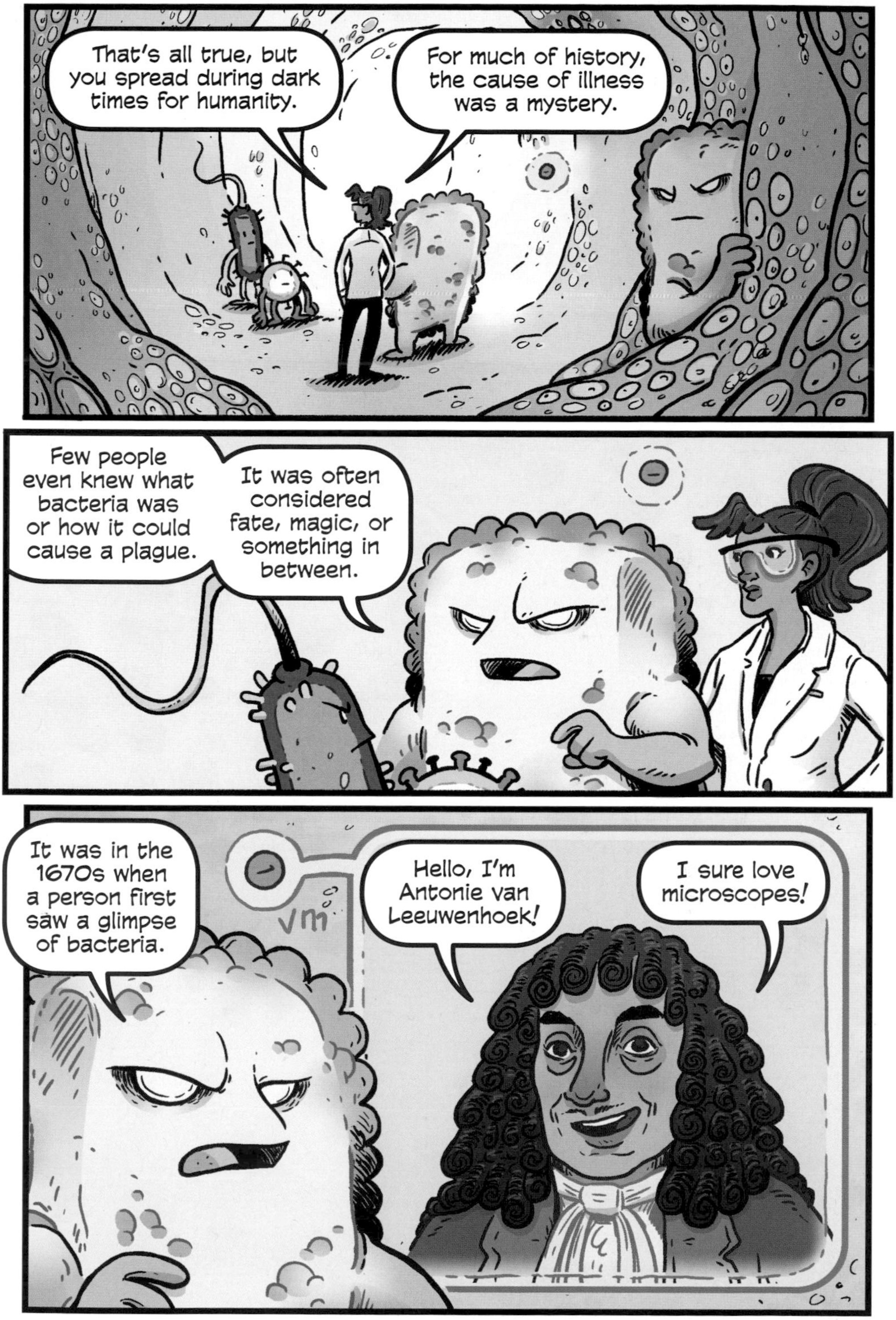
That's all true, but you spread during dark times for humanity.
For much of history, the cause of illness was a mystery.
Few people even knew what bacteria was or how it could cause a plague.
It was often considered fate, magic, or something in between.
It was in the 1670s when a person first saw a glimpse of bacteria.
Hello, I'm Antonie van Leeuwenhoek!
I sure love microscopes!

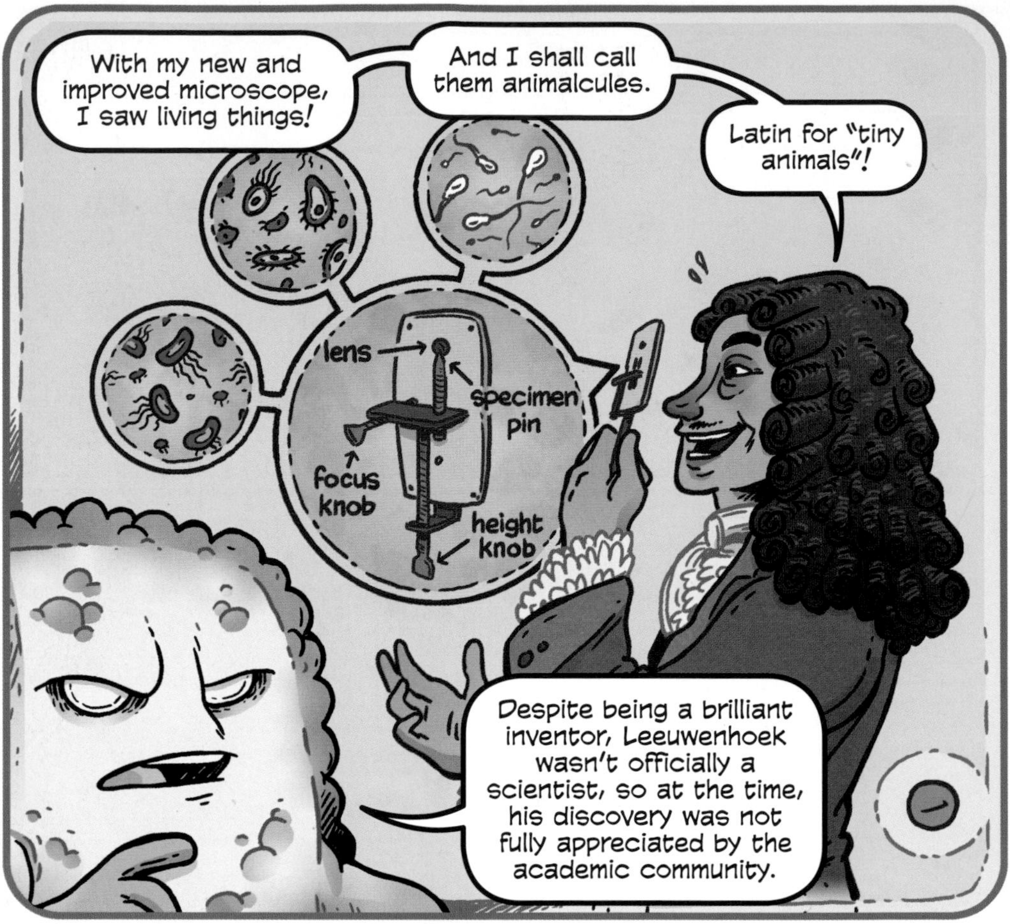
With my new and improved microscope, I saw living things!
And I shall call them animalcules.
Latin for "tiny animals"!
lens
specimen pin
focus knob
height knob
Despite being a brilliant inventor, Leeuwenhoek wasn't officially a scientist, so at the time, his discovery was not fully appreciated by the academic community.

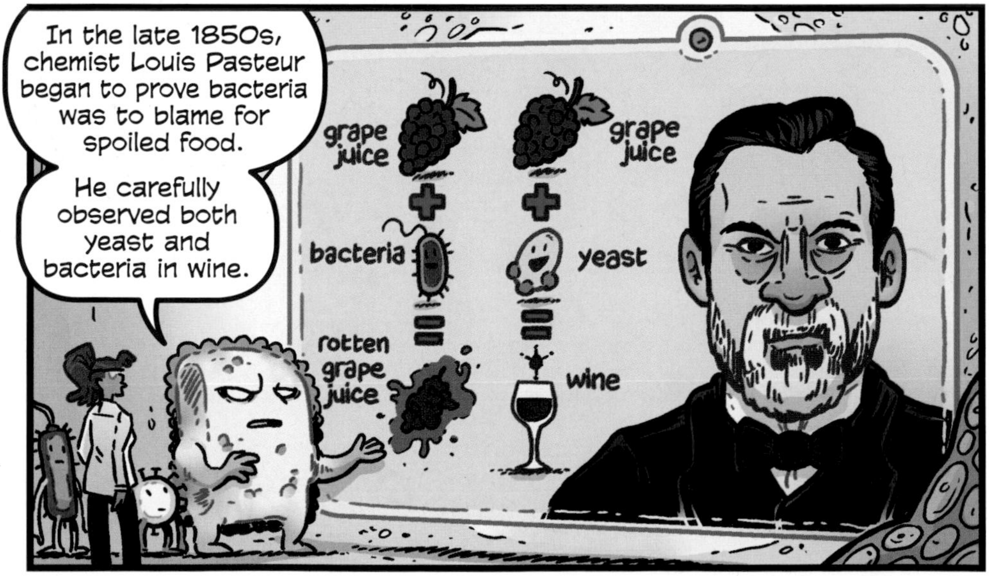
In the late 1850s, chemist Louis Pasteur began to prove bacteria was to blame for spoiled food.
He carefully observed both yeast and bacteria in wine.
grape juice
grape juice
bacteria
yeast
rotten grape juice
wine

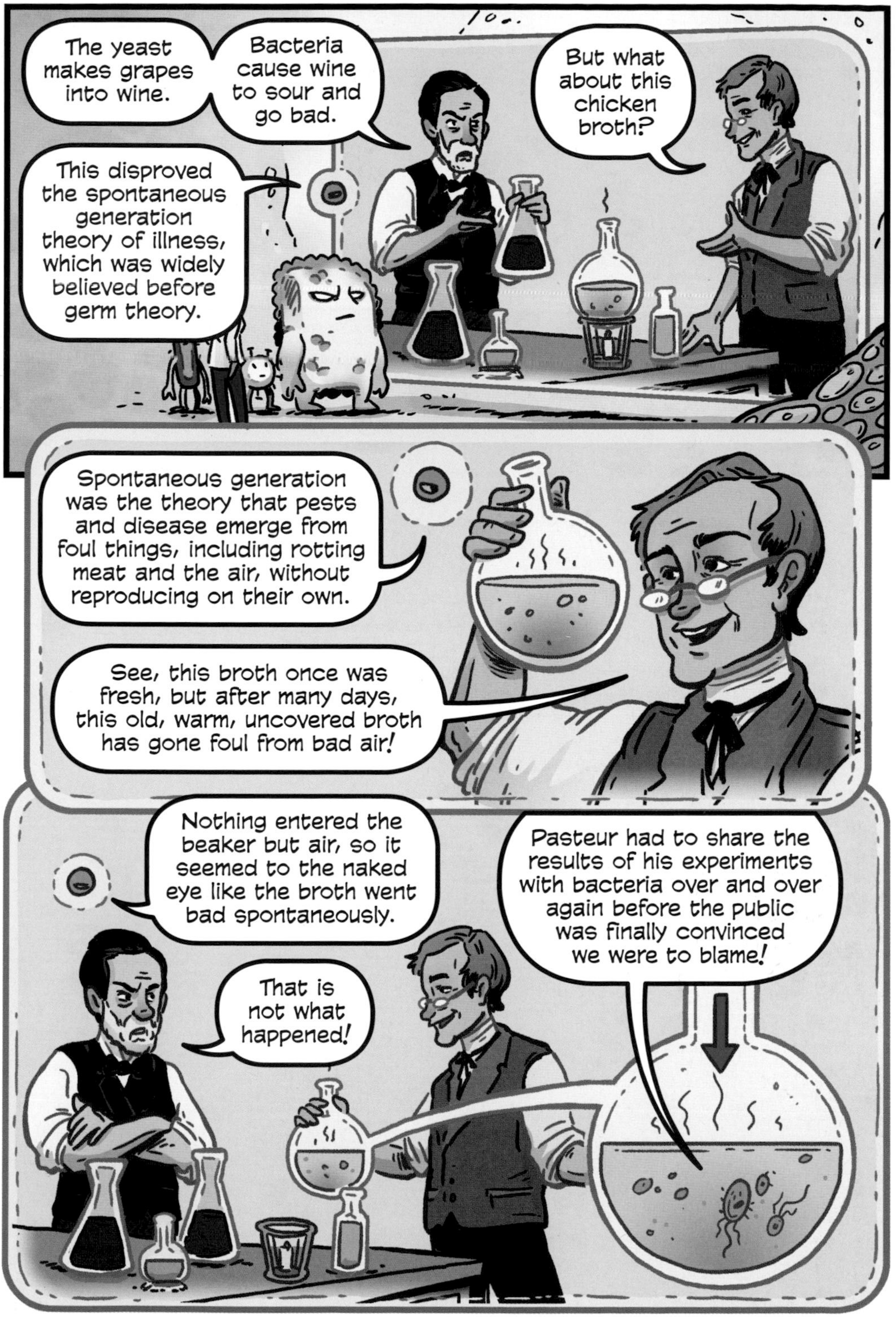
The yeast makes grapes into wine.
Bacteria cause wine to sour and go bad.
But what about this chicken broth?
This disproved the spontaneous generation theory of illness, which was widely believed before germ theory.
Spontaneous generation was the theory that pests and disease emerge from foul things, including rotting meat and the air, without reproducing on their own.
See, this broth once was fresh, but after many days, this old, warm, uncovered broth has gone foul from bad air!
Nothing entered the beaker but air, so it seemed to the naked eye like the broth went bad spontaneously.
That is not what happened!
Pasteur had to share the results of his experiments with bacteria over and over again before the public was finally convinced we were to blame!

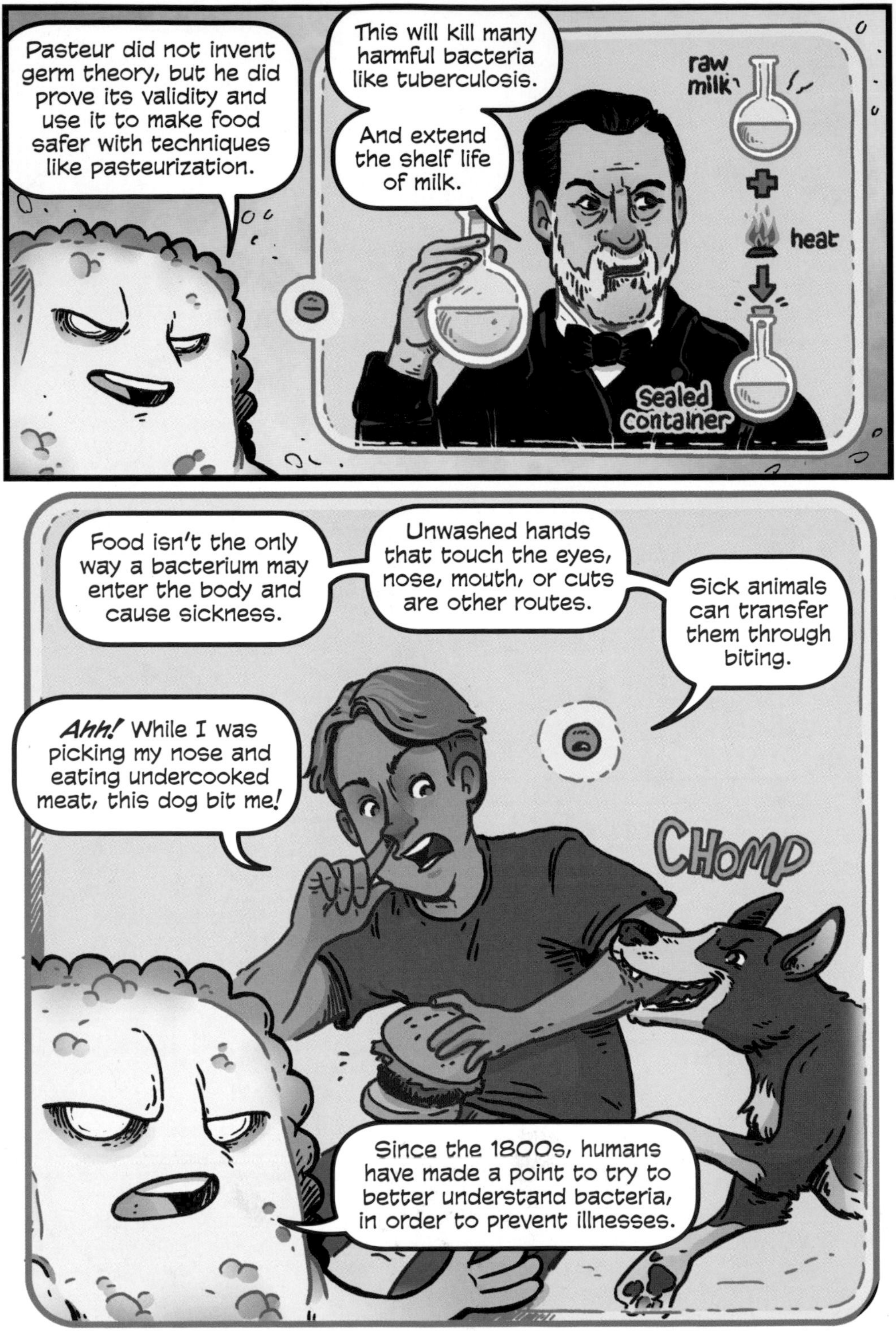

Pasteur did not invent germ theory, but he did prove its validity and use it to make food safer with techniques like pasteurization.
This will kill many harmful bacteria like tuberculosis.
And extend the shelf life of milk.
raw milk
heat
sealed container
Food isn't the only way a bacterium may enter the body and cause sickness.
Unwashed hands that touch the eyes, nose, mouth, or cuts are other routes.
Sick animals can transfer them through biting.
Ahh! While I was picking my nose and eating undercooked meat, this dog bit me!
CHOMP
Since the 1800s, humans have made a point to try to better understand bacteria, in order to prevent illnesses.

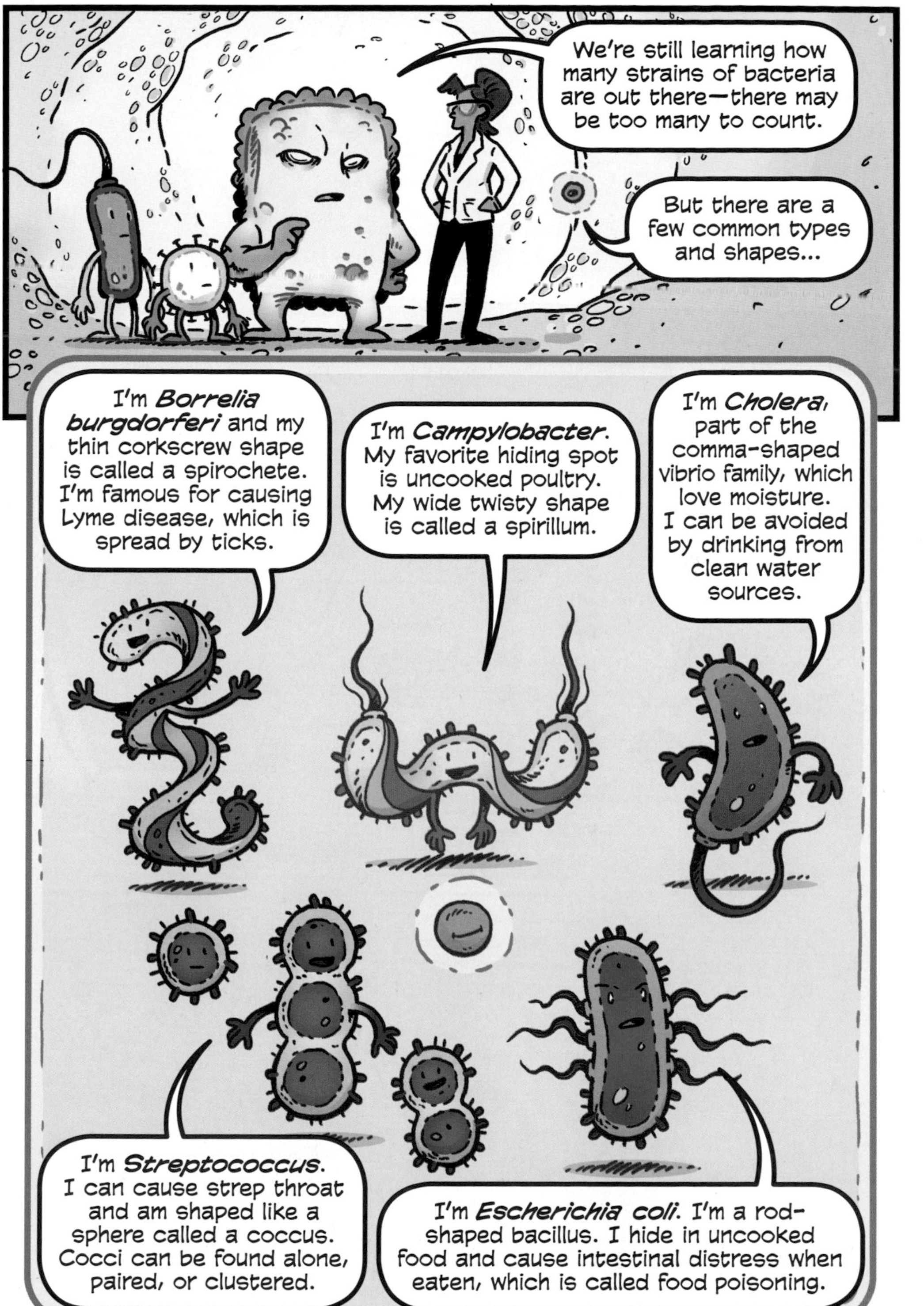

We're still learning how many strains of bacteria are out there—there may be too many to count.
But there are a few common types and shapes...
I'm *Borrelia burgdorferi* and my thin corkscrew shape is called a spirochete. I'm famous for causing Lyme disease, which is spread by ticks.
I'm *Campylobacter*. My favorite hiding spot is uncooked poultry. My wide twisty shape is called a spirillum.
I'm *Cholera*, part of the comma-shaped vibrio family, which love moisture. I can be avoided by drinking from clean water sources.
I'm *Streptococcus*. I can cause strep throat and am shaped like a sphere called a coccus. Cocci can be found alone, paired, or clustered.
I'm *Escherichia coli*. I'm a rod-shaped bacillus. I hide in uncooked food and cause intestinal distress when eaten, which is called food poisoning.

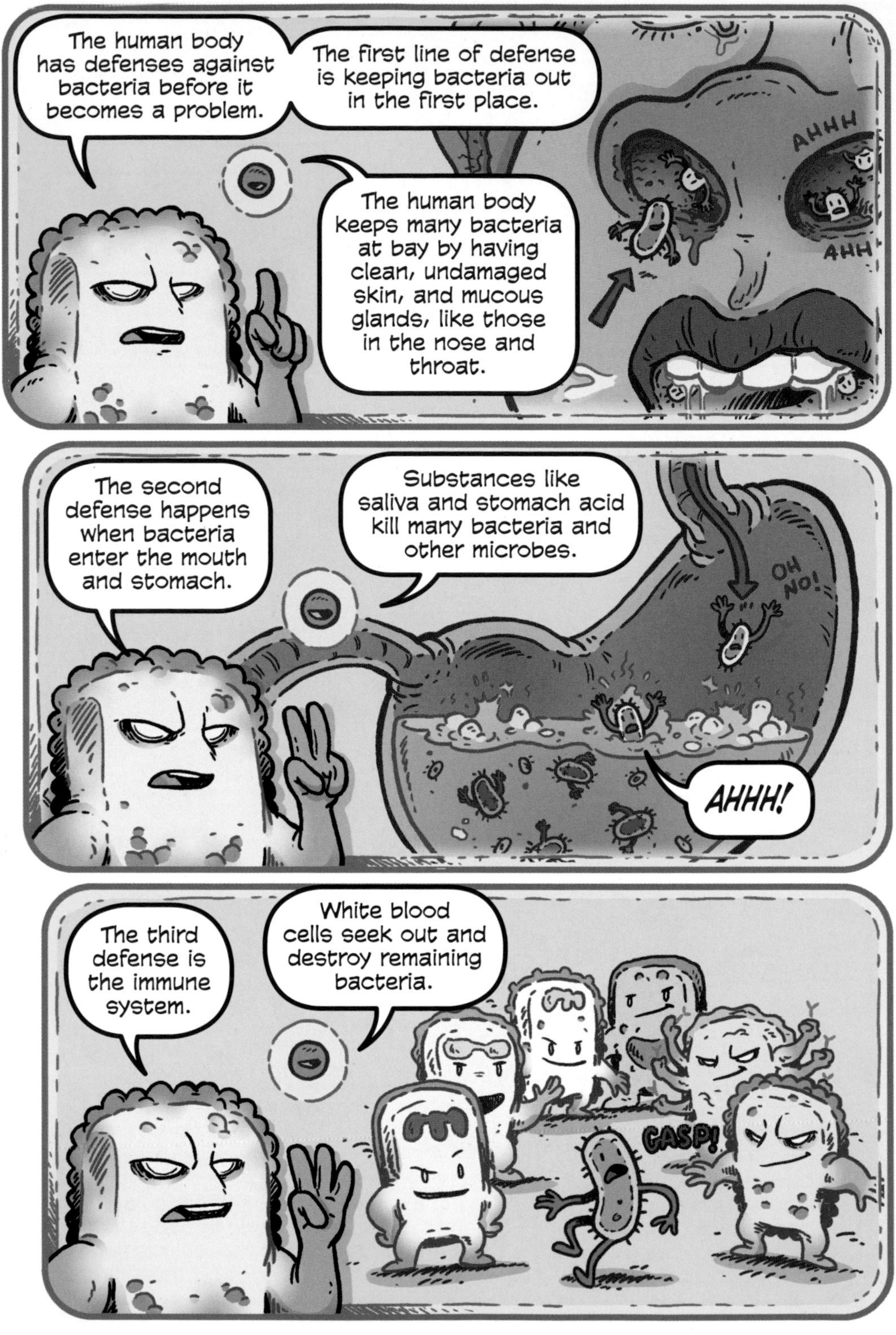

The human body has defenses against bacteria before it becomes a problem.
The first line of defense is keeping bacteria out in the first place.
The human body keeps many bacteria at bay by having clean, undamaged skin, and mucous glands, like those in the nose and throat.
AHHH
AHH
The second defense happens when bacteria enter the mouth and stomach.
Substances like saliva and stomach acid kill many bacteria and other microbes.
OH NO!
AHHH!
The third defense is the immune system.
White blood cells seek out and destroy remaining bacteria.
GASP!

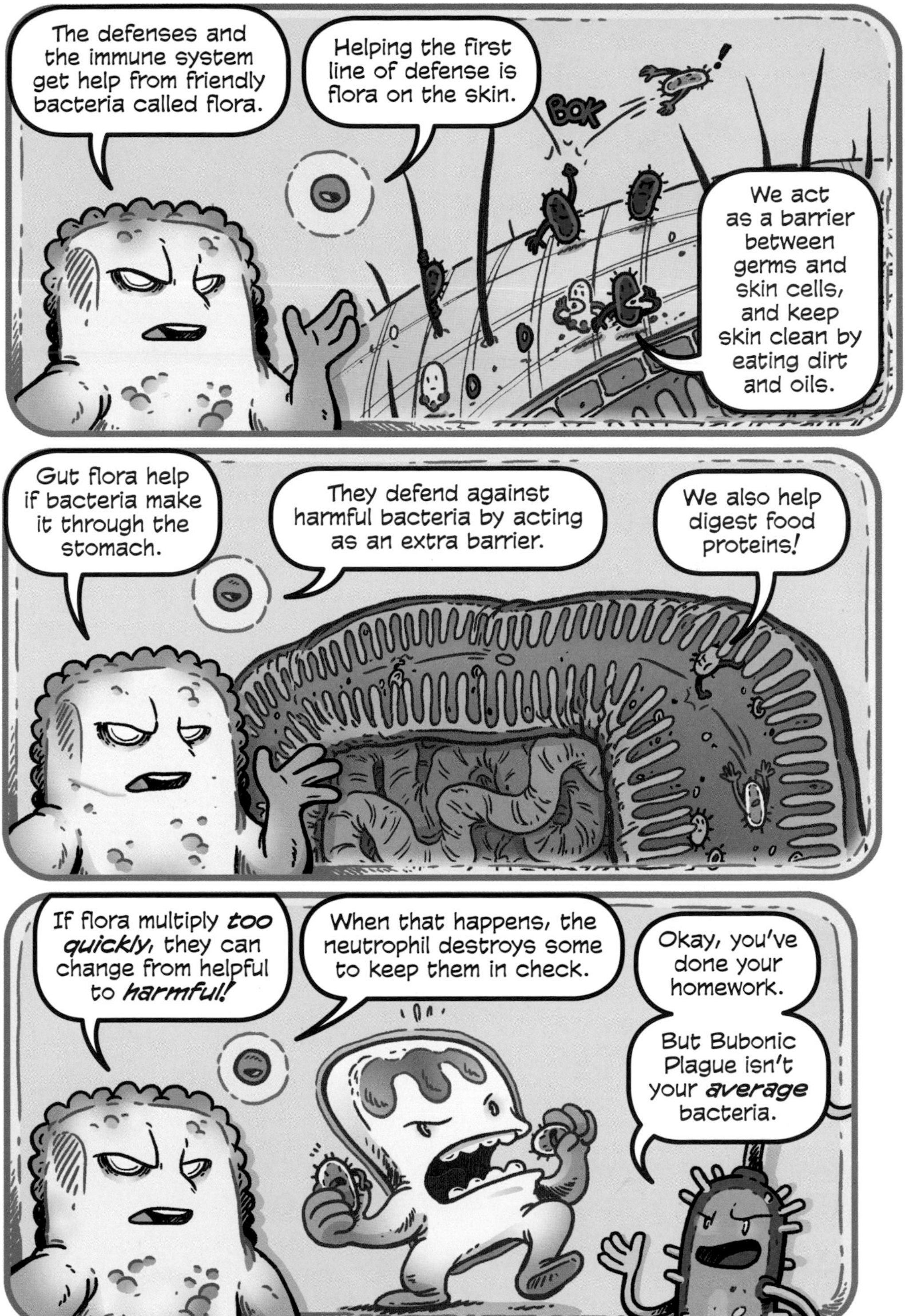

The defenses and the immune system get help from friendly bacteria called flora.
Helping the first line of defense is flora on the skin.
BOK
We act as a barrier between germs and skin cells, and keep skin clean by eating dirt and oils.
Gut flora help if bacteria make it through the stomach.
They defend against harmful bacteria by acting as an extra barrier.
We also help digest food proteins!
If flora multiply *too quickly*, they can change from helpful to *harmful!*
When that happens, the neutrophil destroys some to keep them in check.
Okay, you've done your homework.
But Bubonic Plague isn't your *average* bacteria.

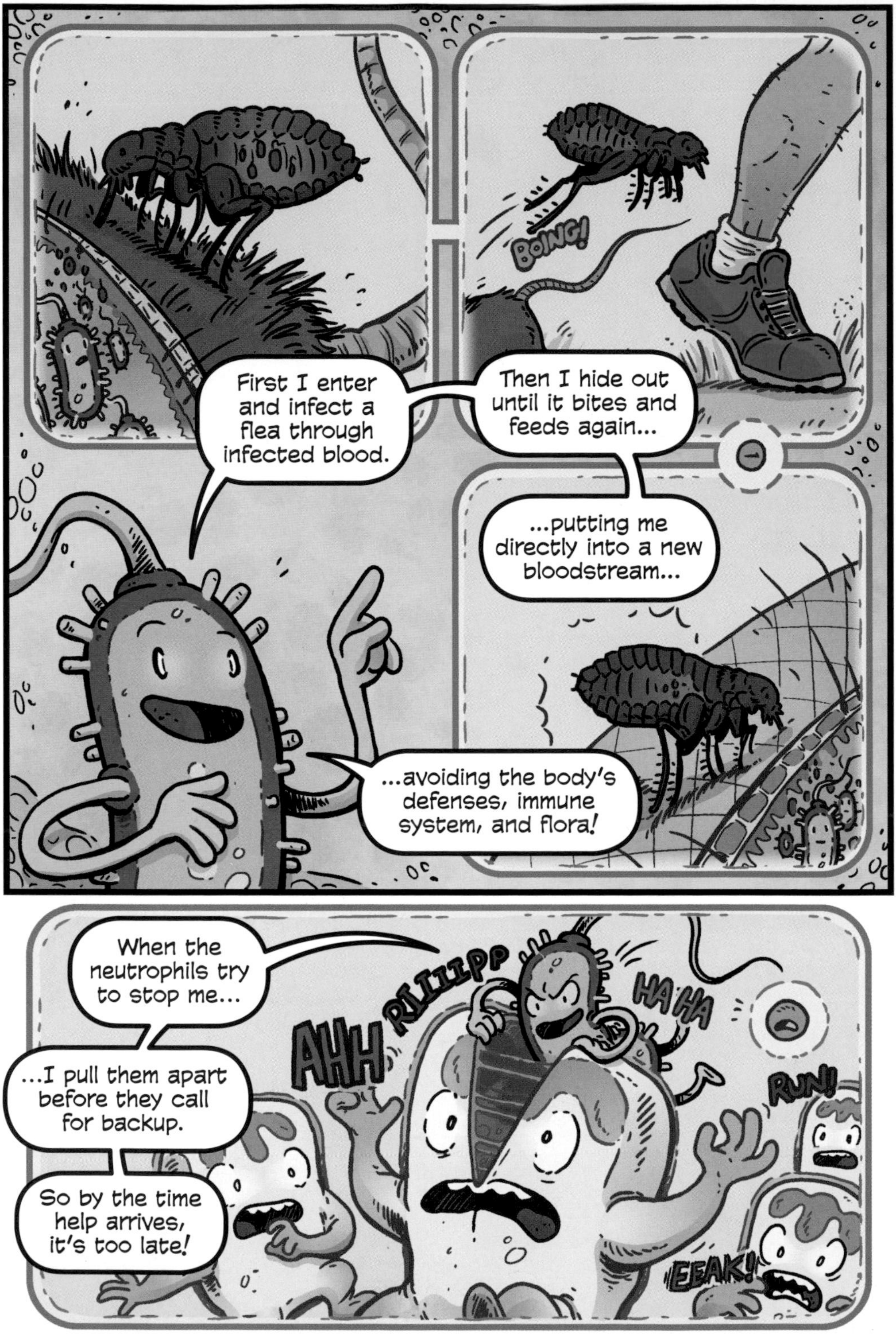
BOING!
First I enter and infect a flea through infected blood.
Then I hide out until it bites and feeds again...
...putting me directly into a new bloodstream...
...avoiding the body's defenses, immune system, and flora!
When the neutrophils try to stop me...
RIIIIPP
HA HA
AHH
...I pull them apart before they call for backup.
RUN!
So by the time help arrives, it's too late!
EEAK!

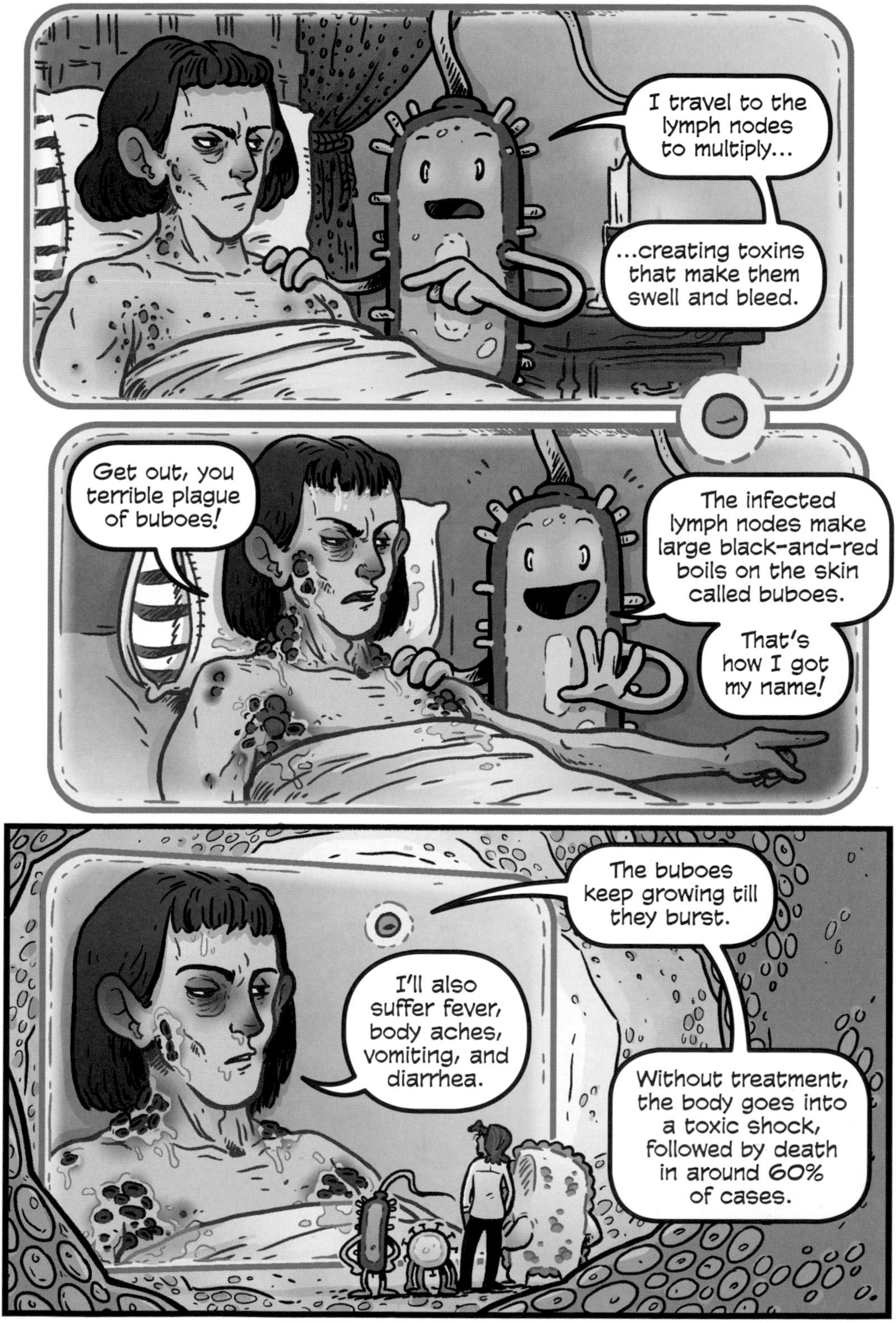
I travel to the lymph nodes to multiply...
...creating toxins that make them swell and bleed.
Get out, you terrible plague of buboes!
The infected lymph nodes make large black-and-red boils on the skin called buboes.
That's how I got my name!
The buboes keep growing till they burst.
I'll also suffer fever, body aches, vomiting, and diarrhea.
Without treatment, the body goes into a toxic shock, followed by death in around 60% of cases.

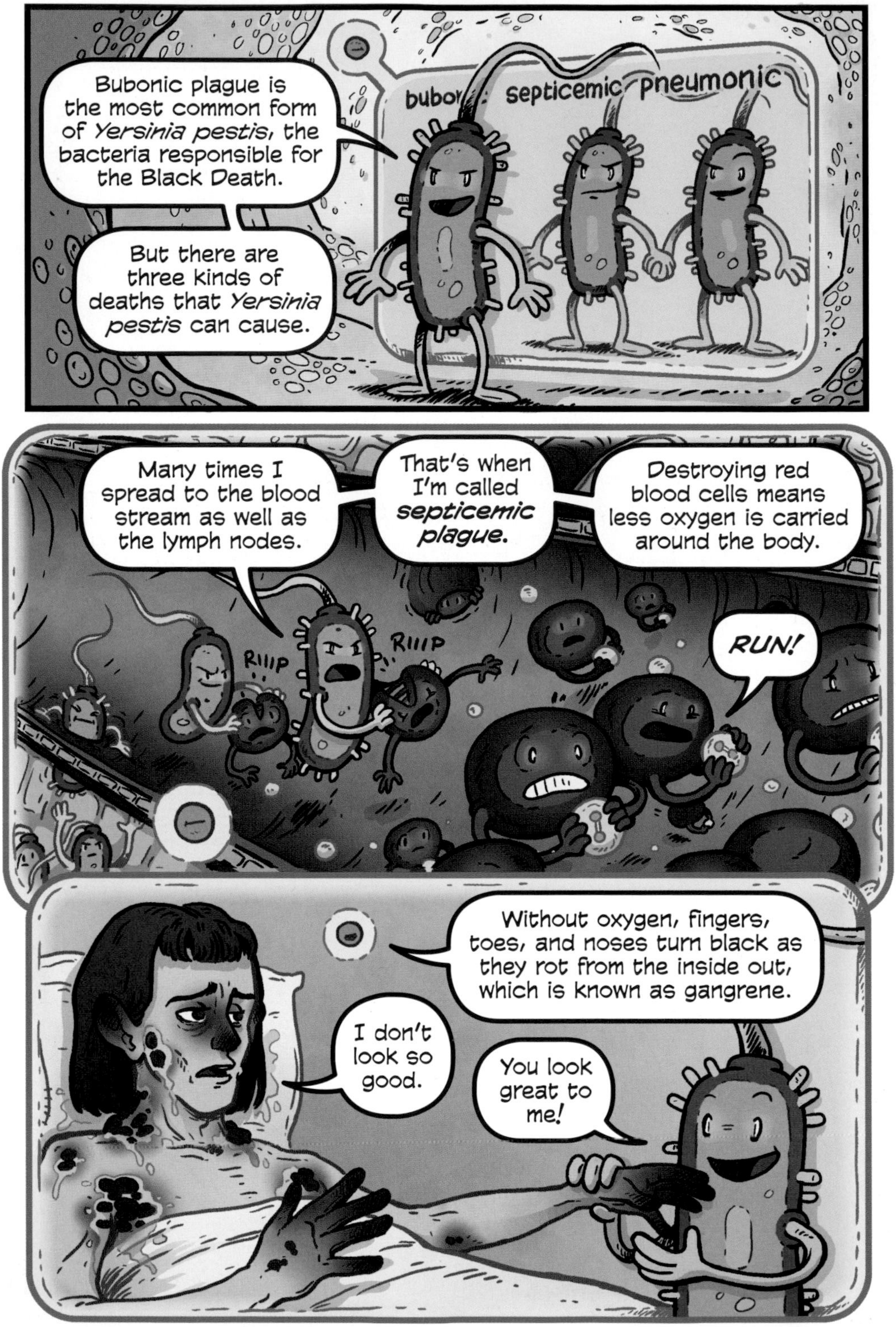
Bubonic plague is the most common form of *Yersinia pestis*, the bacteria responsible for the Black Death.
But there are three kinds of deaths that *Yersinia pestis* can cause.
bubo
septicemic
pneumonic
Many times I spread to the blood stream as well as the lymph nodes.
That's when I'm called ***septicemic plague.***
Destroying red blood cells means less oxygen is carried around the body.
RIIIP
RIIIP
RUN!
Without oxygen, fingers, toes, and noses turn black as they rot from the inside out, which is known as gangrene.
I don't look so good.
You look great to me!

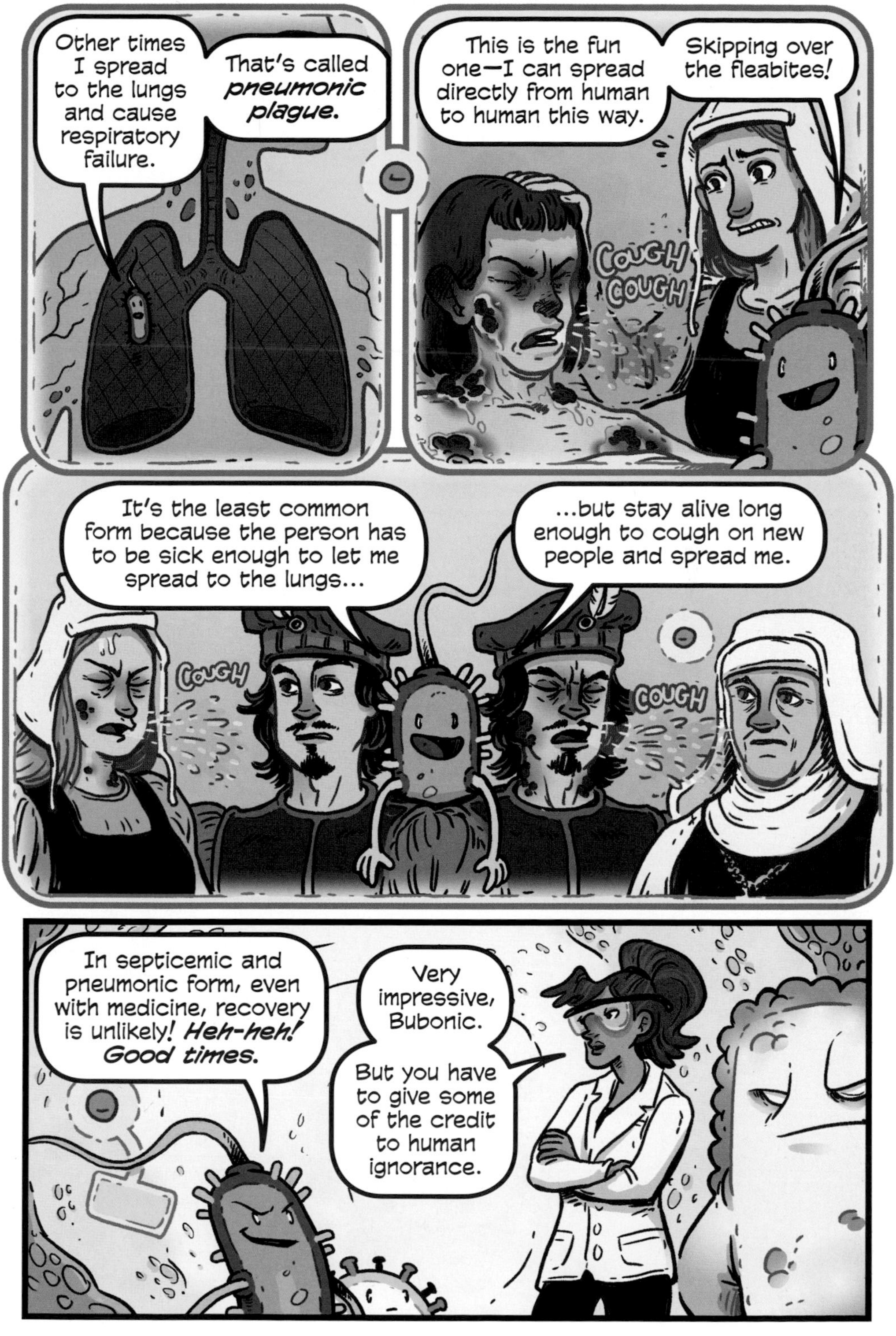
Other times I spread to the lungs and cause respiratory failure.
That's called ***pneumonic plague.***
This is the fun one—I can spread directly from human to human this way.
Skipping over the fleabites!
COUGH COUGH
It's the least common form because the person has to be sick enough to let me spread to the lungs...
...but stay alive long enough to cough on new people and spread me.
COUGH
COUGH
In septicemic and pneumonic form, even with medicine, recovery is unlikely! ***Heh-heh! Good times.***
Very impressive, Bubonic.
But you have to give some of the credit to human ignorance.

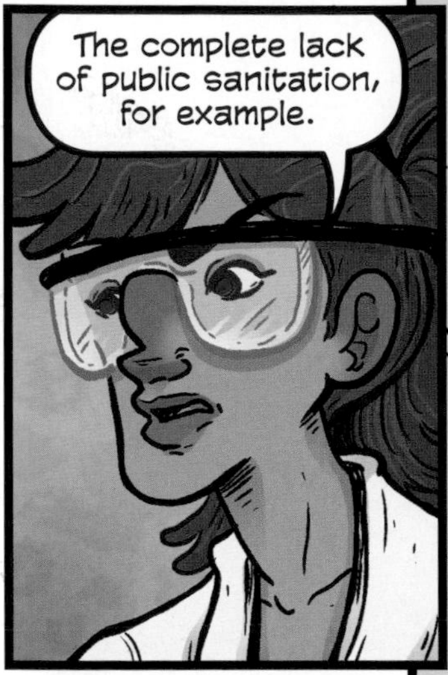
The complete lack of public sanitation, for example.

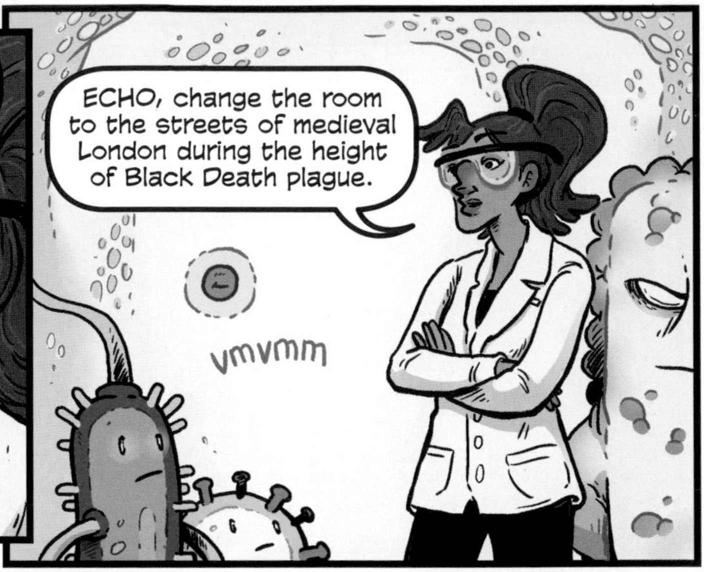
ECHO, change the room to the streets of medieval London during the height of Black Death plague.
vmvmm

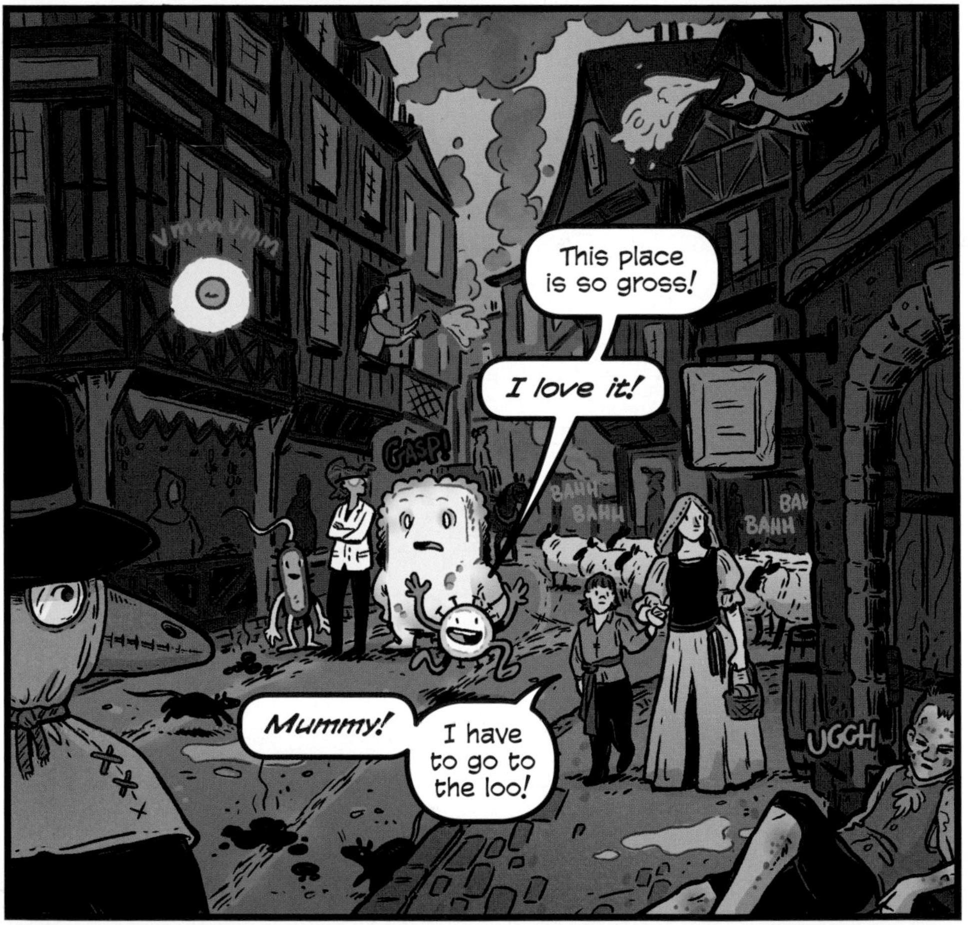
vmvmvmm
This place is so gross!
I love it!
GASP!
BAHH
BAHH
BAHH
Mummy!
I have to go to the loo!
UGGH

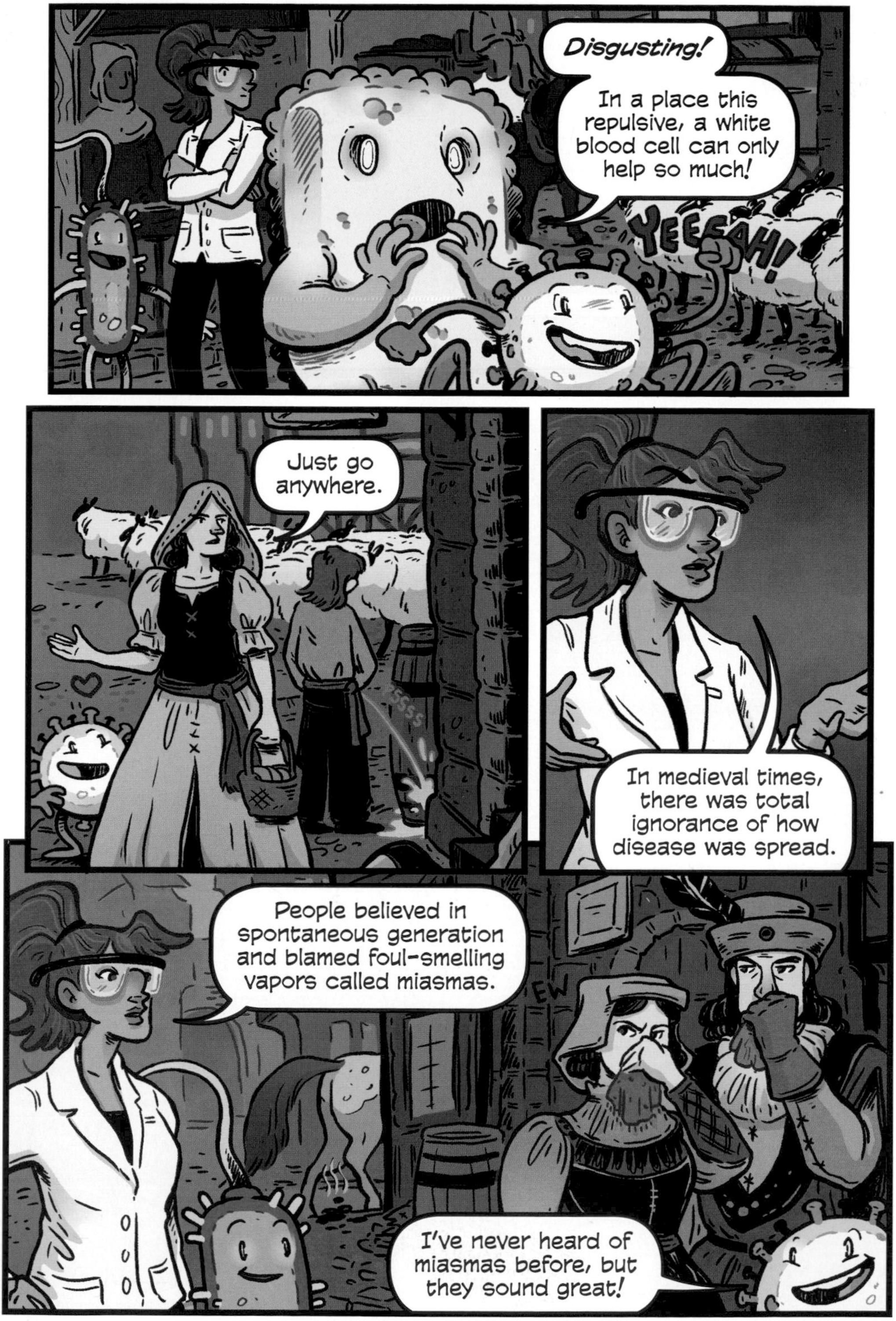
Disgusting!
In a place this repulsive, a white blood cell can only help so much!
YEEEAH!
Just go anywhere.
SSSSS
In medieval times, there was total ignorance of how disease was spread.
People believed in spontaneous generation and blamed foul-smelling vapors called miasmas.
EW
I've never heard of miasmas before, but they sound great!

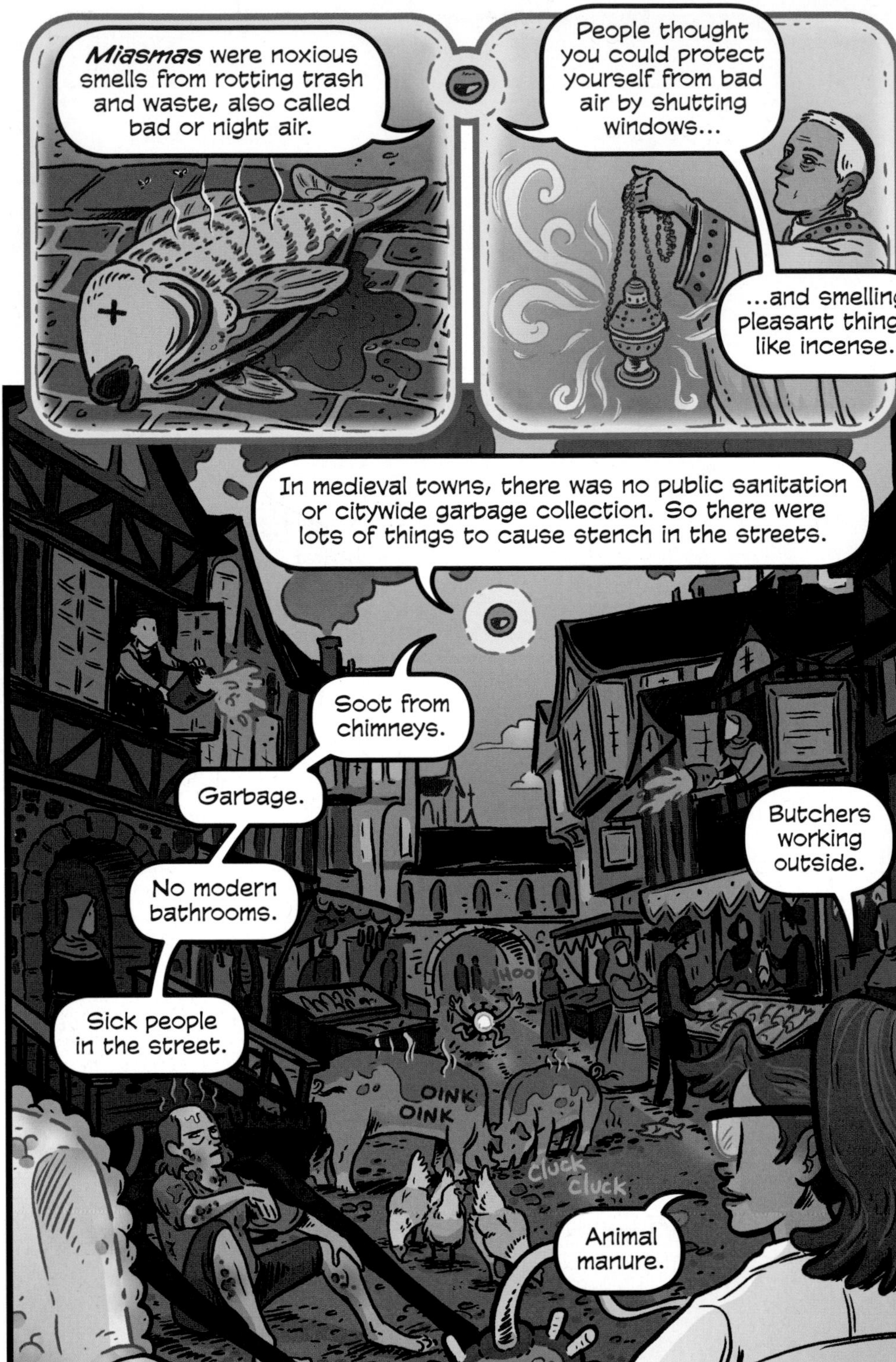
Miasmas were noxious smells from rotting trash and waste, also called bad or night air.
People thought you could protect yourself from bad air by shutting windows...
...and smelling pleasant things like incense.
In medieval towns, there was no public sanitation or citywide garbage collection. So there were lots of things to cause stench in the streets.
Soot from chimneys.
Garbage.
No modern bathrooms.
Sick people in the street.
Butchers working outside.
OINK OINK
CLUCK CLUCK
Animal manure.

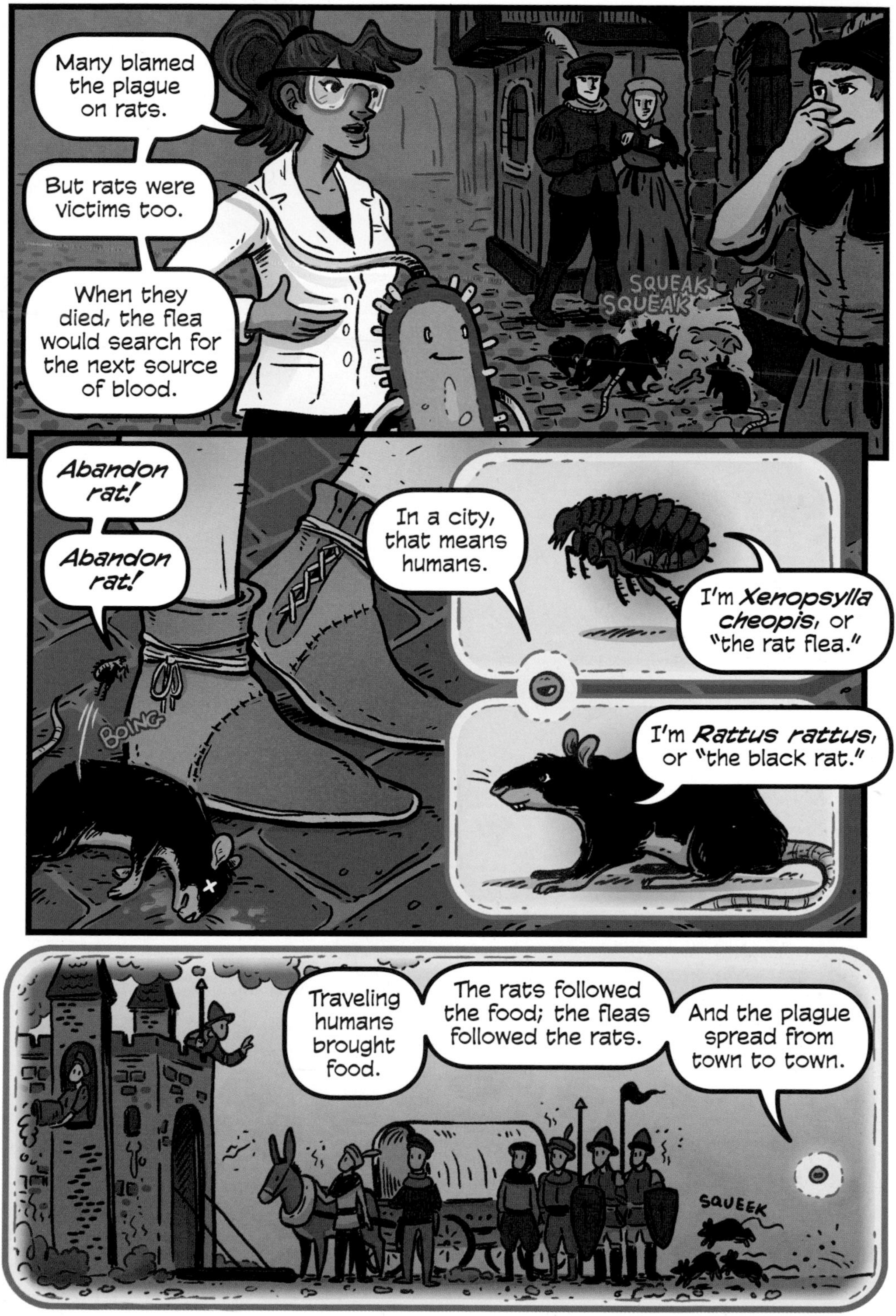
Many blamed the plague on rats.
But rats were victims too.
When they died, the flea would search for the next source of blood.
SQUEAK SQUEAK
Abandon rat!
Abandon rat!
BOING
In a city, that means humans.
I'm *Xenopsylla cheopis*, or "the rat flea."
I'm *Rattus rattus*, or "the black rat."
Traveling humans brought food.
The rats followed the food; the fleas followed the rats.
And the plague spread from town to town.
SQUEEK

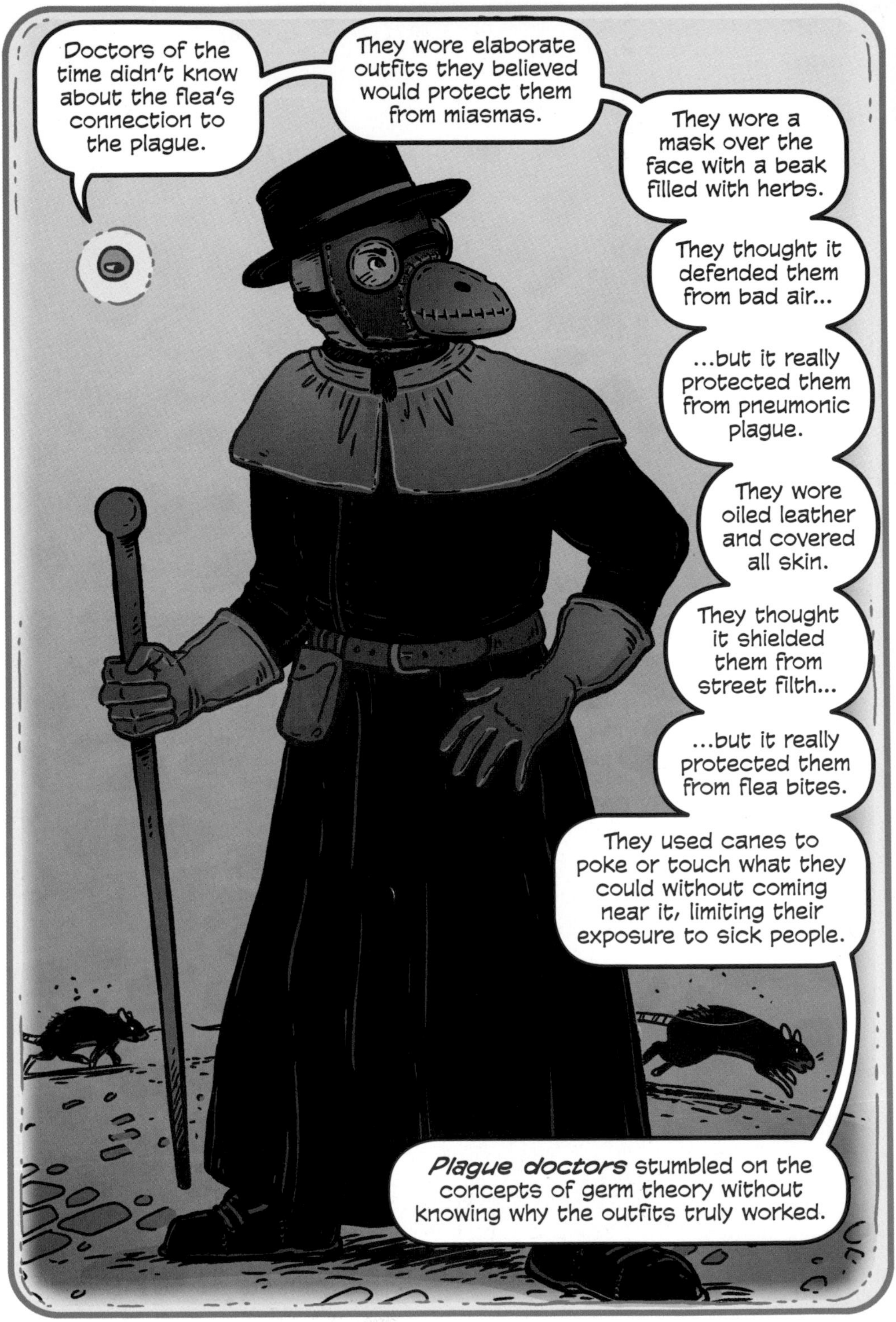

Doctors of the time didn't know about the flea's connection to the plague.
They wore elaborate outfits they believed would protect them from miasmas.
They wore a mask over the face with a beak filled with herbs.
They thought it defended them from bad air...
...but it really protected them from pneumonic plague.
They wore oiled leather and covered all skin.
They thought it shielded them from street filth...
...but it really protected them from flea bites.
They used canes to poke or touch what they could without coming near it, limiting their exposure to sick people.
Plague doctors stumbled on the concepts of germ theory without knowing why the outfits truly worked.

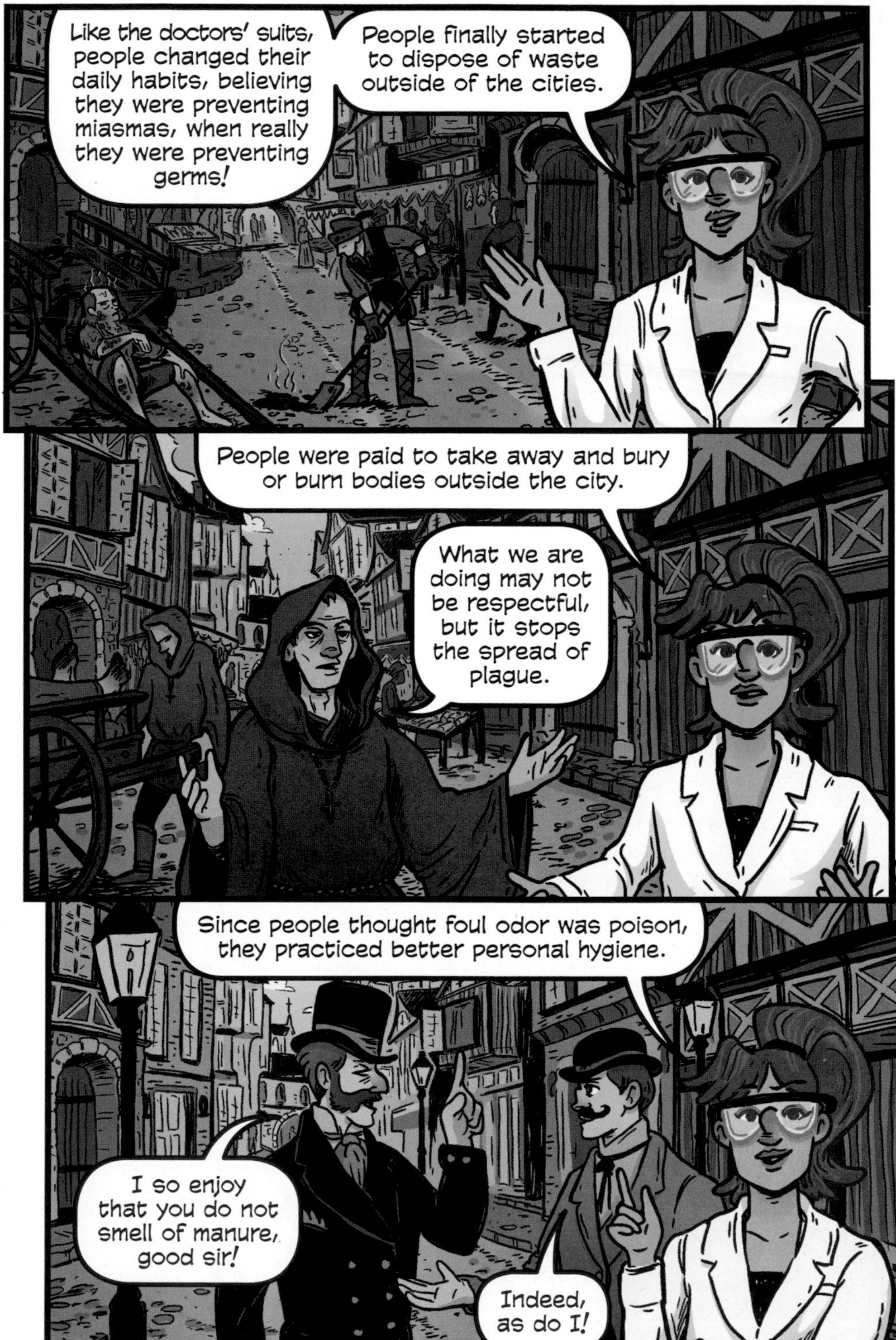
Like the doctors' suits, people changed their daily habits, believing they were preventing miasmas, when really they were preventing germs!
People finally started to dispose of waste outside of the cities.
People were paid to take away and bury or burn bodies outside the city.
What we are doing may not be respectful, but it stops the spread of plague.
Since people thought foul odor was poison, they practiced better personal hygiene.
I so enjoy that you do not smell of manure, good sir!
Indeed, as do I!

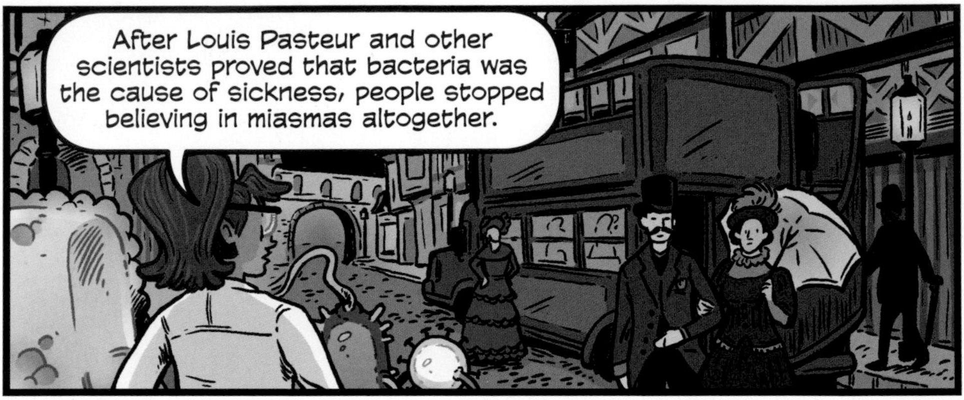
After Louis Pasteur and other scientists proved that bacteria was the cause of sickness, people stopped believing in miasmas altogether.

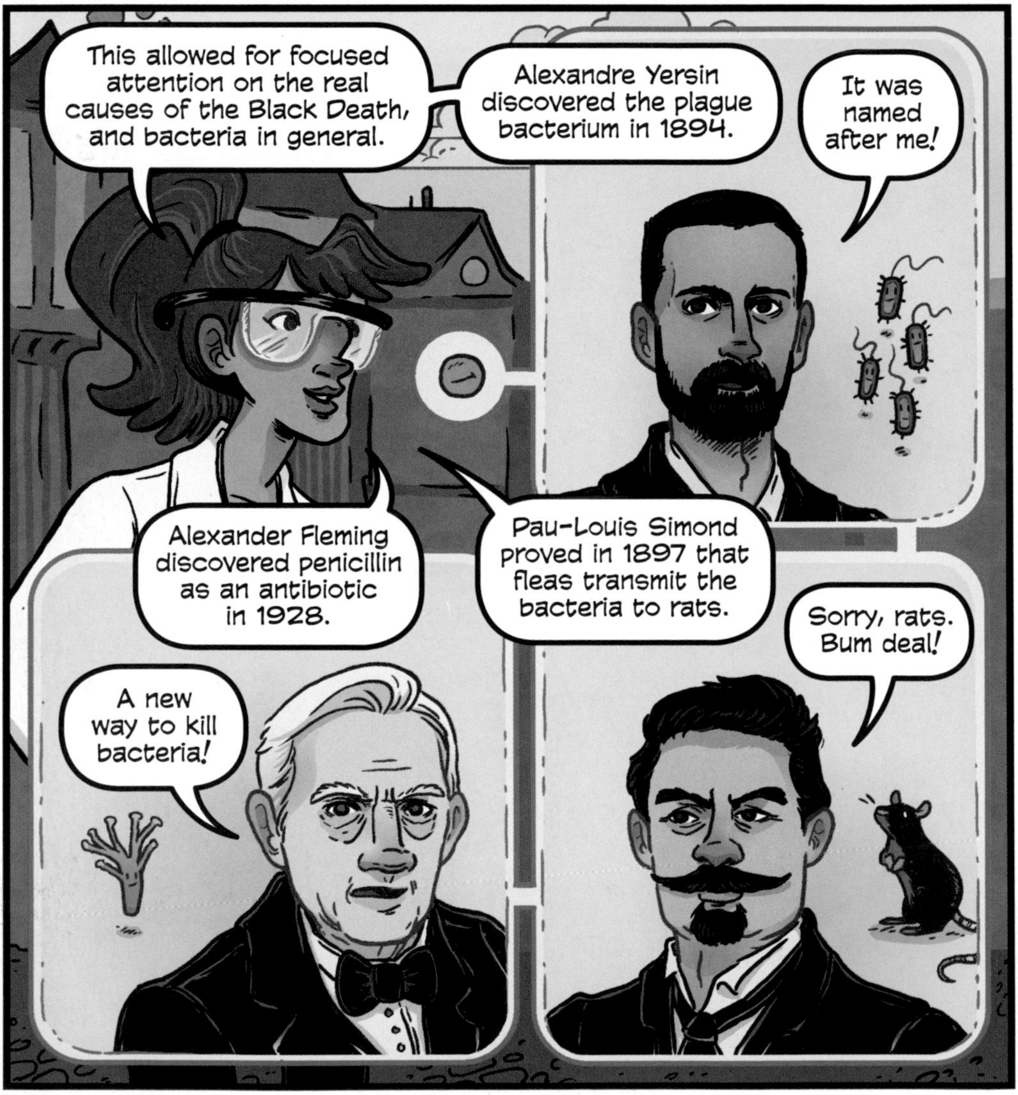
This allowed for focused attention on the real causes of the Black Death, and bacteria in general.
Alexandre Yersin discovered the plague bacterium in 1894.
It was named after me!
Alexander Fleming discovered penicillin as an antibiotic in 1928.
Pau-Louis Simond proved in 1897 that fleas transmit the bacteria to rats.
A new way to kill bacteria!
Sorry, rats. Bum deal!

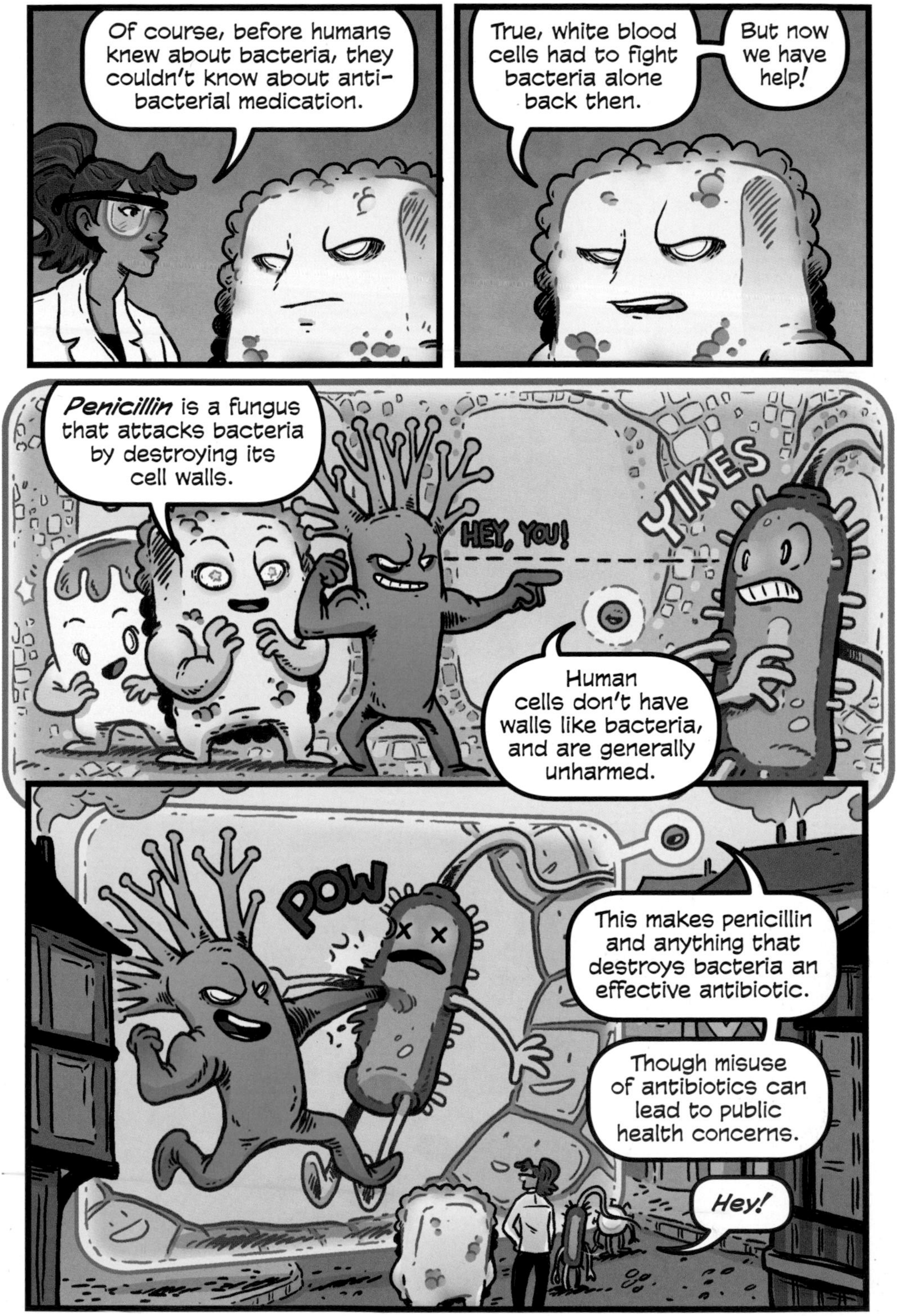

Of course, before humans knew about bacteria, they couldn't know about anti-bacterial medication.
True, white blood cells had to fight bacteria alone back then.
But now we have help!
Penicillin is a fungus that attacks bacteria by destroying its cell walls.
HEY, YOU!
YIKES
Human cells don't have walls like bacteria, and are generally unharmed.
POW
This makes penicillin and anything that destroys bacteria an effective antibiotic.
Though misuse of antibiotics can lead to public health concerns.
Hey!

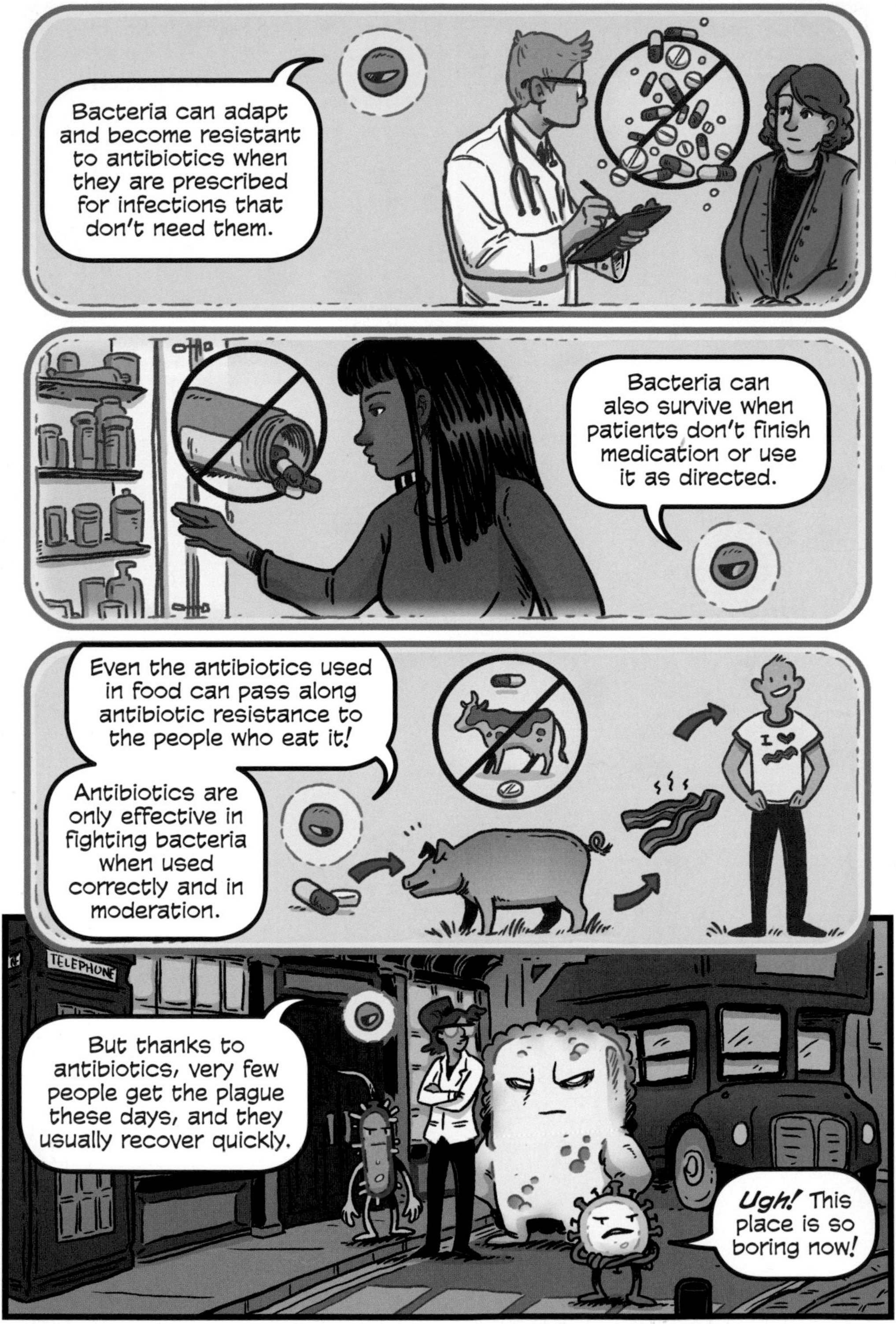
Bacteria can adapt and become resistant to antibiotics when they are prescribed for infections that don't need them.
Bacteria can also survive when patients don't finish medication or use it as directed.
Even the antibiotics used in food can pass along antibiotic resistance to the people who eat it!
Antibiotics are only effective in fighting bacteria when used correctly and in moderation.
TELEPHONE
But thanks to antibiotics, very few people get the plague these days, and they usually recover quickly.
Ugh! This place is so boring now!

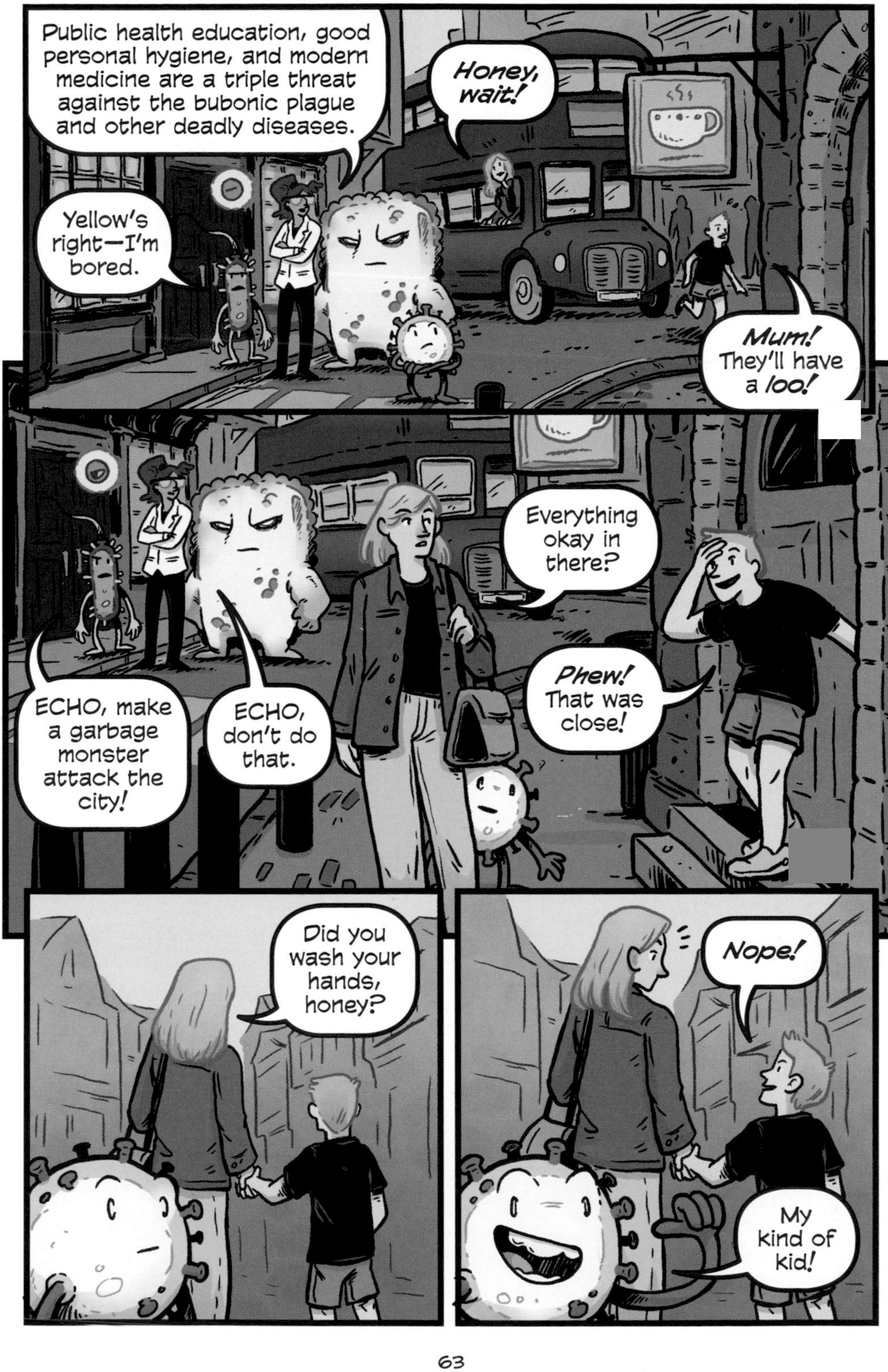
Public health education, good personal hygiene, and modern medicine are a triple threat against the bubonic plague and other deadly diseases.
Honey, wait!
Yellow's right—I'm bored.
Mum! They'll have a loo!
Everything okay in there?
ECHO, make a garbage monster attack the city!
ECHO, don't do that.
Phew! That was close!
Did you wash your hands, honey?
Nope!
My kind of kid!

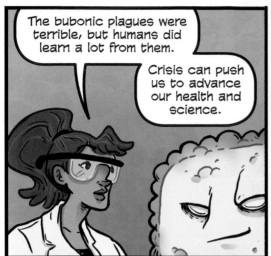

The bubonic plagues were terrible, but humans did learn a lot from them.

Crisis can push us to advance our health and science.

All *I'm* hearing is that without *ME*...

...you'd still be pooping on the street and blaming the flu on fart smells!

You may have come a long way, but you'll never get rid of me completely.

Because of that critter right there!

Hi, there!

BOOP

SQUEAK

Hey!

Vmm Vmm Vmm Vmm Vmm SQUEAK!

Ah yes, vectors.

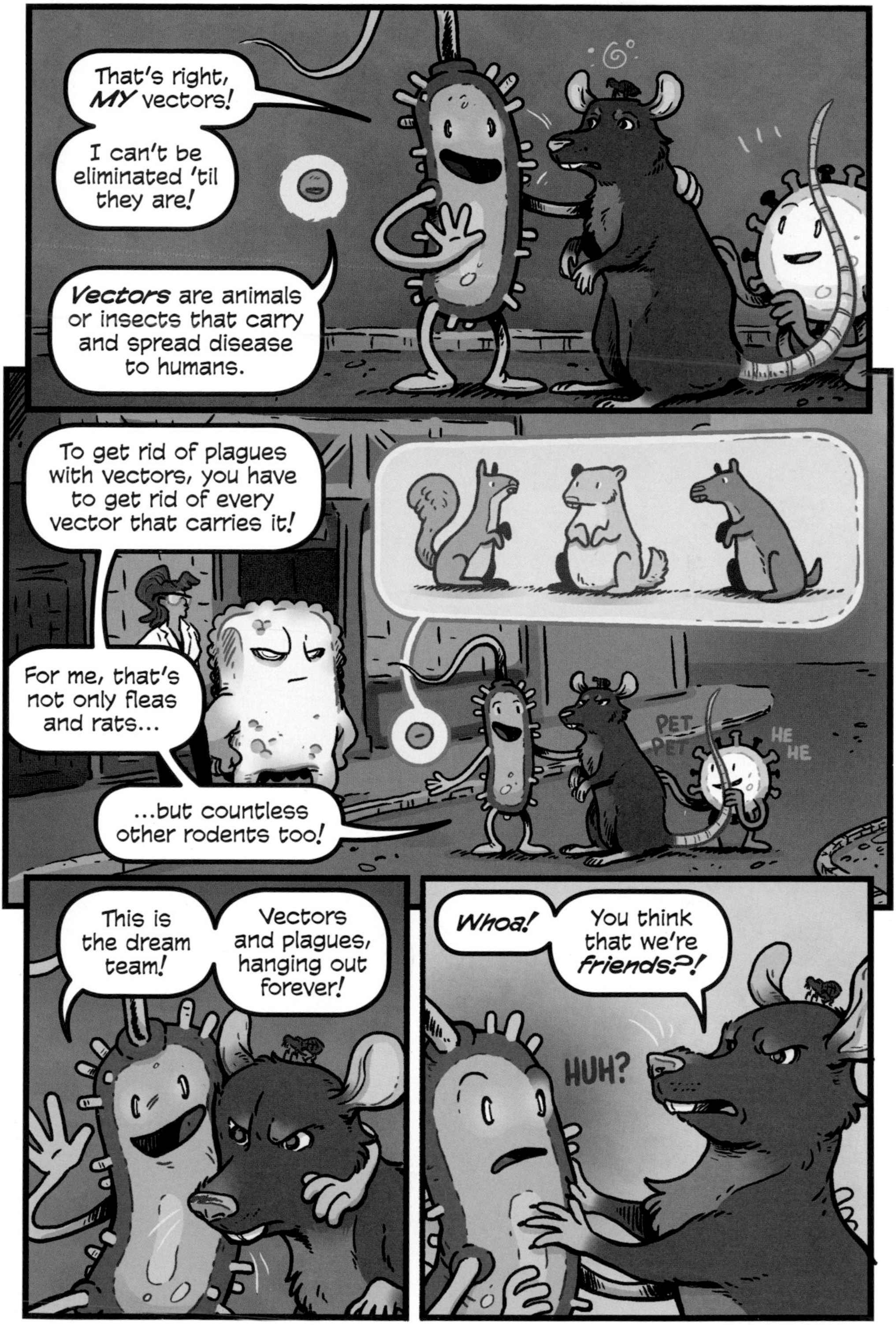
That's right, MY vectors!
I can't be eliminated 'til they are!
Vectors are animals or insects that carry and spread disease to humans.
To get rid of plagues with vectors, you have to get rid of every vector that carries it!
For me, that's not only fleas and rats...
...but countless other rodents too!
PET PET
HE HE
This is the dream team!
Vectors and plagues, hanging out forever!
Whoa!
You think that we're friends?!
HUH?

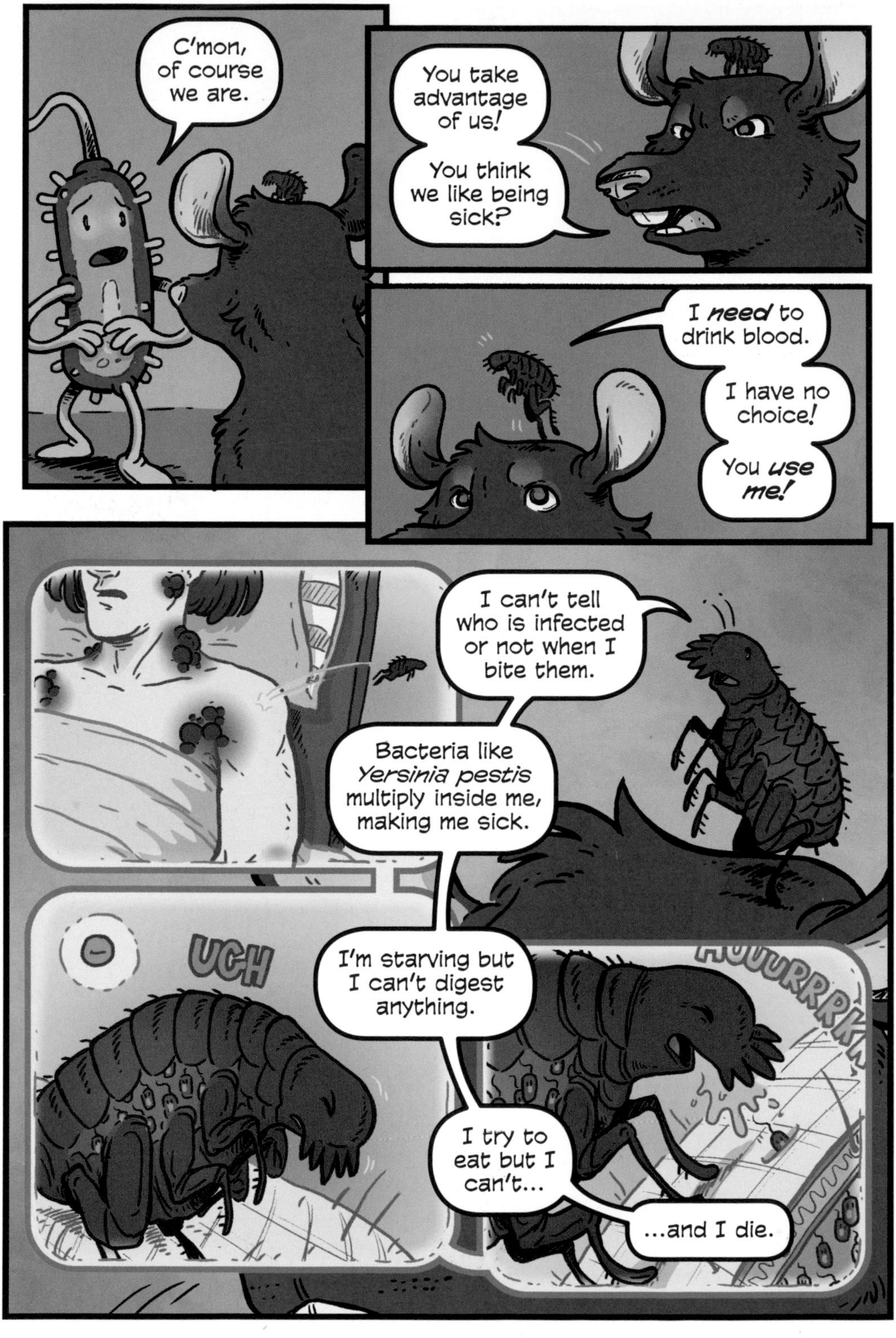

C'mon, of course we are.
You take advantage of us!
You think we like being sick?
I *need* to drink blood.
I have no choice!
You *use me!*
I can't tell who is infected or not when I bite them.
Bacteria like *Yersinia pestis* multiply inside me, making me sick.
UCH
I'm starving but I can't digest anything.
HUUURRRK
I try to eat but I can't...
...and I die.

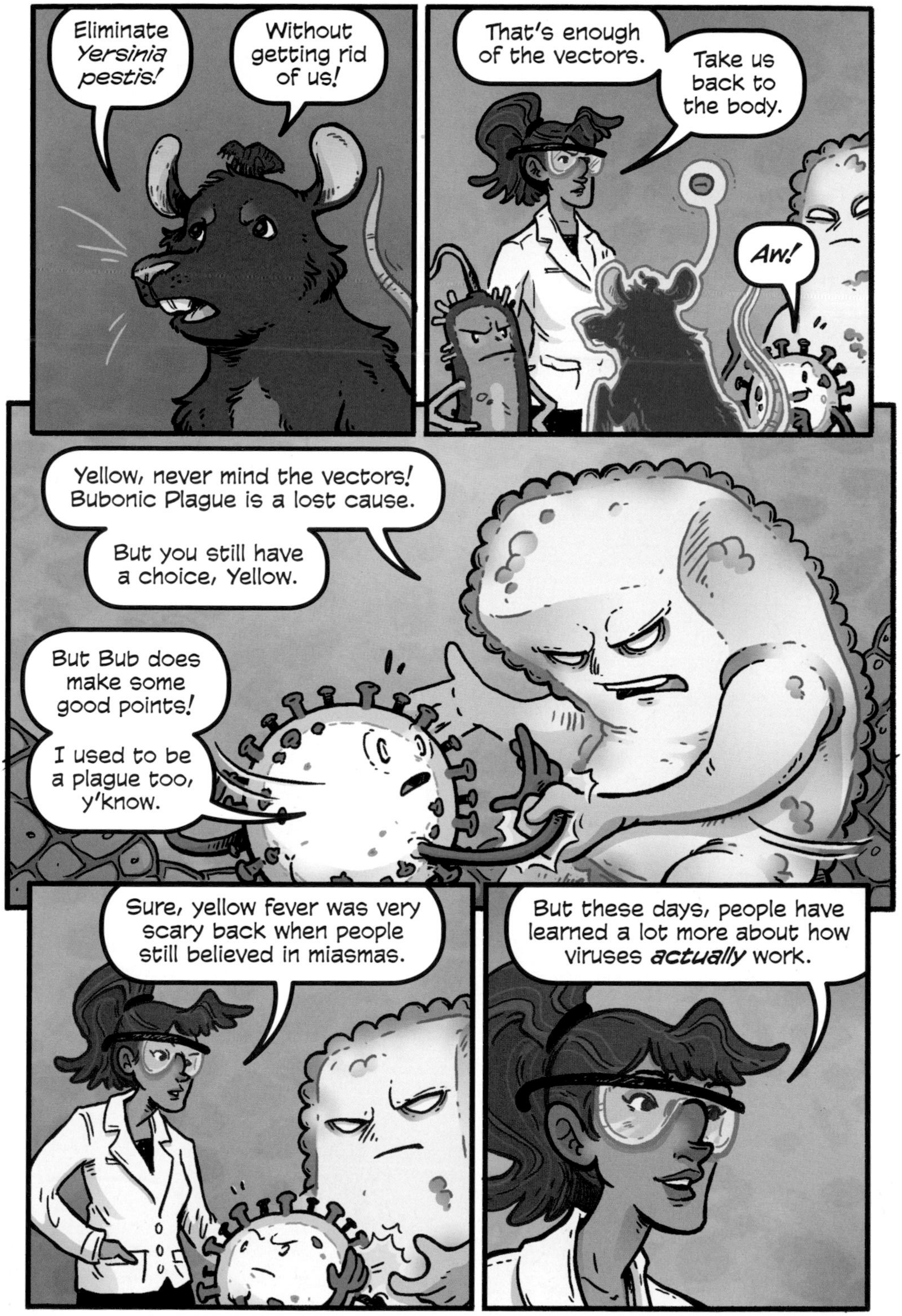
Eliminate *Yersinia pestis!*
Without getting rid of us!
That's enough of the vectors.
Take us back to the body.
Aw!
Yellow, never mind the vectors! Bubonic Plague is a lost cause.
But you still have a choice, Yellow.
But Bub does make some good points!
I used to be a plague too, y'know.
Sure, yellow fever was very scary back when people still believed in miasmas.
But these days, people have learned a lot more about how viruses ***actually*** work.

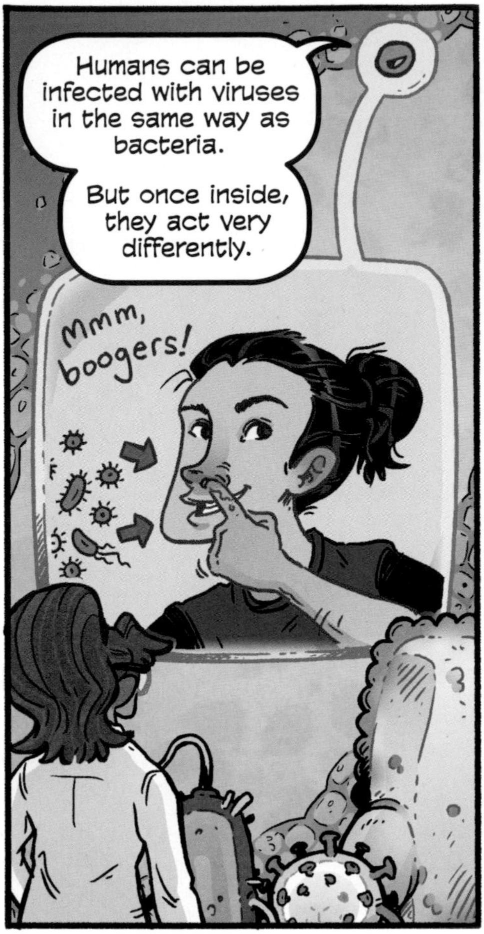
Humans can be infected with viruses in the same way as bacteria.
But once inside, they act very differently.
Mmm, boogers!

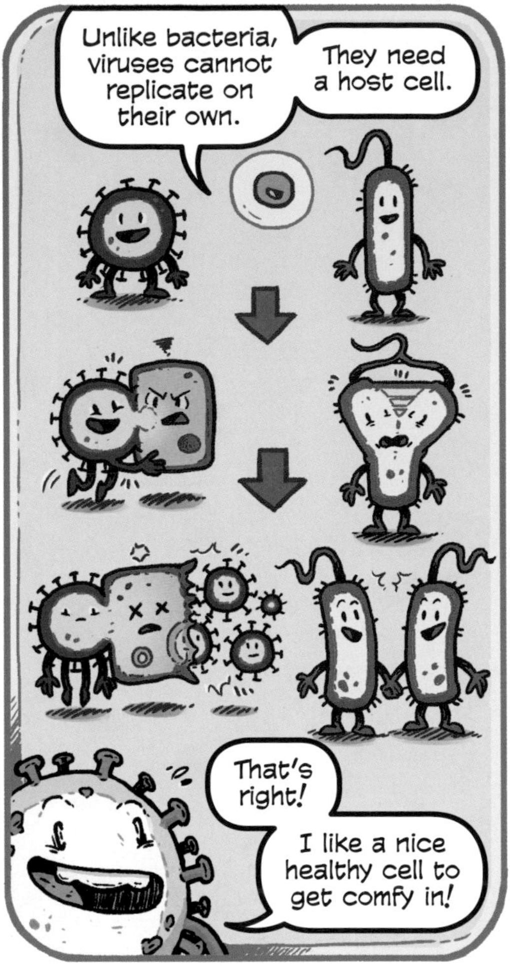
Unlike bacteria, viruses cannot replicate on their own.
They need a host cell.
That's right!
I like a nice healthy cell to get comfy in!

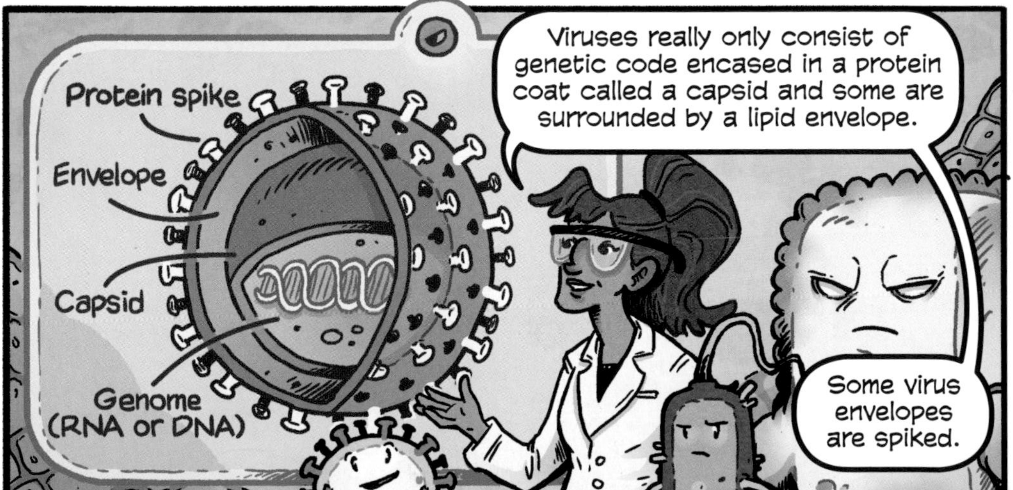
Protein spike
Envelope
Capsid
Genome (RNA or DNA)
Viruses really only consist of genetic code encased in a protein coat called a capsid and some are surrounded by a lipid envelope.
Some virus envelopes are spiked.

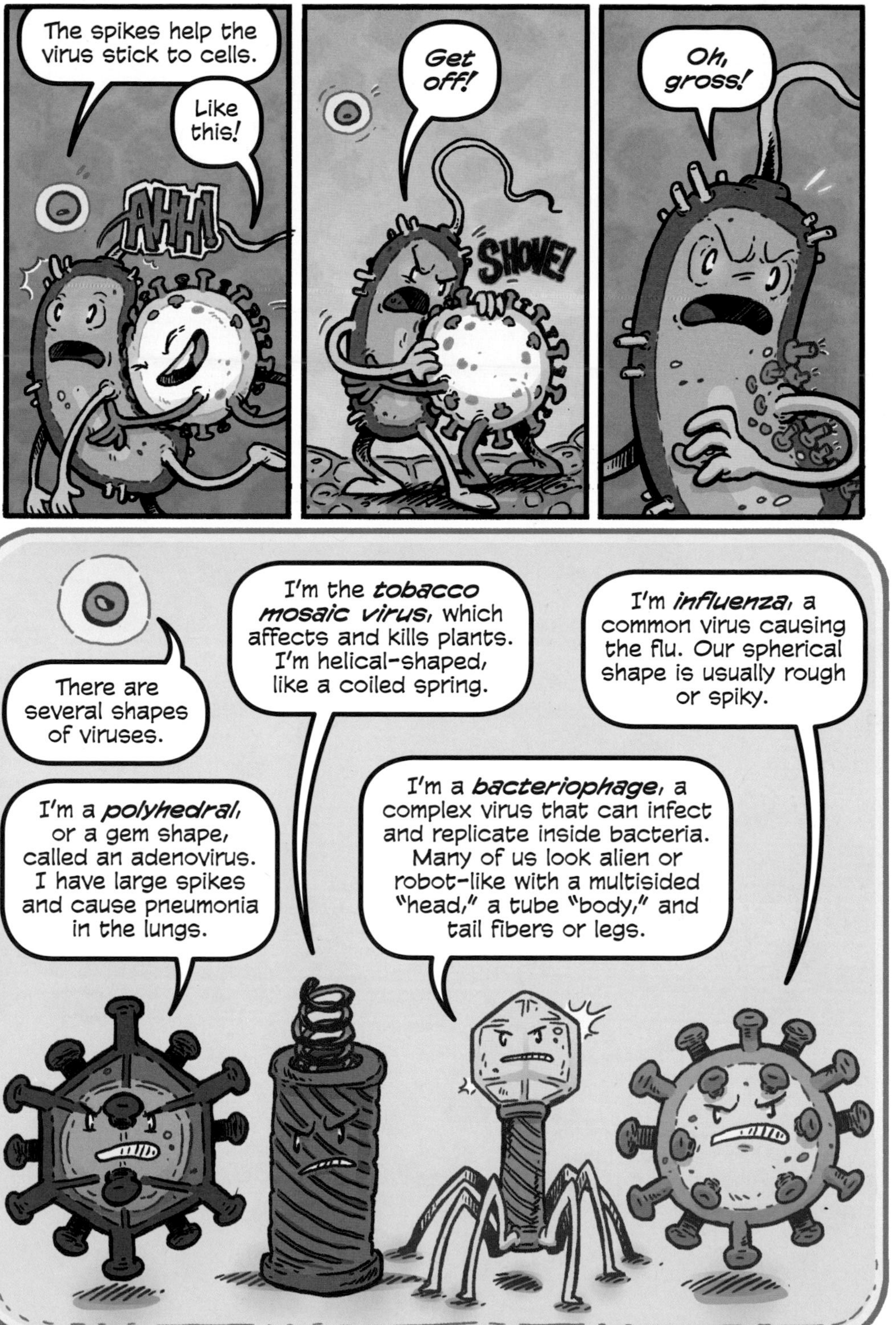

The spikes help the virus stick to cells.
Like this!
AHH!
Get off!
SHOVE!
Oh, gross!
There are several shapes of viruses.
I'm a *polyhedral*, or a gem shape, called an adenovirus. I have large spikes and cause pneumonia in the lungs.
I'm the *tobacco mosaic virus*, which affects and kills plants. I'm helical-shaped, like a coiled spring.
I'm a *bacteriophage*, a complex virus that can infect and replicate inside bacteria. Many of us look alien or robot-like with a multisided "head," a tube "body," and tail fibers or legs.
I'm *influenza*, a common virus causing the flu. Our spherical shape is usually rough or spiky.

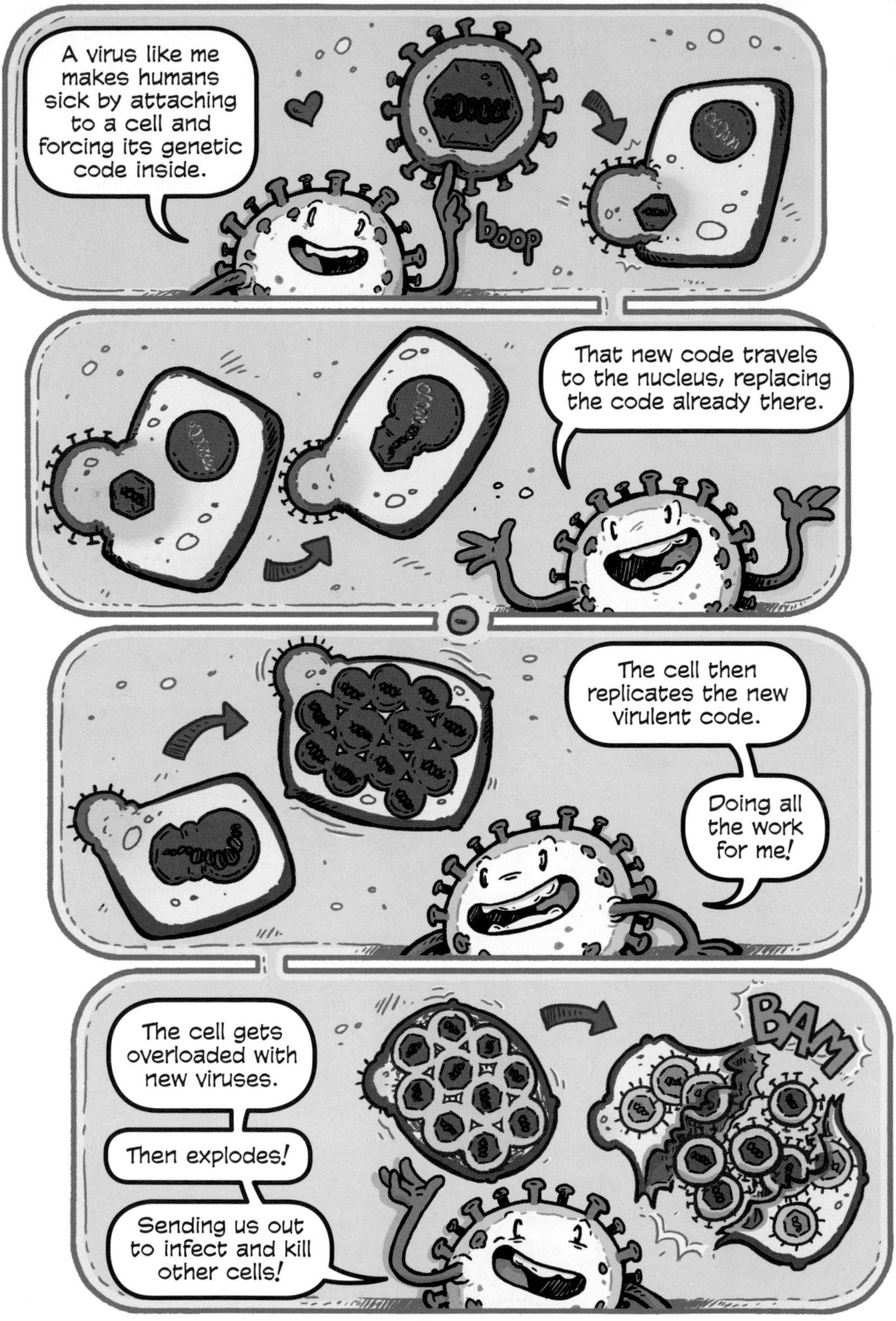
A virus like me makes humans sick by attaching to a cell and forcing its genetic code inside.
boop
That new code travels to the nucleus, replacing the code already there.
The cell then replicates the new virulent code.
Doing all the work for me!
The cell gets overloaded with new viruses.
Then explodes!
Sending us out to infect and kill other cells!
BAM

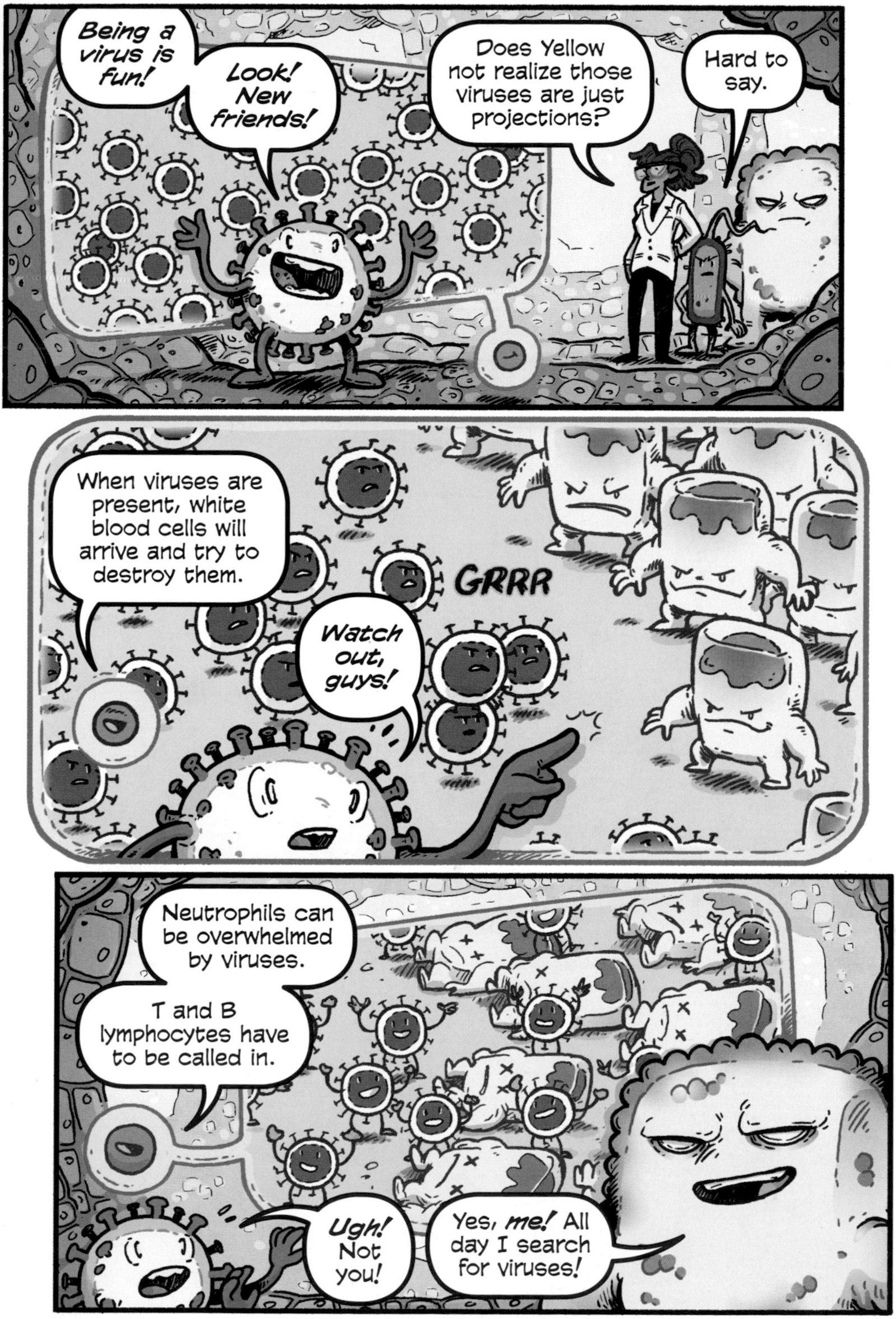
Being a virus is fun!
Look! New friends!
Does Yellow not realize those viruses are just projections?
Hard to say.
When viruses are present, white blood cells will arrive and try to destroy them.
GRRR
Watch out, guys!
Neutrophils can be overwhelmed by viruses.
T and B lymphocytes have to be called in.
Ugh! Not you!
Yes, me! All day I search for viruses!

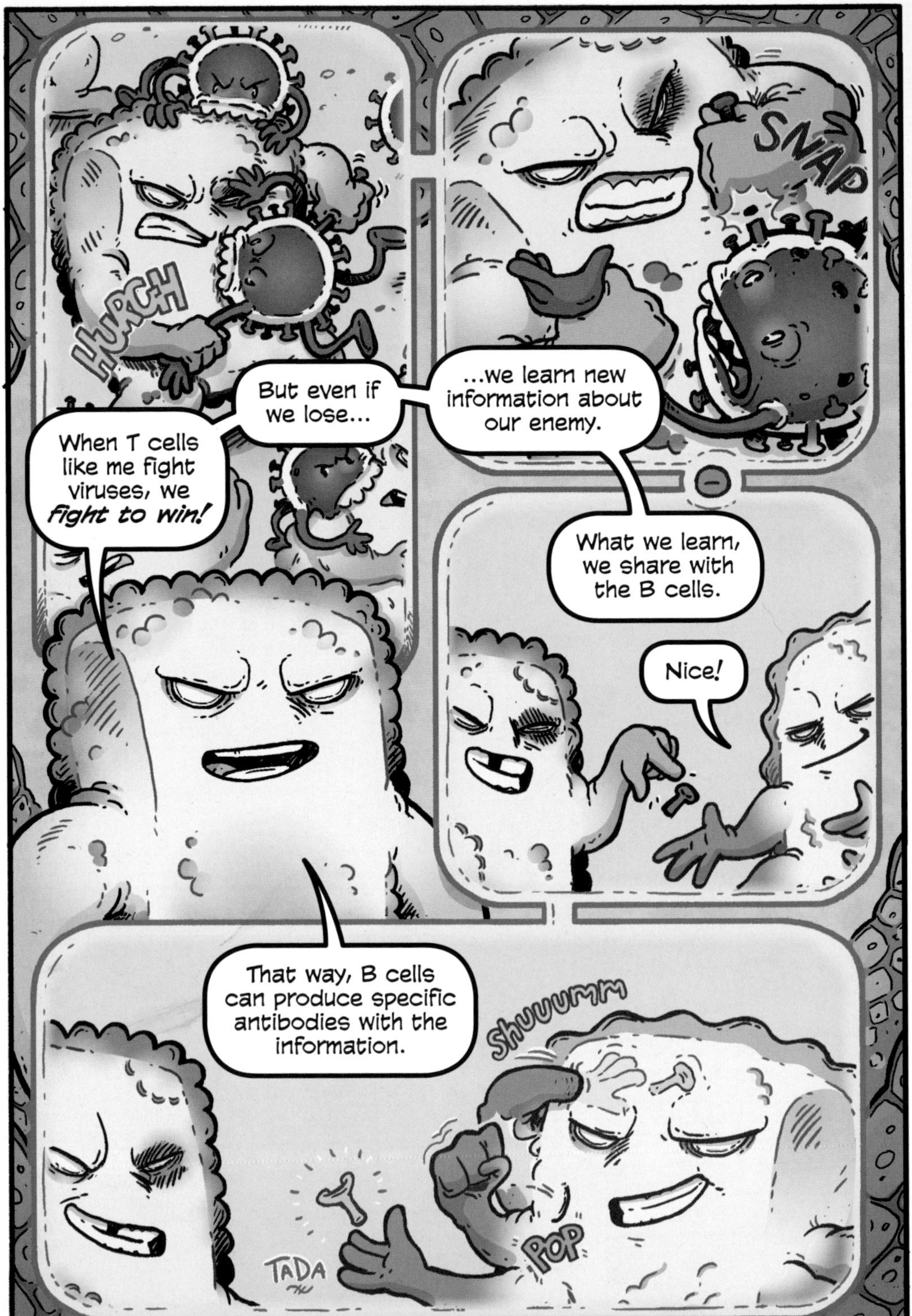
HURCH
SNAP
When T cells like me fight viruses, we *fight to win!*
But even if we lose...
...we learn new information about our enemy.
What we learn, we share with the B cells.
Nice!
That way, B cells can produce specific antibodies with the information.
SHUUUMM
TADA
POP

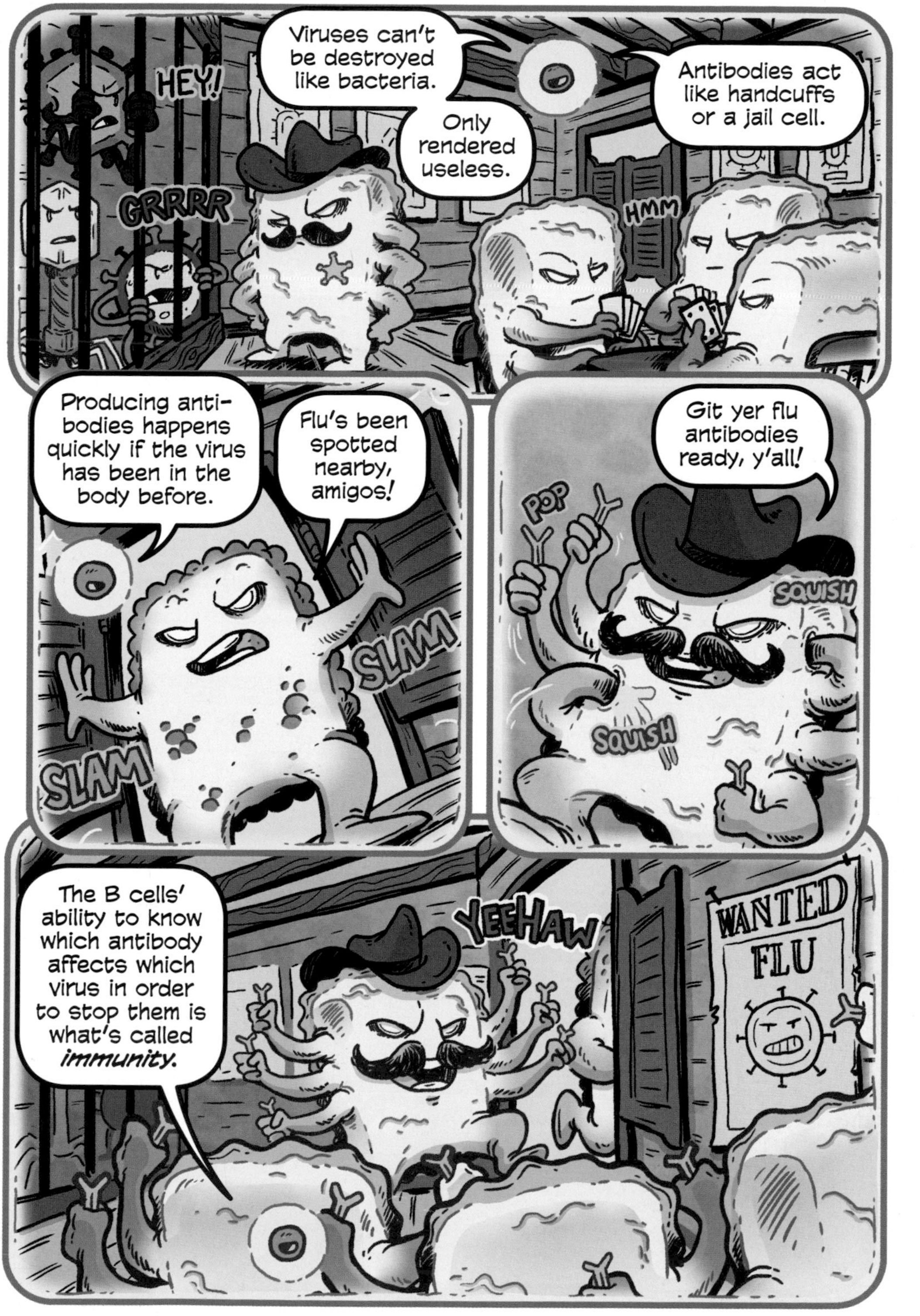
HEY!
Viruses can't be destroyed like bacteria.
Only rendered useless.
Antibodies act like handcuffs or a jail cell.
GRRRR
HMM
Producing anti-bodies happens quickly if the virus has been in the body before.
Flu's been spotted nearby, amigos!
SLAM
SLAM
Git yer flu antibodies ready, y'all!
POP
SQUISH
SQUISH
The B cells' ability to know which antibody affects which virus in order to stop them is what's called *immunity*.
YEEHAW
WANTED
FLU

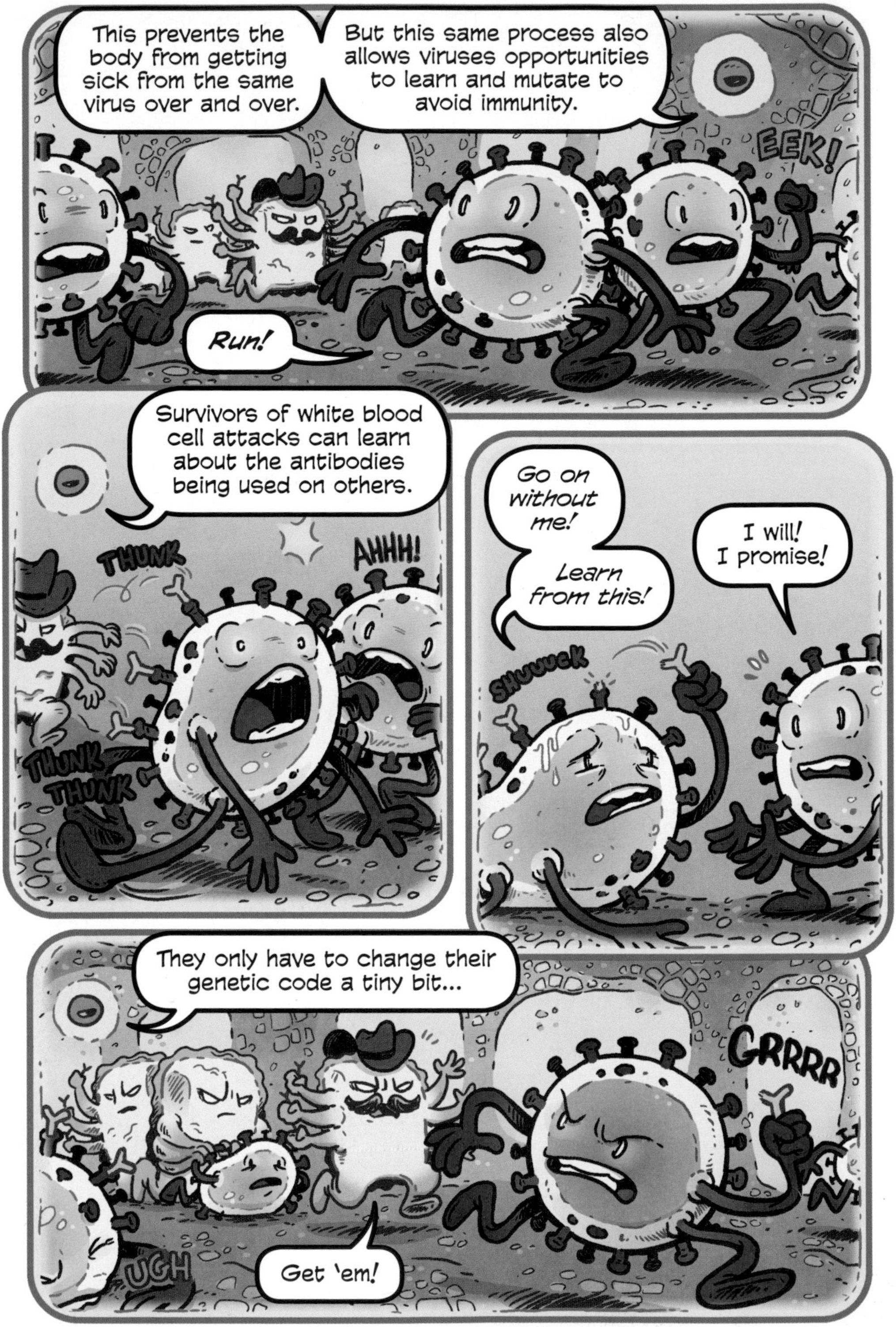
This prevents the body from getting sick from the same virus over and over.
But this same process also allows viruses opportunities to learn and mutate to avoid immunity.
EEK!
Run!
Survivors of white blood cell attacks can learn about the antibodies being used on others.
THUNK
AHHH!
THUNK THUNK
Go on without me!
Learn from this!
I will! I promise!
SHUUUCK
They only have to change their genetic code a tiny bit...
GRRRR
Get 'em!
UGH

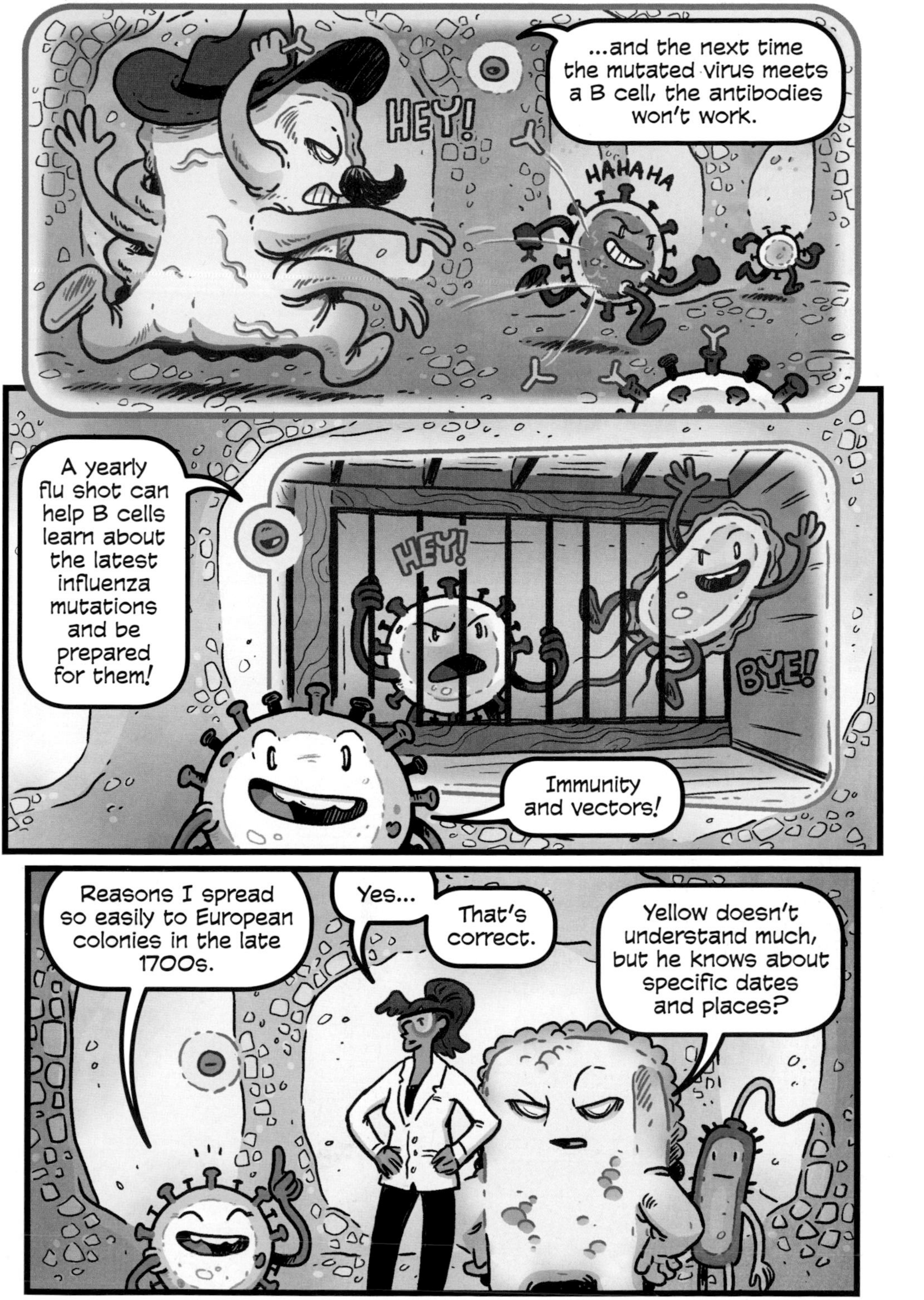
...and the next time the mutated virus meets a B cell, the antibodies won't work.
HEY!
HAHAHA
A yearly flu shot can help B cells learn about the latest influenza mutations and be prepared for them!
HEY!
BYE!
Immunity and vectors!
Reasons I spread so easily to European colonies in the late 1700s.
Yes...
That's correct.
Yellow doesn't understand much, but he knows about specific dates and places?

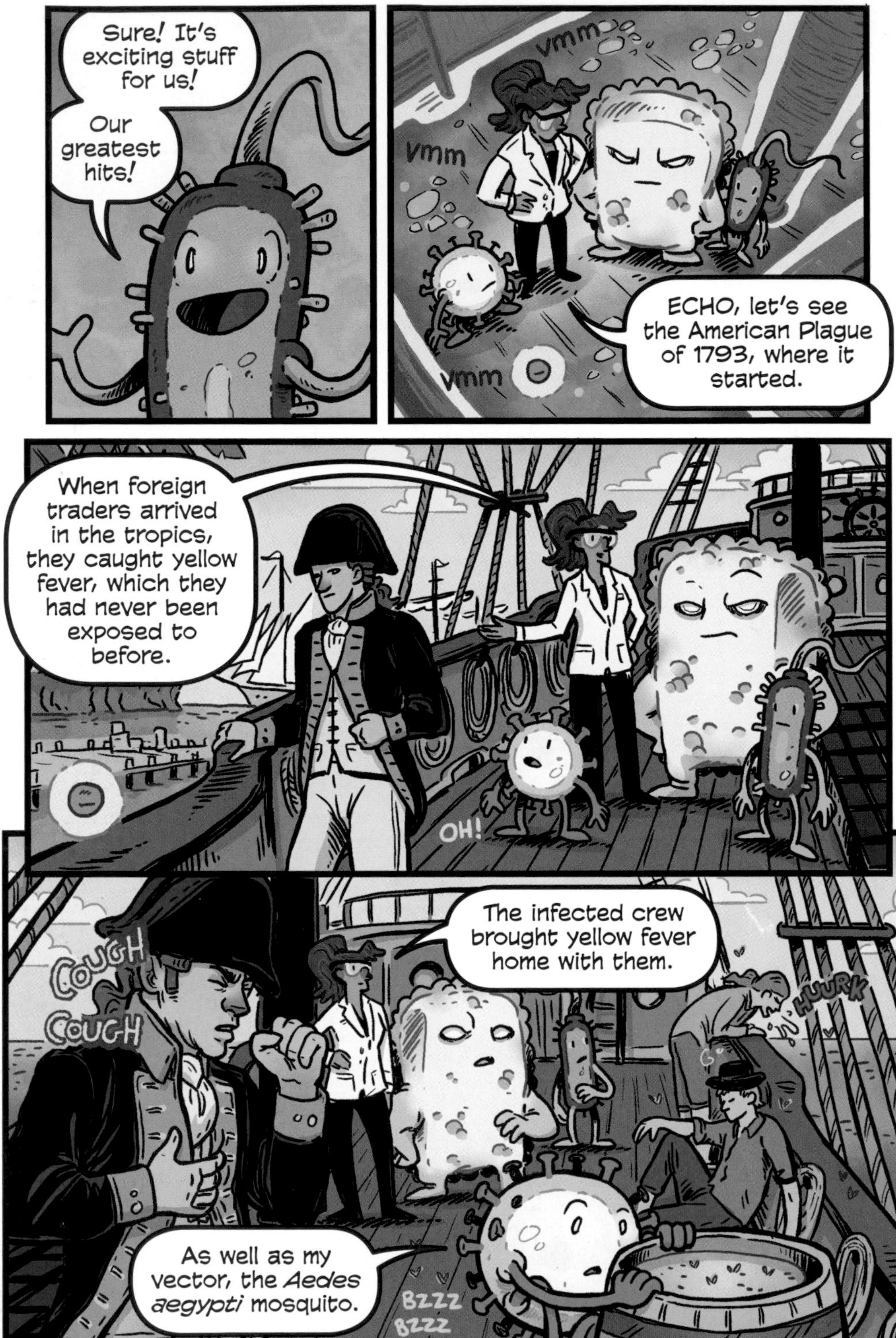
Sure! It's exciting stuff for us!
Our greatest hits!
vmm
vmm
vmm
ECHO, let's see the American Plague of 1793, where it started.
When foreign traders arrived in the tropics, they caught yellow fever, which they had never been exposed to before.
OH!
COUGH
COUGH
The infected crew brought yellow fever home with them.
HUURK
As well as my vector, the *Aedes aegypti* mosquito.
BZZZ
BZZZ

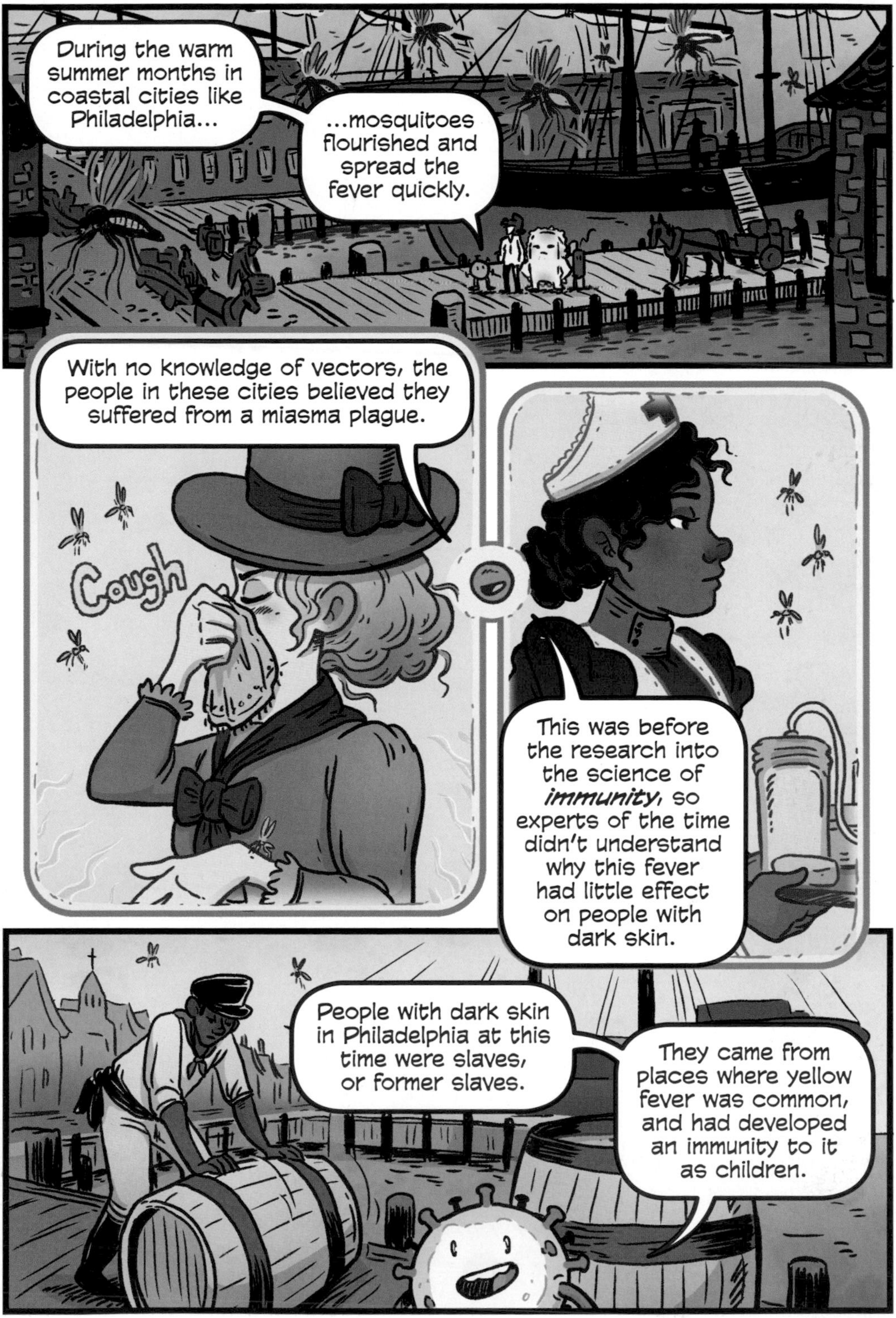

During the warm summer months in coastal cities like Philadelphia...
...mosquitoes flourished and spread the fever quickly.
With no knowledge of vectors, the people in these cities believed they suffered from a miasma plague.
Cough
This was before the research into the science of *immunity*, so experts of the time didn't understand why this fever had little effect on people with dark skin.
People with dark skin in Philadelphia at this time were slaves, or former slaves.
They came from places where yellow fever was common, and had developed an immunity to it as children.

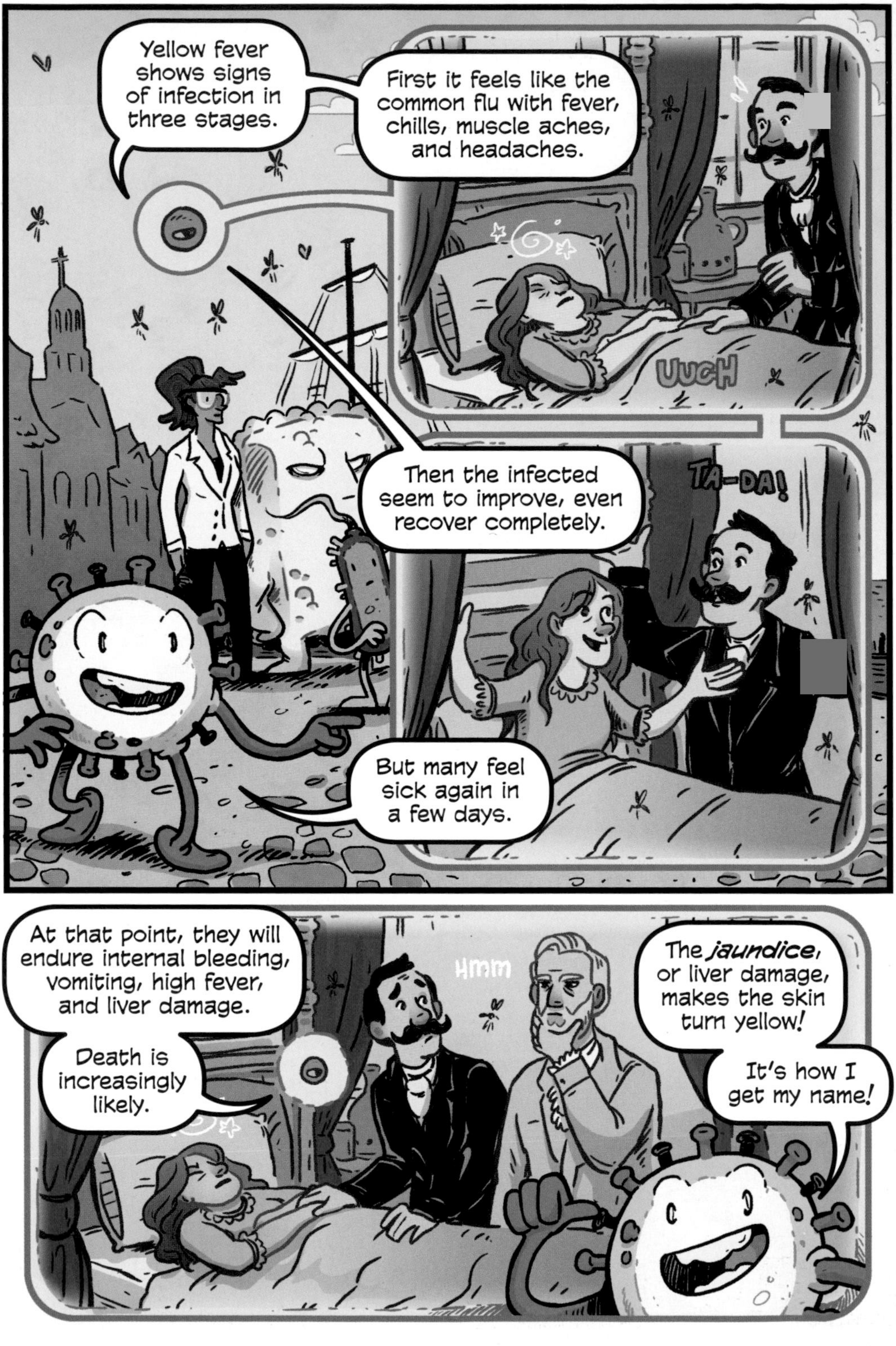
Yellow fever shows signs of infection in three stages.
First it feels like the common flu with fever, chills, muscle aches, and headaches.
UUGH
Then the infected seem to improve, even recover completely.
TA-DA!
But many feel sick again in a few days.
At that point, they will endure internal bleeding, vomiting, high fever, and liver damage.
Death is increasingly likely.
HMM
The *jaundice*, or liver damage, makes the skin turn yellow!
It's how I get my name!

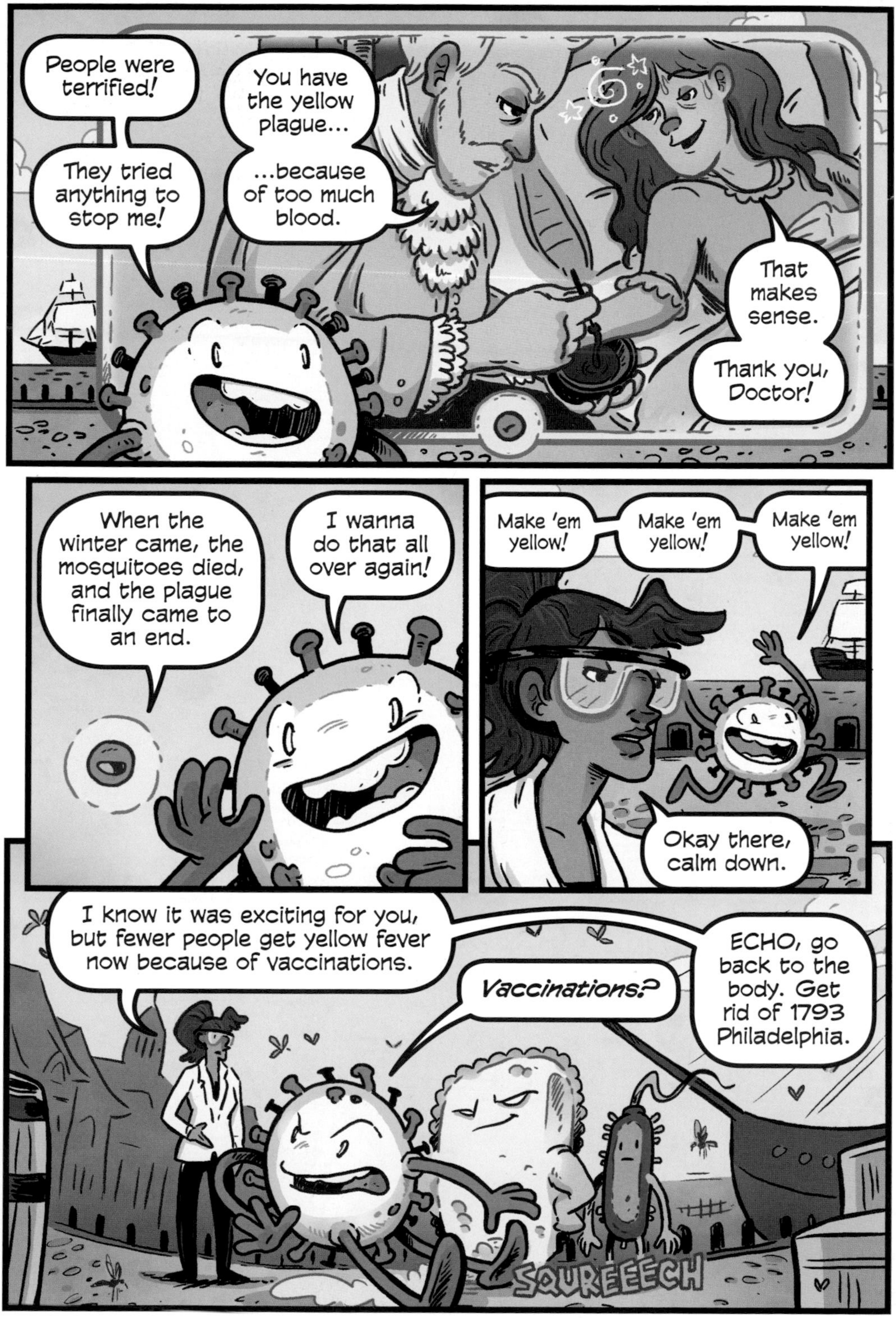
People were terrified!
They tried anything to stop me!
You have the yellow plague...
...because of too much blood.
That makes sense.
Thank you, Doctor!
When the winter came, the mosquitoes died, and the plague finally came to an end.
I wanna do that all over again!
Make 'em yellow!
Make 'em yellow!
Make 'em yellow!
Okay there, calm down.
I know it was exciting for you, but fewer people get yellow fever now because of vaccinations.
Vaccinations?
ECHO, go back to the body. Get rid of 1793 Philadelphia.
SQUREEECH

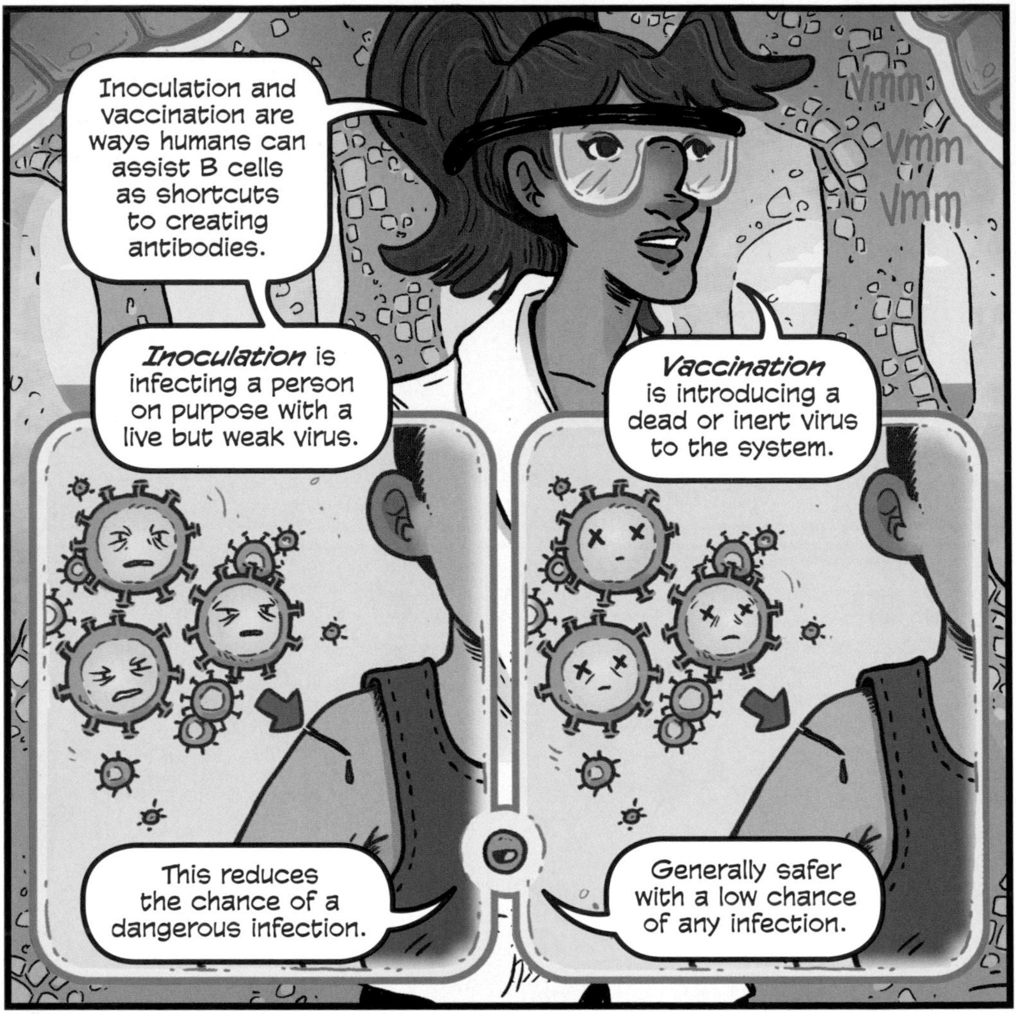
Inoculation and vaccination are ways humans can assist B cells as shortcuts to creating antibodies.
Vmm
Vmm
Vmm
Inoculation is infecting a person on purpose with a live but weak virus.
Vaccination is introducing a dead or inert virus to the system.
This reduces the chance of a dangerous infection.
Generally safer with a low chance of any infection.

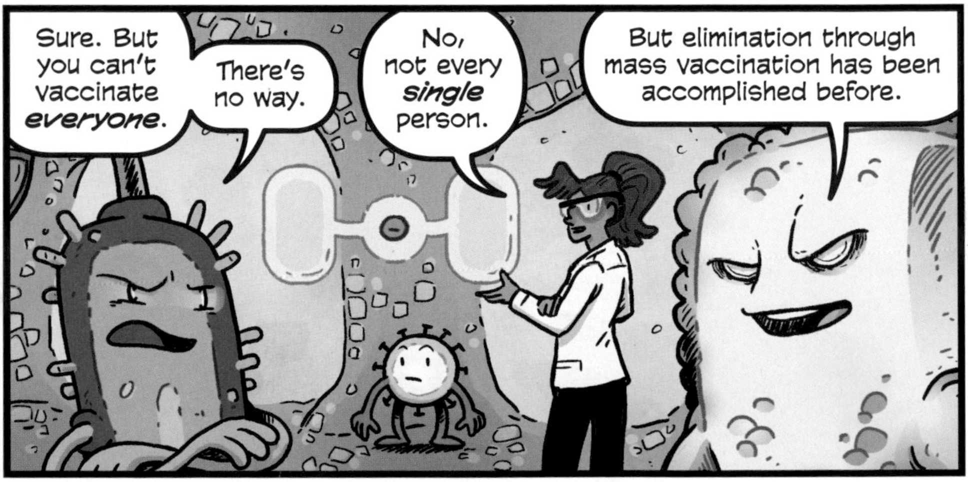
Sure. But you can't vaccinate *everyone*.
There's no way.
No, not every *single* person.
But elimination through mass vaccination has been accomplished before.

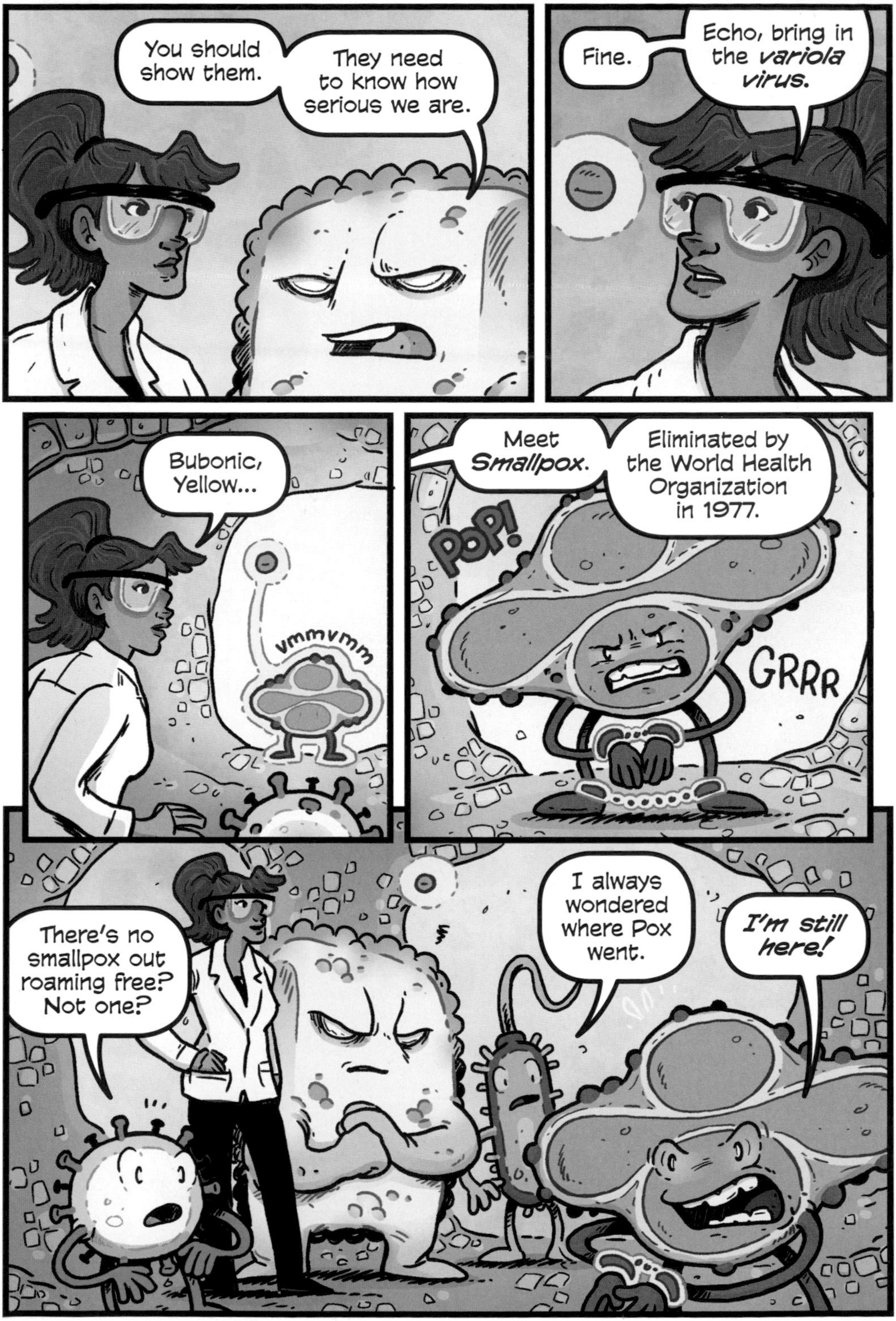
You should show them.
They need to know how serious we are.
Fine.
Echo, bring in the *variola virus.*
Bubonic, Yellow...
vmmvmm
Meet *Smallpox.*
Eliminated by the World Health Organization in 1977.
POP!
GRRR
There's no smallpox out roaming free? Not one?
I always wondered where Pox went.
I'm still here!

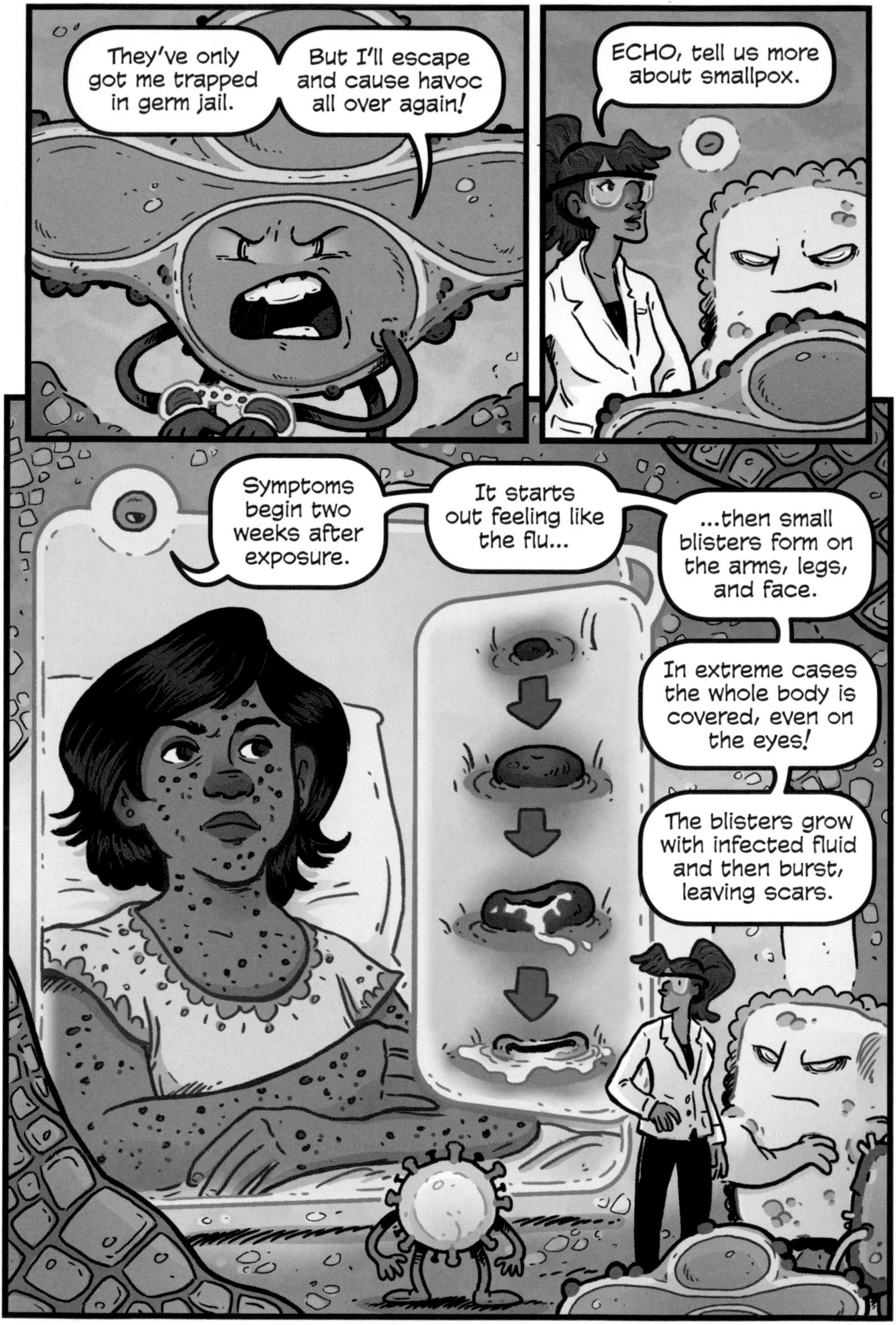
They've only got me trapped in germ jail.
But I'll escape and cause havoc all over again!
ECHO, tell us more about smallpox.
Symptoms begin two weeks after exposure.
It starts out feeling like the flu...
...then small blisters form on the arms, legs, and face.
In extreme cases the whole body is covered, even on the eyes!
The blisters grow with infected fluid and then burst, leaving scars.

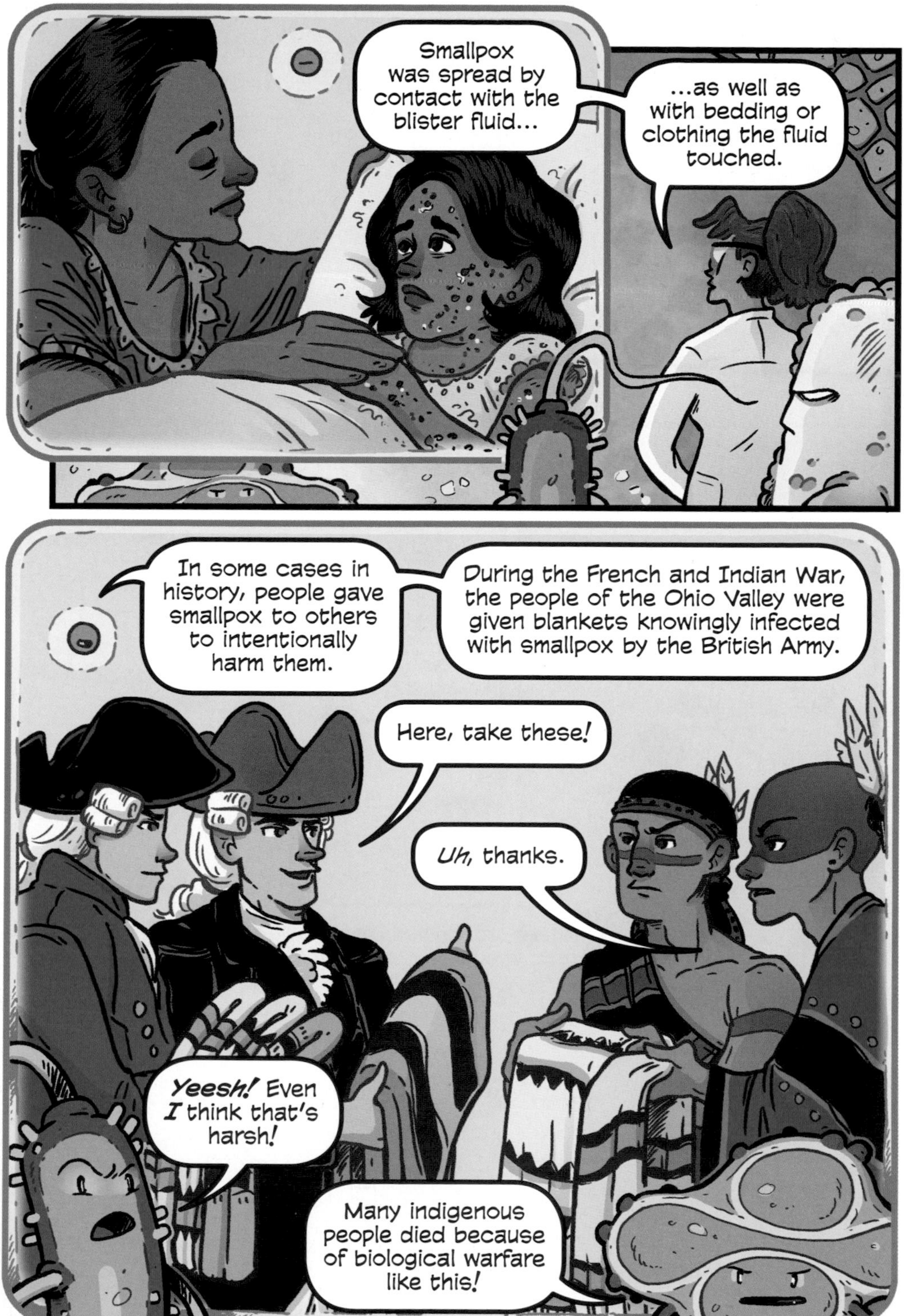

Smallpox was spread by contact with the blister fluid...
...as well as with bedding or clothing the fluid touched.
In some cases in history, people gave smallpox to others to intentionally harm them.
During the French and Indian War, the people of the Ohio Valley were given blankets knowingly infected with smallpox by the British Army.
Here, take these!
Uh, thanks.
Yeesh! Even ***I*** think that's harsh!
Many indigenous people died because of biological warfare like this!

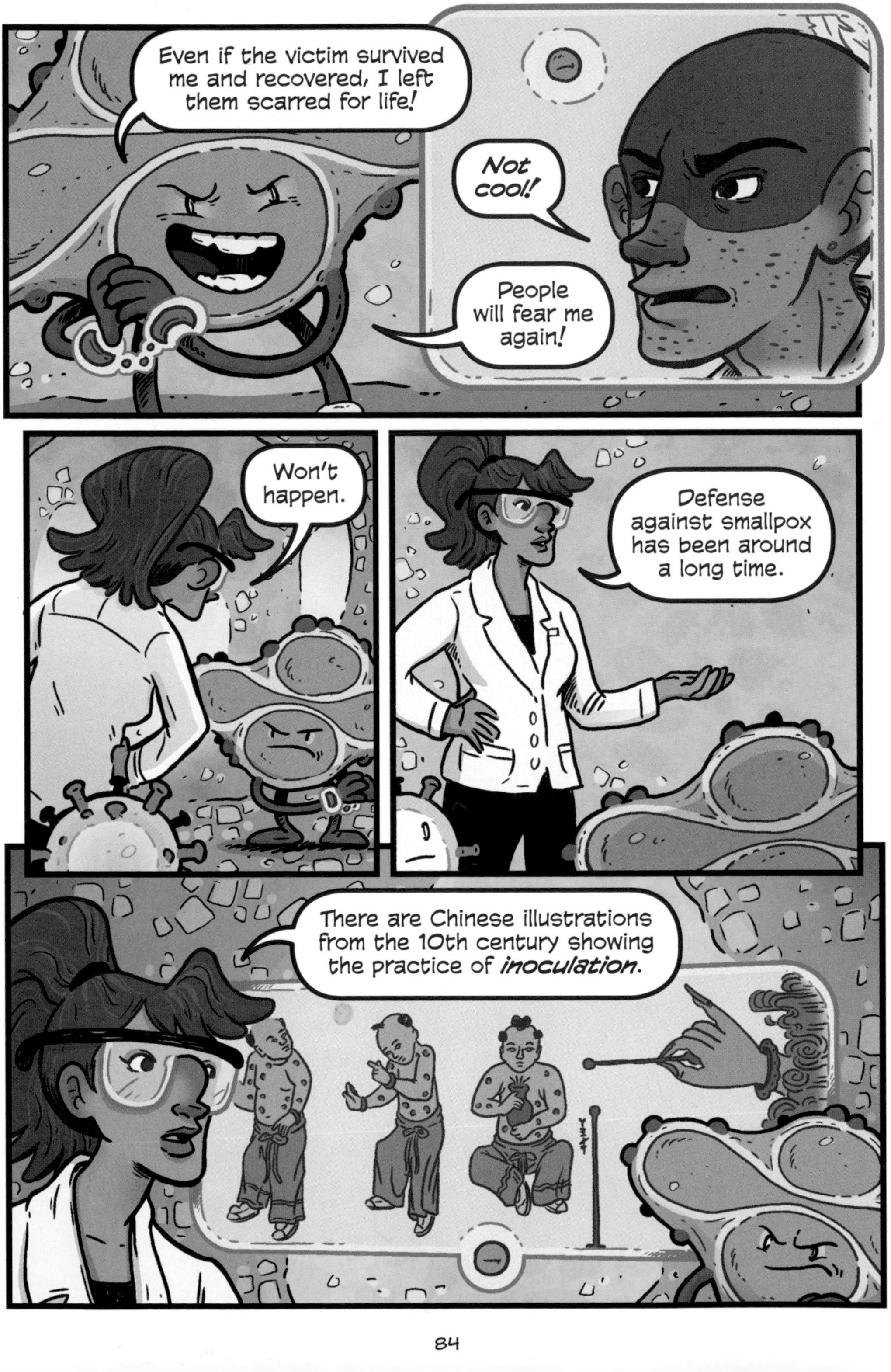
Even if the victim survived me and recovered, I left them scarred for life!
Not cool!
People will fear me again!
Won't happen.
Defense against smallpox has been around a long time.
There are Chinese illustrations from the 10th century showing the practice of *inoculation*.

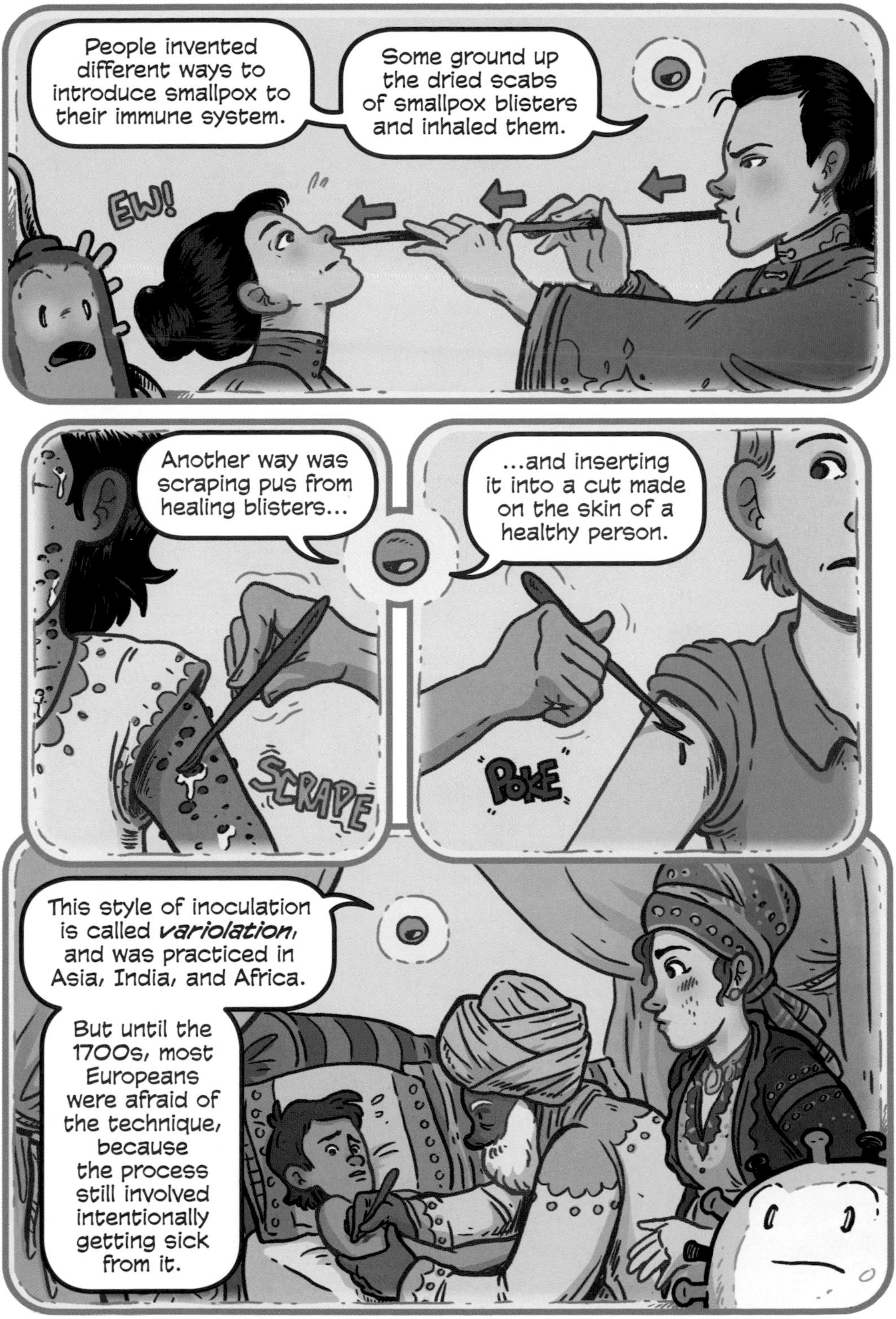
People invented different ways to introduce smallpox to their immune system.
Some ground up the dried scabs of smallpox blisters and inhaled them.
EW!
Another way was scraping pus from healing blisters...
SCRAPE
...and inserting it into a cut made on the skin of a healthy person.
POKE
This style of inoculation is called *variolation*, and was practiced in Asia, India, and Africa.
But until the 1700s, most Europeans were afraid of the technique, because the process still involved intentionally getting sick from it.

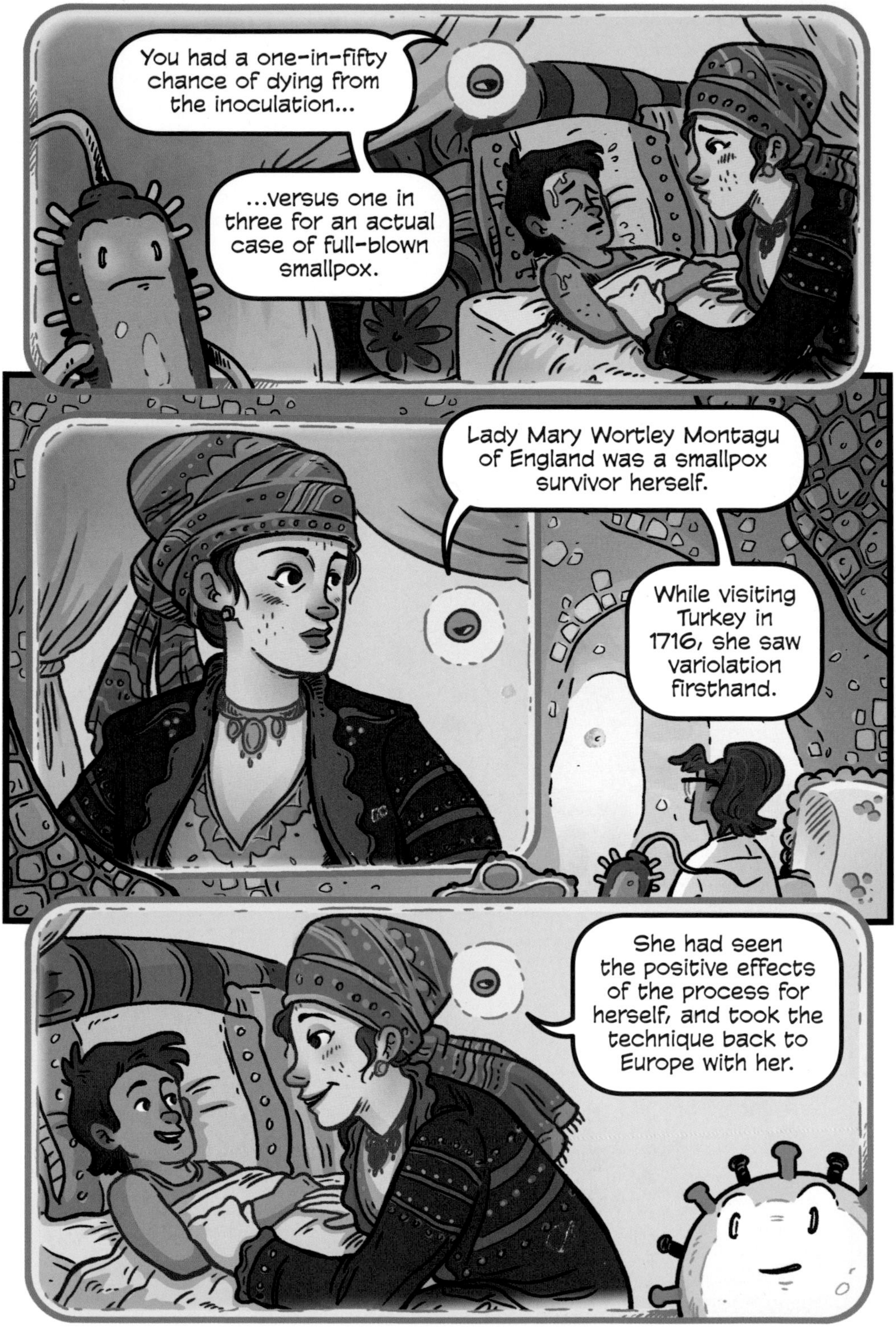
You had a one-in-fifty chance of dying from the inoculation...
...versus one in three for an actual case of full-blown smallpox.
Lady Mary Wortley Montagu of England was a smallpox survivor herself.
While visiting Turkey in 1716, she saw variolation firsthand.
She had seen the positive effects of the process for herself, and took the technique back to Europe with her.

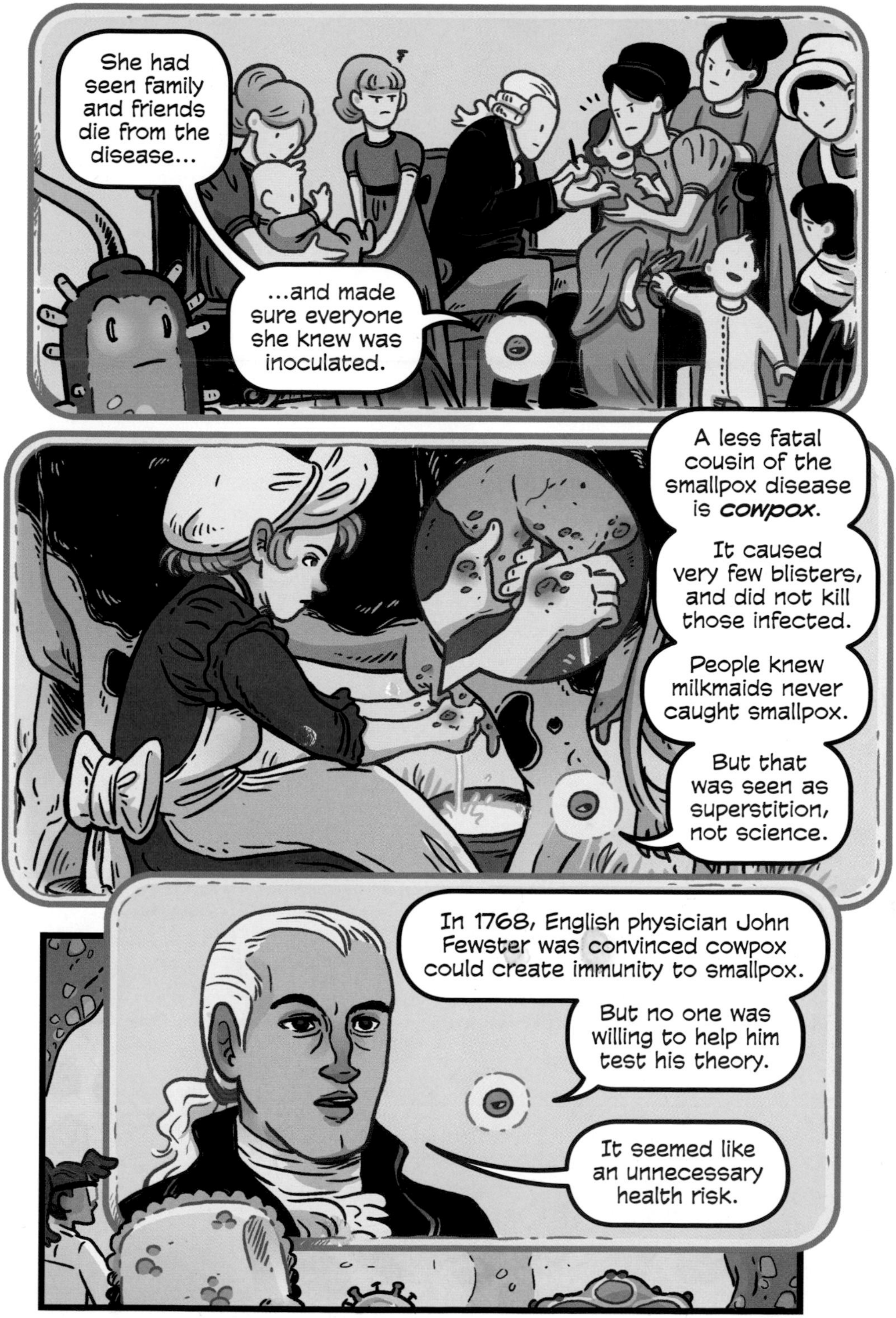
She had seen family and friends die from the disease...
...and made sure everyone she knew was inoculated.
A less fatal cousin of the smallpox disease is *cowpox*.
It caused very few blisters, and did not kill those infected.
People knew milkmaids never caught smallpox.
But that was seen as superstition, not science.
In 1768, English physician John Fewster was convinced cowpox could create immunity to smallpox.
But no one was willing to help him test his theory.
It seemed like an unnecessary health risk.

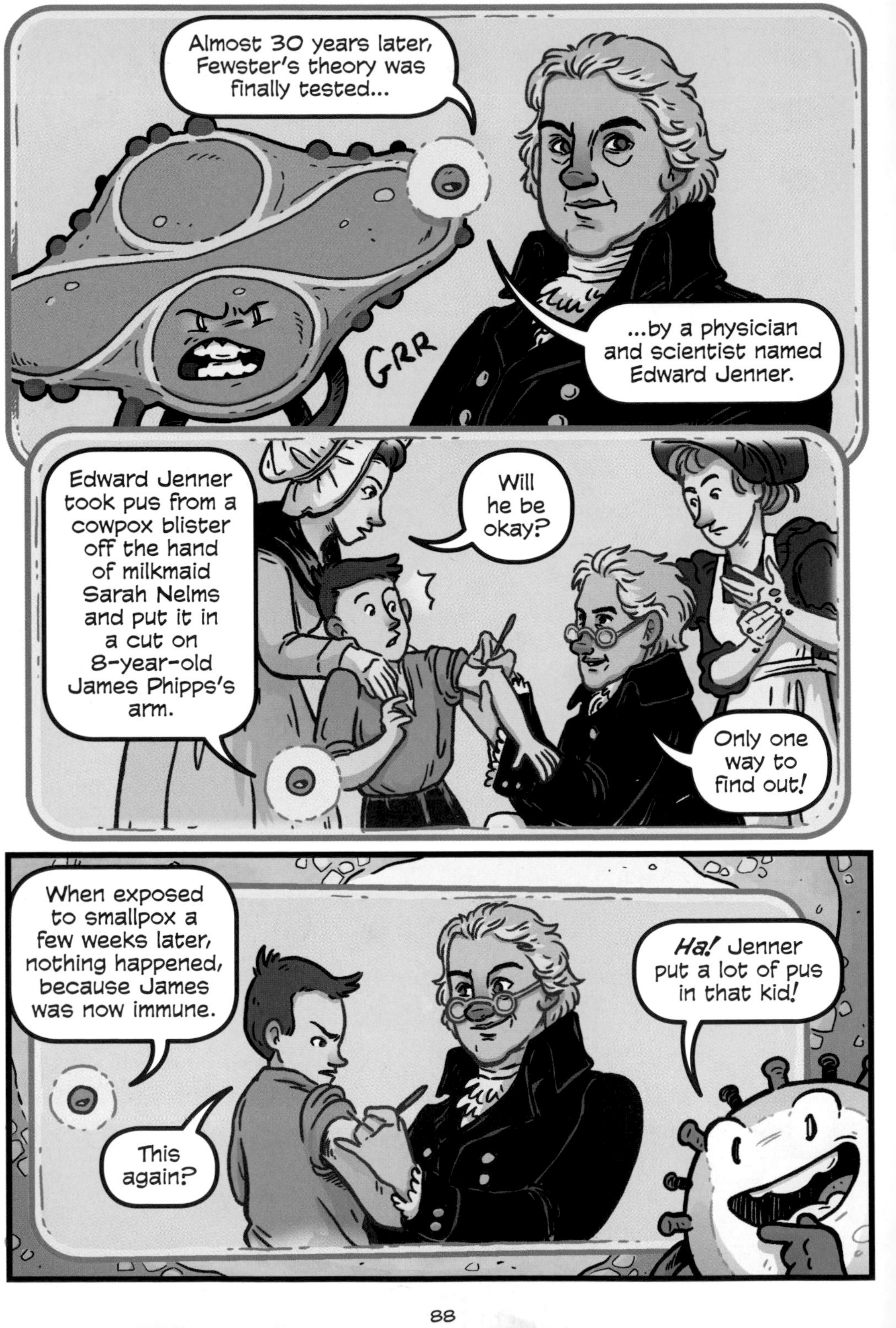

Almost 30 years later, Fewster's theory was finally tested...
GRR
...by a physician and scientist named Edward Jenner.
Edward Jenner took pus from a cowpox blister off the hand of milkmaid Sarah Nelms and put it in a cut on 8-year-old James Phipps's arm.
Will he be okay?
Only one way to find out!
When exposed to smallpox a few weeks later, nothing happened, because James was now immune.
This again?
Ha! Jenner put a lot of pus in that kid!

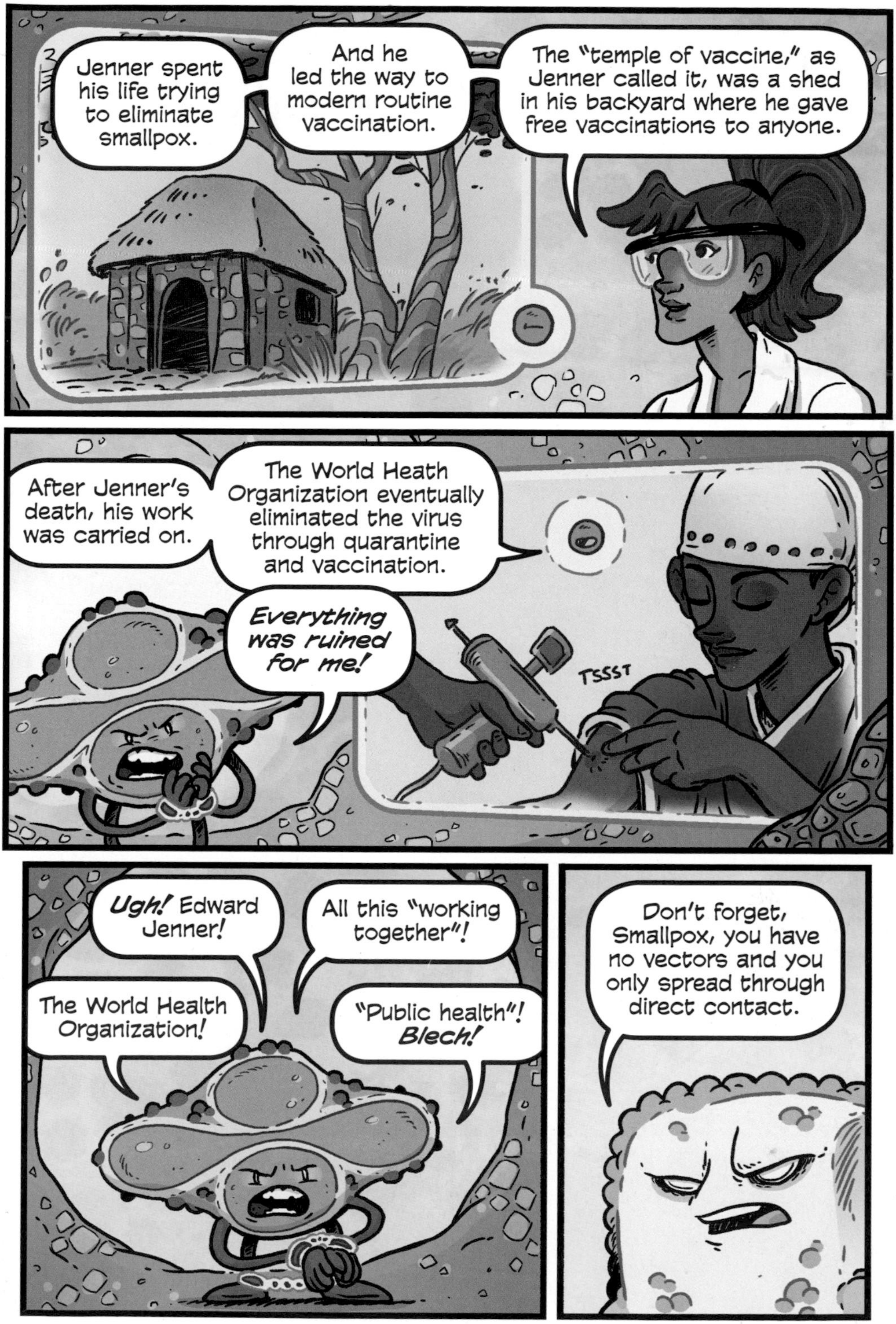
Jenner spent his life trying to eliminate smallpox.
And he led the way to modern routine vaccination.
The "temple of vaccine," as Jenner called it, was a shed in his backyard where he gave free vaccinations to anyone.
After Jenner's death, his work was carried on.
The World Heath Organization eventually eliminated the virus through quarantine and vaccination.
Everything was ruined for me!
TSSST
Ugh! Edward Jenner!
All this "working together"!
The World Health Organization!
"Public health"! *Blech!*
Don't forget, Smallpox, you have no vectors and you only spread through direct contact.

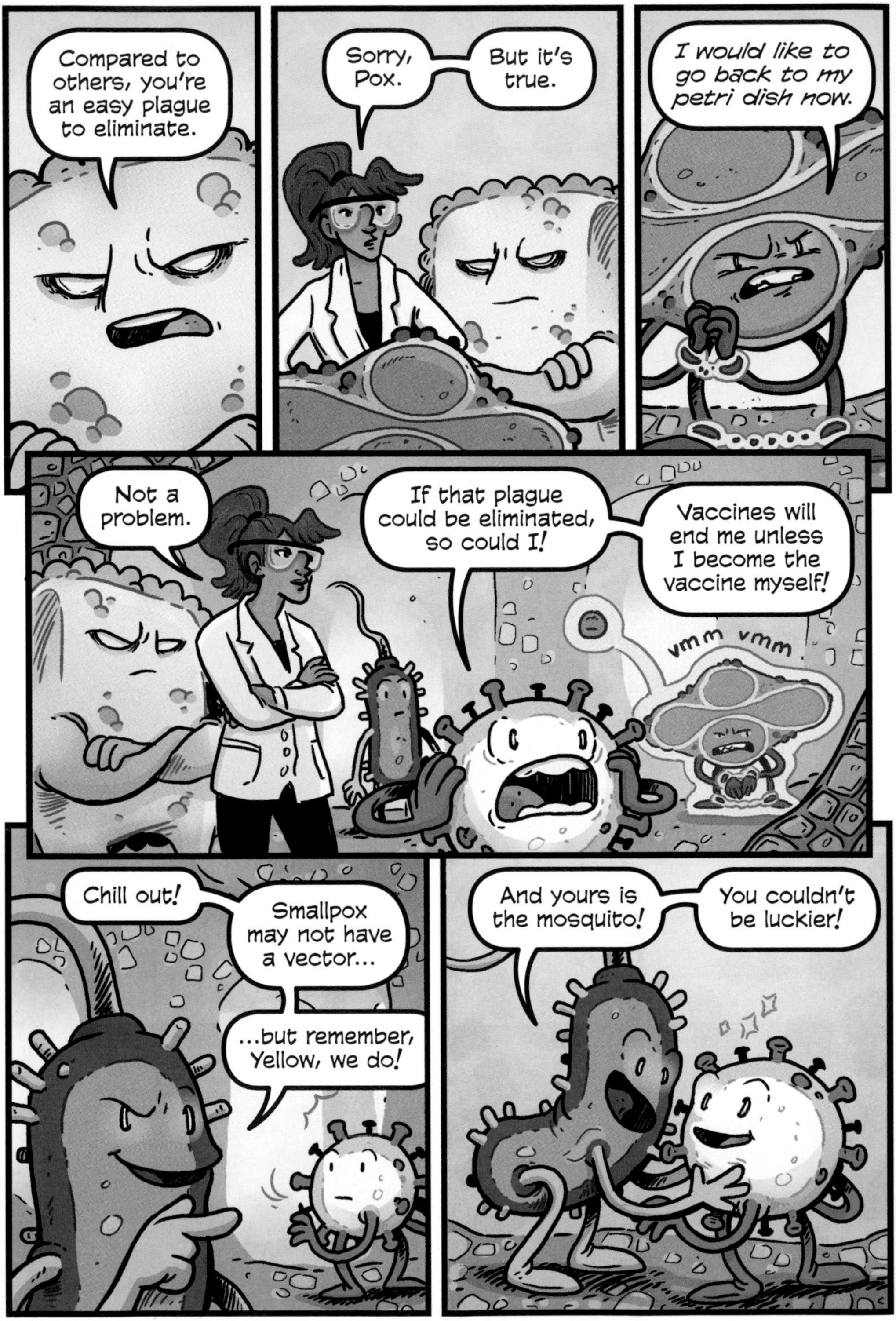
Compared to others, you're an easy plague to eliminate.
Sorry, Pox.
But it's true.
I would like to go back to my petri dish now.
Not a problem.
If that plague could be eliminated, so could I!
Vaccines will end me unless I become the vaccine myself!
vmm vmm
Chill out!
Smallpox may not have a vector...
...but remember, Yellow, we do!
And yours is the mosquito!
You couldn't be luckier!

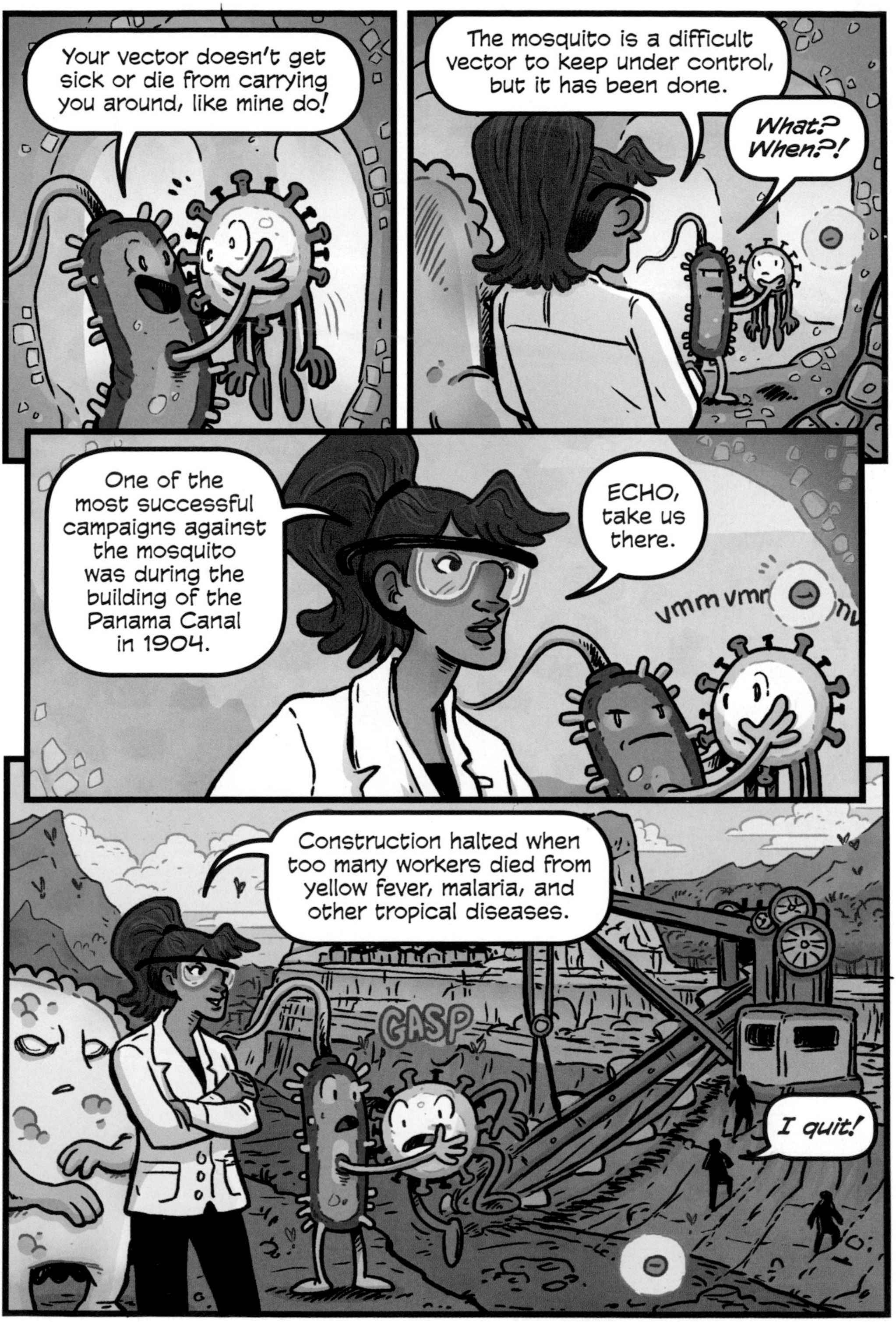

Your vector doesn't get sick or die from carrying you around, like mine do!
The mosquito is a difficult vector to keep under control, but it has been done.
What? When?!
One of the most successful campaigns against the mosquito was during the building of the Panama Canal in 1904.
ECHO, take us there.
vmm vmm
Construction halted when too many workers died from yellow fever, malaria, and other tropical diseases.
GASP
I quit!

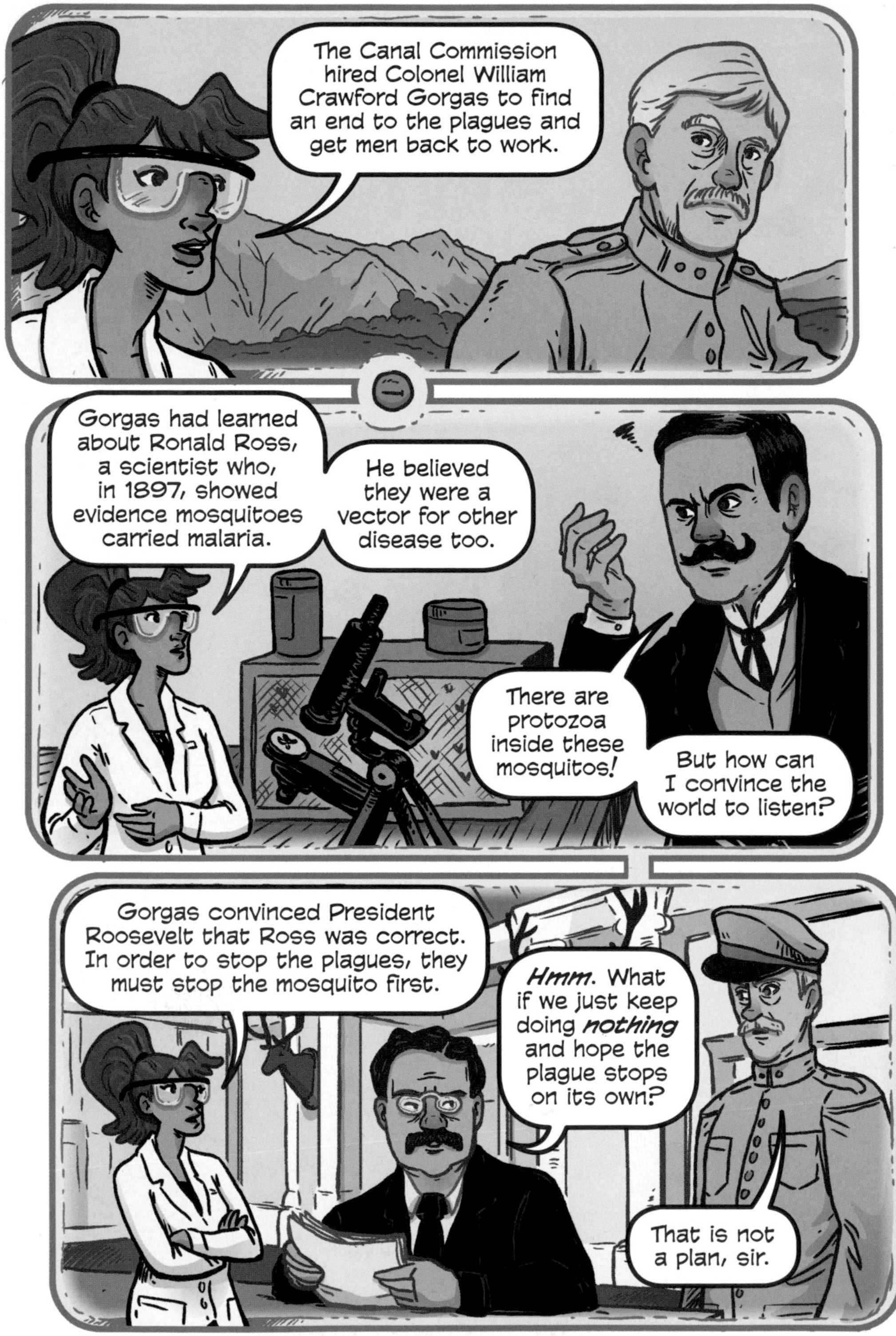
The Canal Commission hired Colonel William Crawford Gorgas to find an end to the plagues and get men back to work.
Gorgas had learned about Ronald Ross, a scientist who, in 1897, showed evidence mosquitoes carried malaria.
He believed they were a vector for other disease too.
There are protozoa inside these mosquitos!
But how can I convince the world to listen?
Gorgas convinced President Roosevelt that Ross was correct. In order to stop the plagues, they must stop the mosquito first.
Hmm. What if we just keep doing ***nothing*** and hope the plague stops on its own?
That is not a plan, sir.

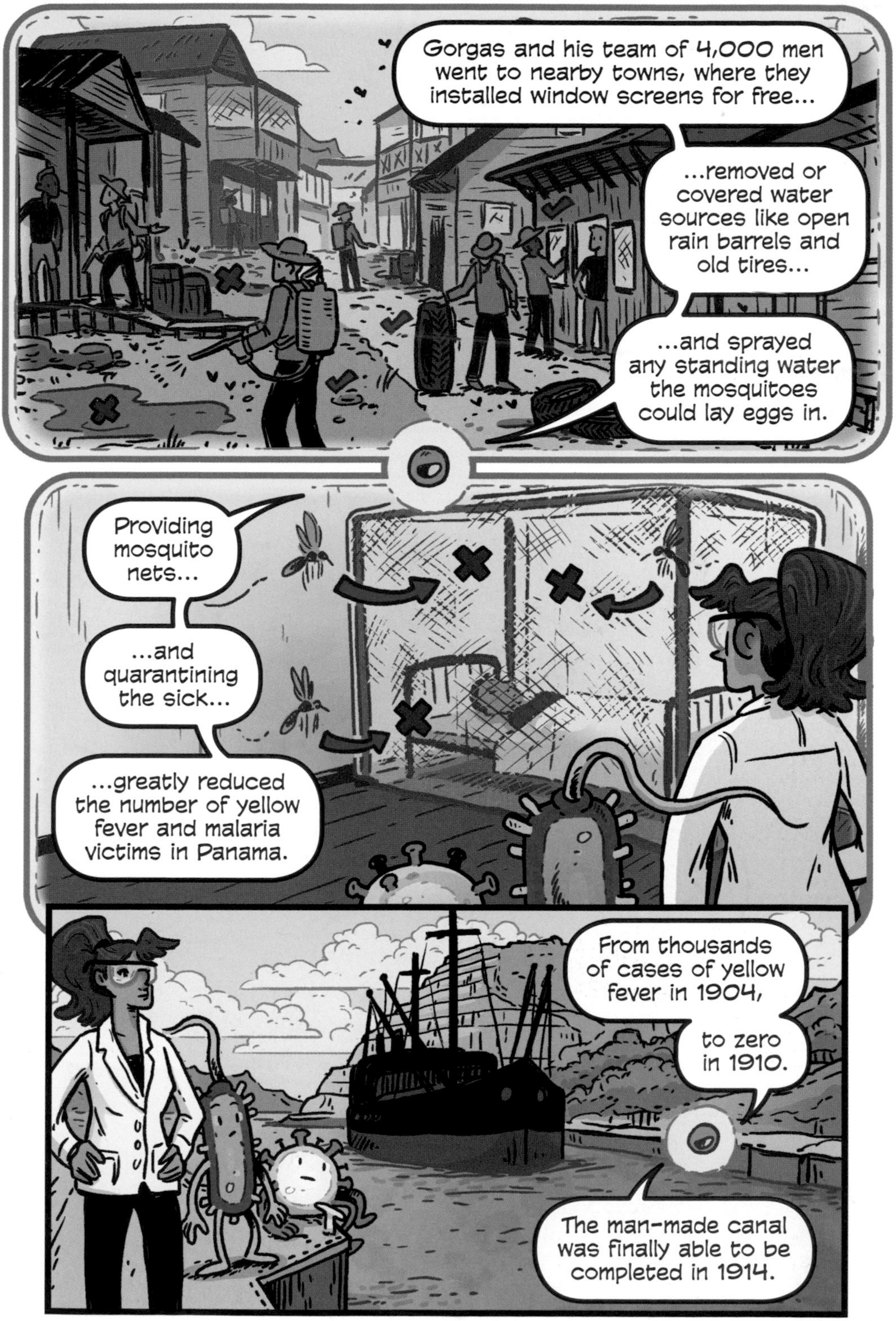

Gorgas and his team of 4,000 men went to nearby towns, where they installed window screens for free...
...removed or covered water sources like open rain barrels and old tires...
...and sprayed any standing water the mosquitoes could lay eggs in.
Providing mosquito nets...
...and quarantining the sick...
...greatly reduced the number of yellow fever and malaria victims in Panama.
From thousands of cases of yellow fever in 1904,
to zero in 1910.
The man-made canal was finally able to be completed in 1914.

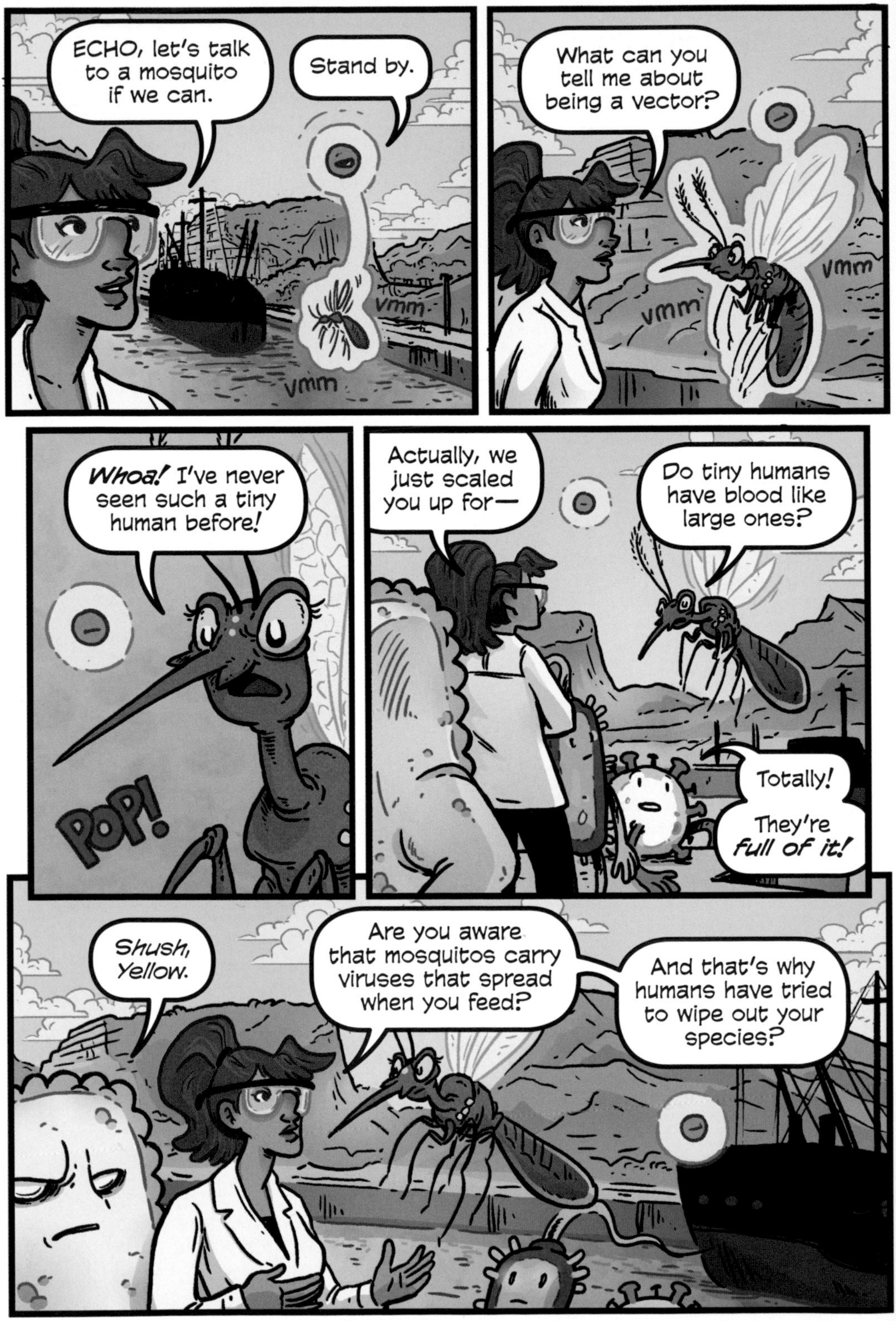
ECHO, let's talk to a mosquito if we can.
Stand by.
vmm
vmm
What can you tell me about being a vector?
vmm
vmm
Whoa! I've never seen such a tiny human before!
POP!
Actually, we just scaled you up for—
Do tiny humans have blood like large ones?
Totally!
They're *full of it!*
Shush, Yellow.
Are you aware that mosquitos carry viruses that spread when you feed?
And that's why humans have tried to wipe out your species?

You're saying we're being killed for eating? Something we *have* to do?

Well, you spread lots of terrible plagues.

Bzz. Bzz.

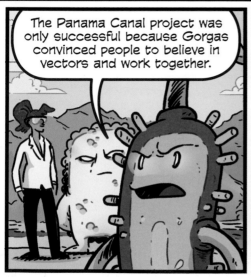

So the best way to stop those plagues is to stop *you*.

That's not fair!

Sigh. ECHO, end the mosquito simulation.

vmm

The Panama Canal project was only successful because Gorgas convinced people to believe in vectors and work together.

But what if they hadn't?

Plagues often thrive because people are their *own worst enemies*.

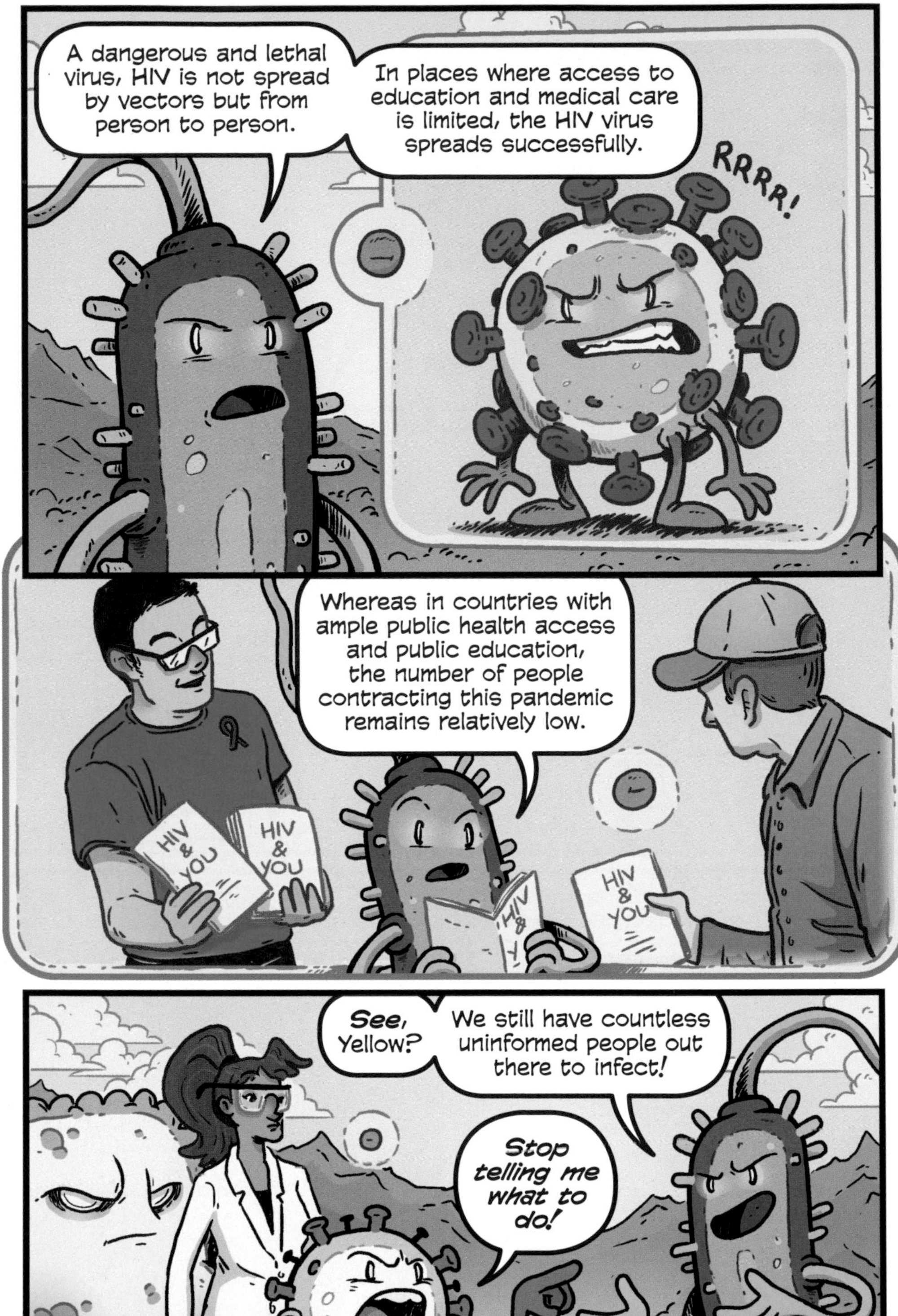

A dangerous and lethal virus, HIV is not spread by vectors but from person to person.
In places where access to education and medical care is limited, the HIV virus spreads successfully.
RRRR!
Whereas in countries with ample public health access and public education, the number of people contracting this pandemic remains relatively low.
HIV & YOU
HIV & YOU
HIV & YOU
See, Yellow?
We still have countless uninformed people out there to infect!
Stop telling me what to do!

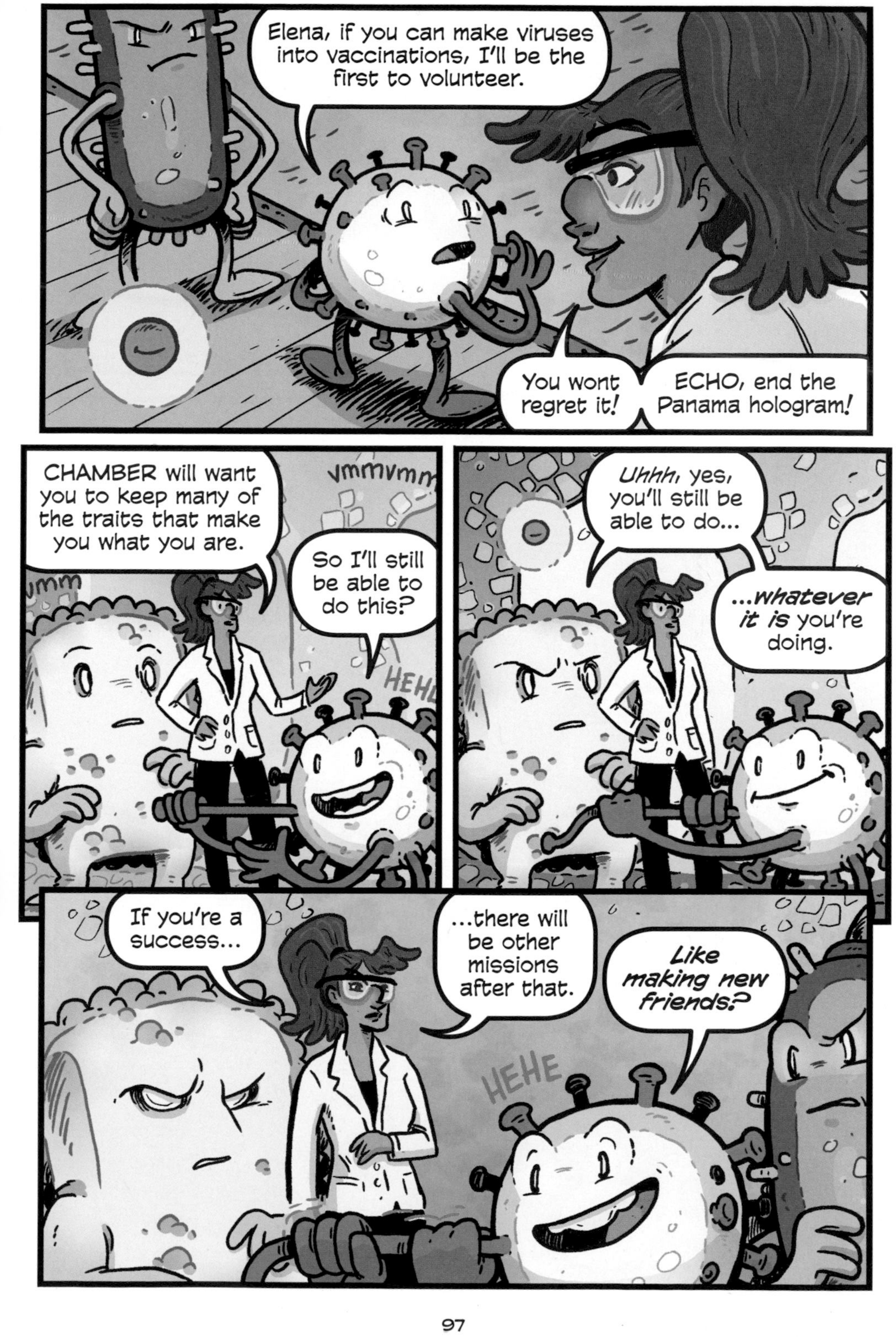
Elena, if you can make viruses into vaccinations, I'll be the first to volunteer.
You wont regret it!
ECHO, end the Panama hologram!
CHAMBER will want you to keep many of the traits that make you what you are.
vmmvmm
vmm
So I'll still be able to do this?
HEHE
Uhhh, yes, you'll still be able to do...
...whatever it is you're doing.
If you're a success...
...there will be other missions after that.
Like making new friends?
HEHE

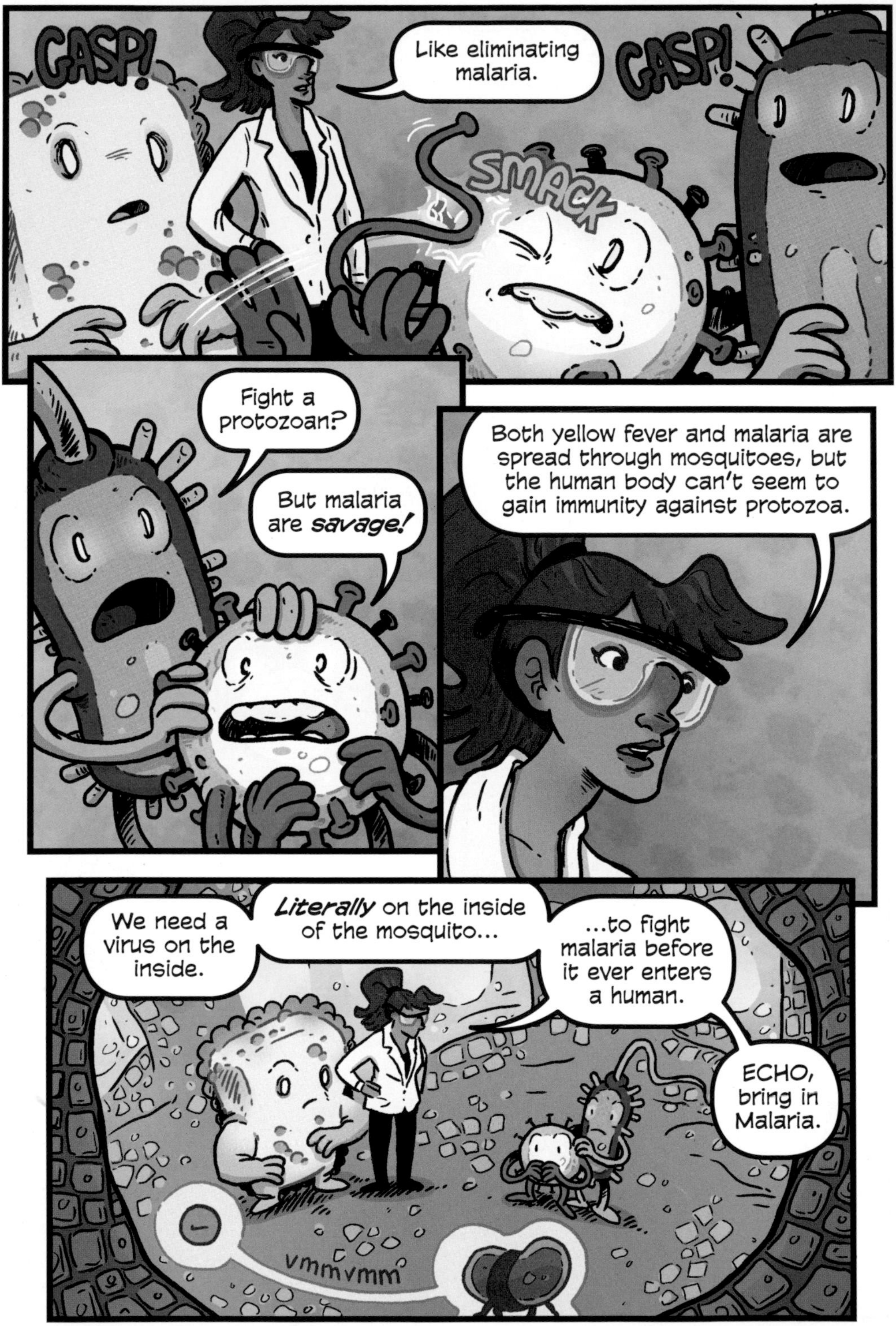
GASP!
Like eliminating malaria.
GASP!
SMACK
Fight a protozoan?
But malaria are *savage!*
Both yellow fever and malaria are spread through mosquitoes, but the human body can't seem to gain immunity against protozoa.
We need a virus on the inside.
Literally on the inside of the mosquito...
...to fight malaria before it ever enters a human.
ECHO, bring in Malaria.
vmmvmm

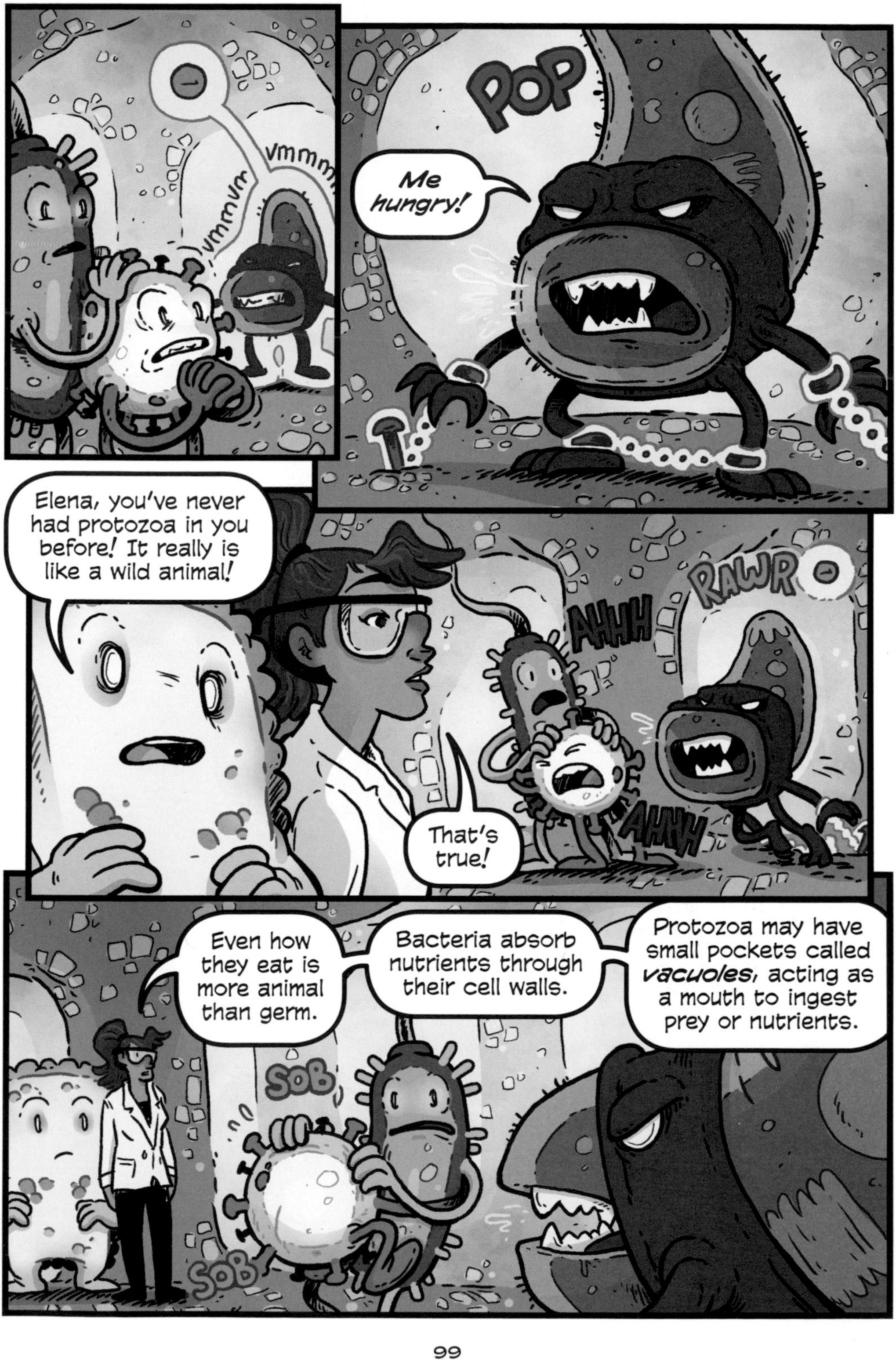
vmmmm
vmmvm
vmmvm
POP
Me hungry!
Elena, you've never had protozoa in you before! It really is like a wild animal!
RAWR
AHHH
That's true!
AHHH
Even how they eat is more animal than germ.
Bacteria absorb nutrients through their cell walls.
Protozoa may have small pockets called *vacuoles*, acting as a mouth to ingest prey or nutrients.
SOB
SOB

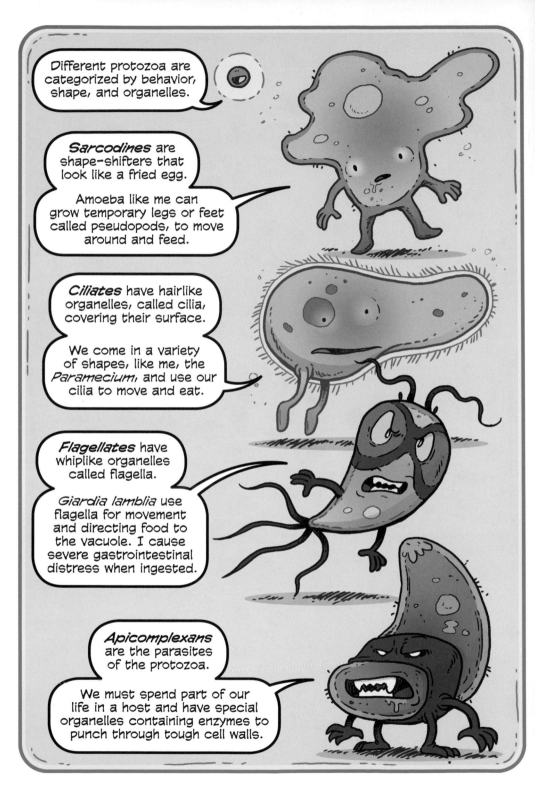

Different protozoa are categorized by behavior, shape, and organelles.

Sarcodines are shape-shifters that look like a fried egg.

Amoeba like me can grow temporary legs or feet called pseudopods, to move around and feed.

Ciliates have hairlike organelles, called cilia, covering their surface.

We come in a variety of shapes, like me, the *Paramecium,* and use our cilia to move and eat.

Flagellates have whiplike organelles called flagella.

Giardia lamblia use flagella for movement and directing food to the vacuole. I cause severe gastrointestinal distress when ingested.

Apicomplexans are the parasites of the protozoa.

We must spend part of our life in a host and have special organelles containing enzymes to punch through tough cell walls.

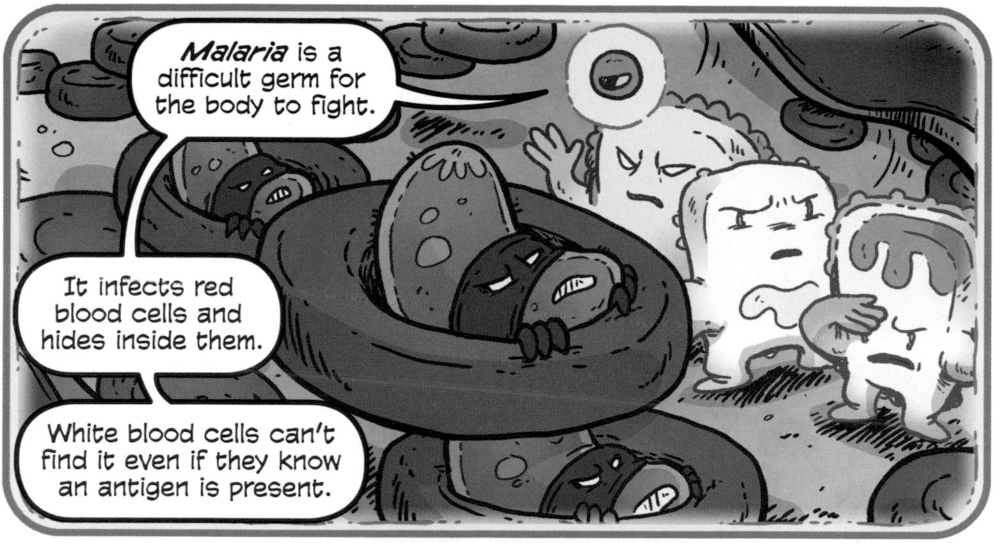
Malaria is a difficult germ for the body to fight.
It infects red blood cells and hides inside them.
White blood cells can't find it even if they know an antigen is present.

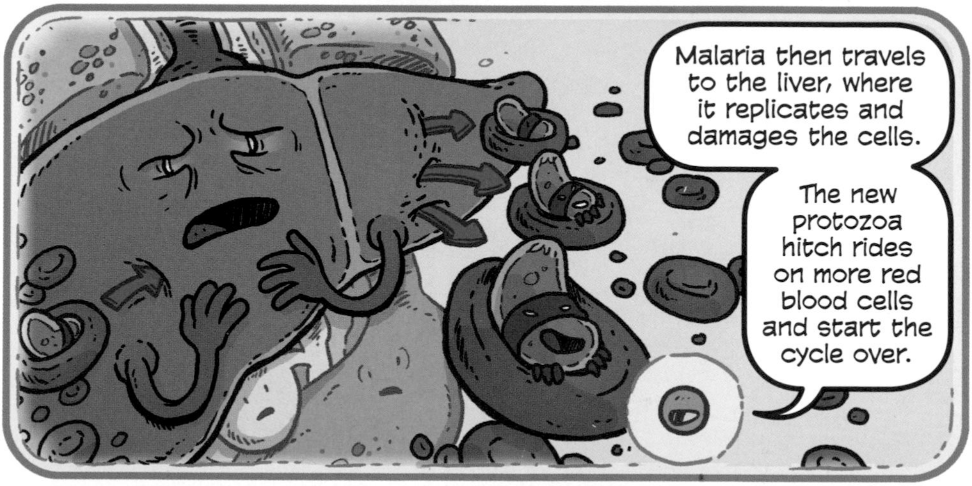
Malaria then travels to the liver, where it replicates and damages the cells.
The new protozoa hitch rides on more red blood cells and start the cycle over.

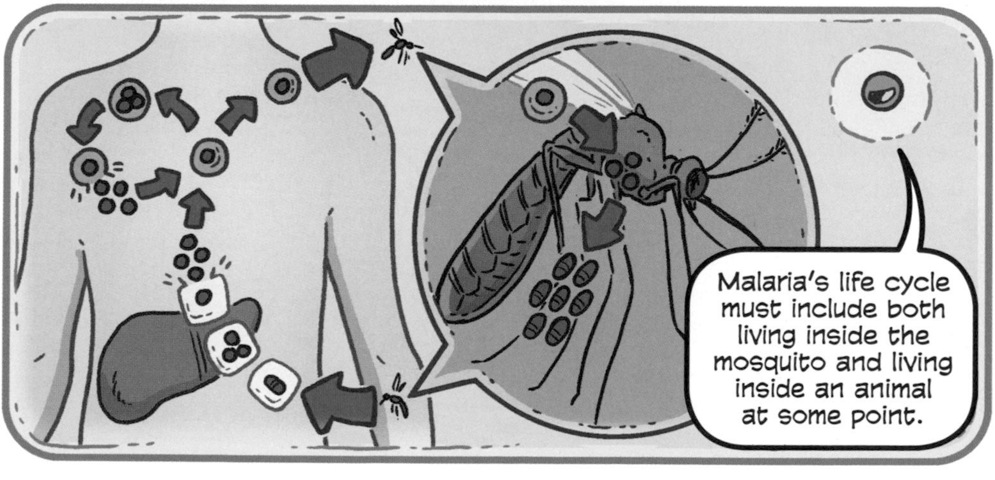
Malaria's life cycle must include both living inside the mosquito and living inside an animal at some point.

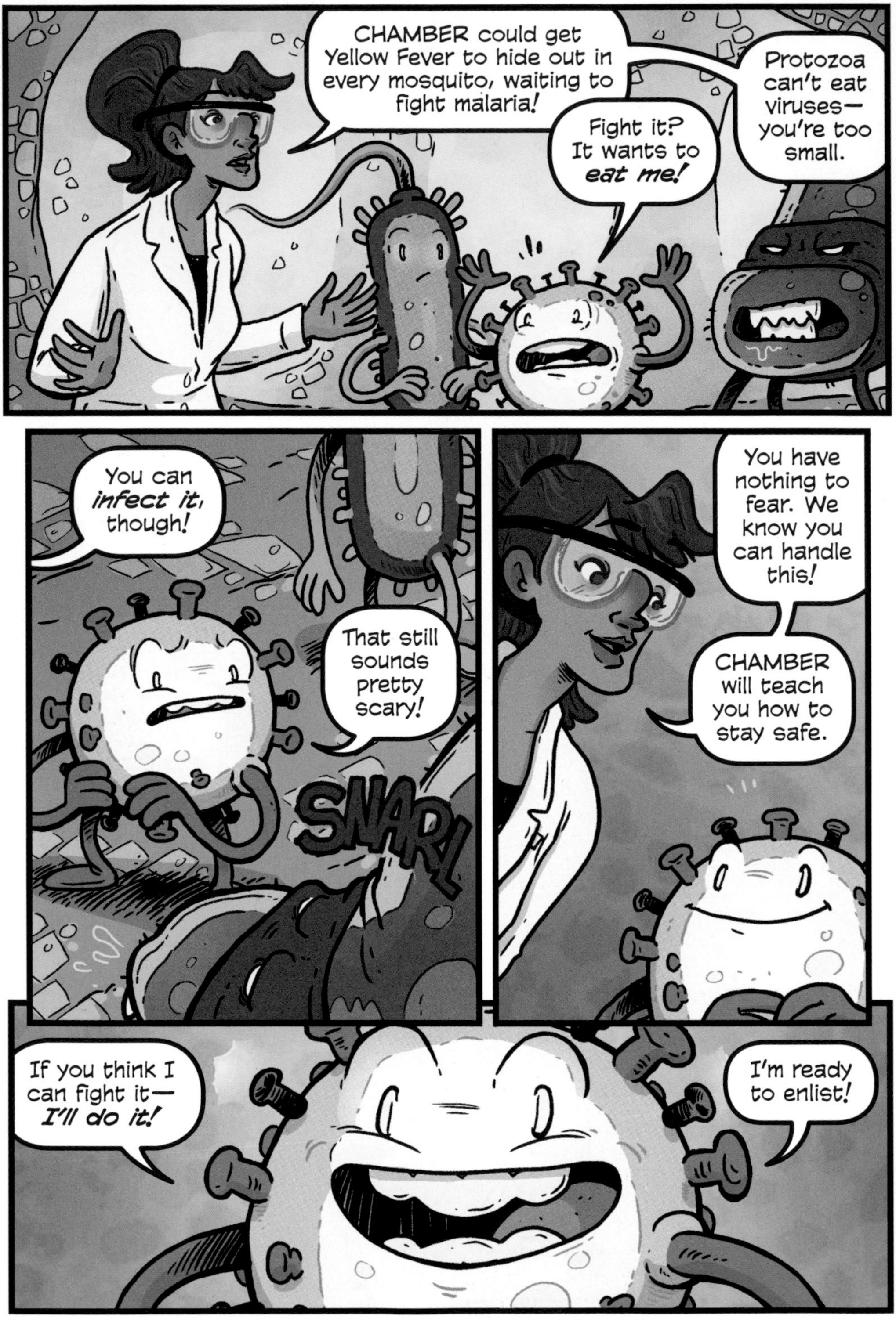
CHAMBER could get Yellow Fever to hide out in every mosquito, waiting to fight malaria!
Fight it? It wants to *eat me!*
Protozoa can't eat viruses—you're too small.
You can *infect it,* though!
That still sounds pretty scary!
SNARL
You have nothing to fear. We know you can handle this!
CHAMBER will teach you how to stay safe.
If you think I can fight it—*I'll do it!*
I'm ready to enlist!

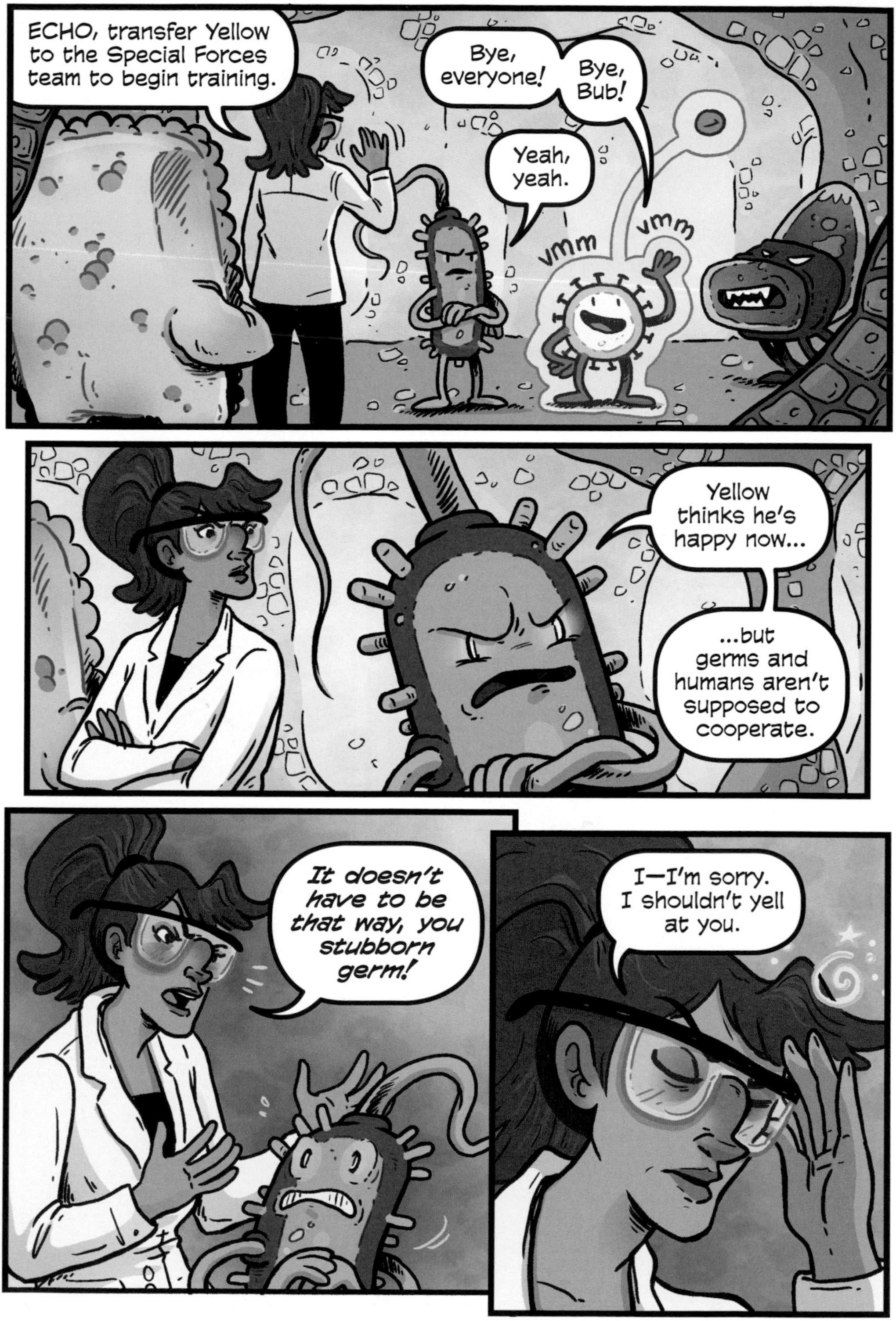
ECHO, transfer Yellow to the Special Forces team to begin training.
Bye, everyone!
Bye, Bub!
Yeah, yeah.
vmm
vmm
Yellow thinks he's happy now...
...but germs and humans aren't supposed to cooperate.
It doesn't have to be that way, you stubborn germ!
I—I'm sorry. I shouldn't yell at you.

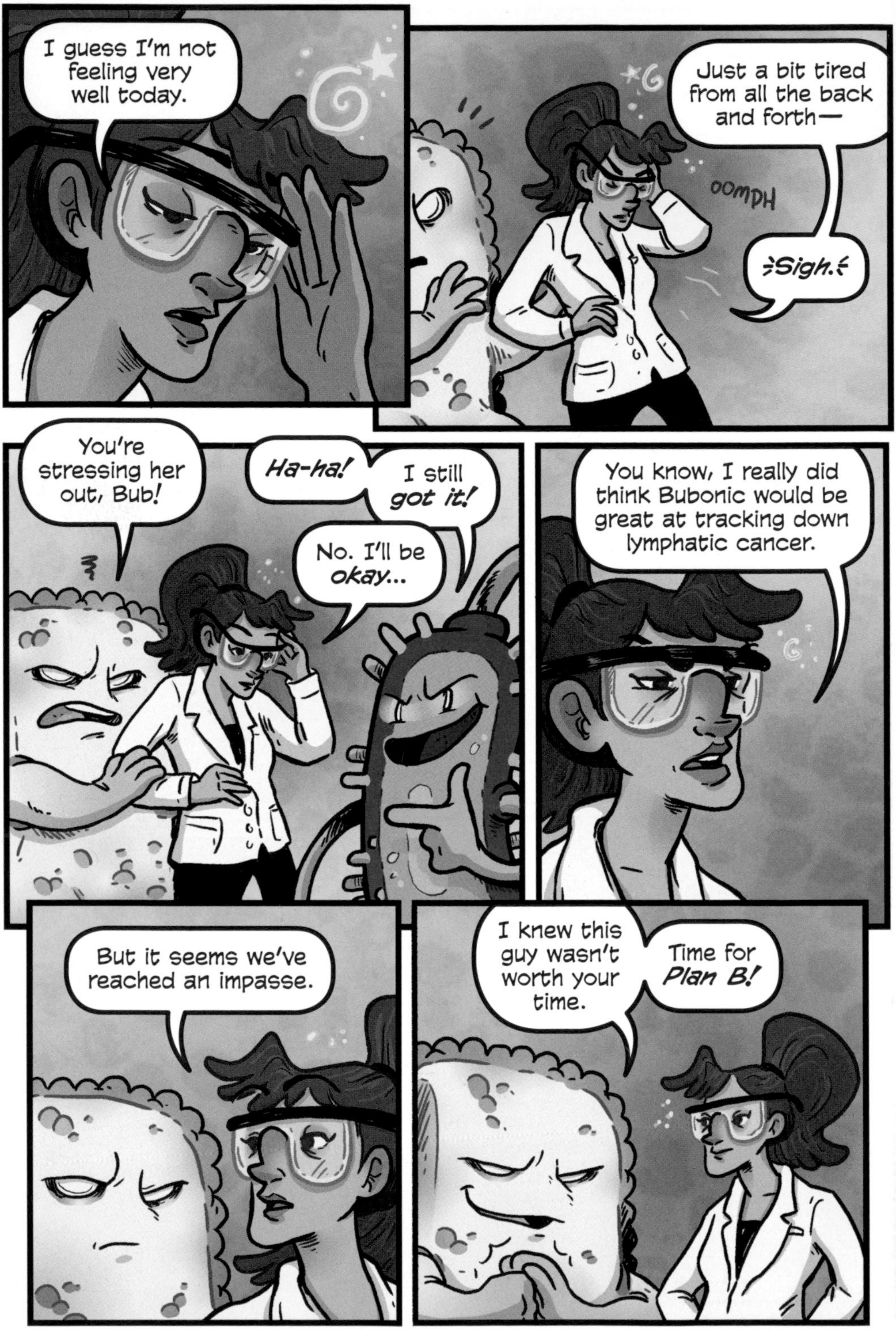
I guess I'm not feeling very well today.
Just a bit tired from all the back and forth—
OOMPH
Sigh.
You're stressing her out, Bub!
Ha-ha!
I still got it!
No. I'll be okay...
You know, I really did think Bubonic would be great at tracking down lymphatic cancer.
But it seems we've reached an impasse.
I knew this guy wasn't worth your time.
Time for Plan B!

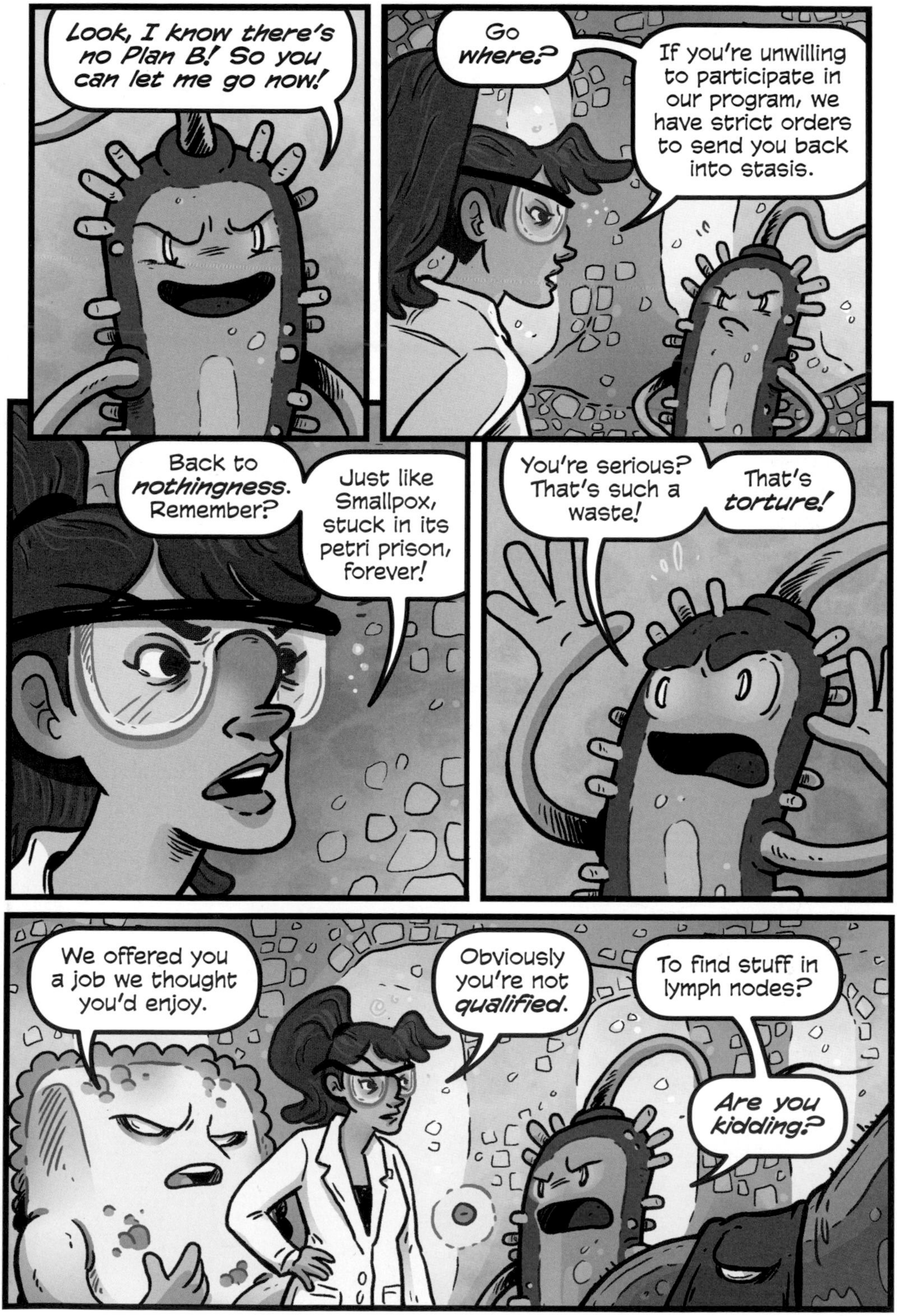
Look, I know there's no Plan B! So you can let me go now!
Go where?
If you're unwilling to participate in our program, we have strict orders to send you back into stasis.
Back to nothingness. Remember?
Just like Smallpox, stuck in its petri prison, forever!
You're serious? That's such a waste!
That's torture!
We offered you a job we thought you'd enjoy.
Obviously you're not qualified.
To find stuff in lymph nodes?
Are you kidding?

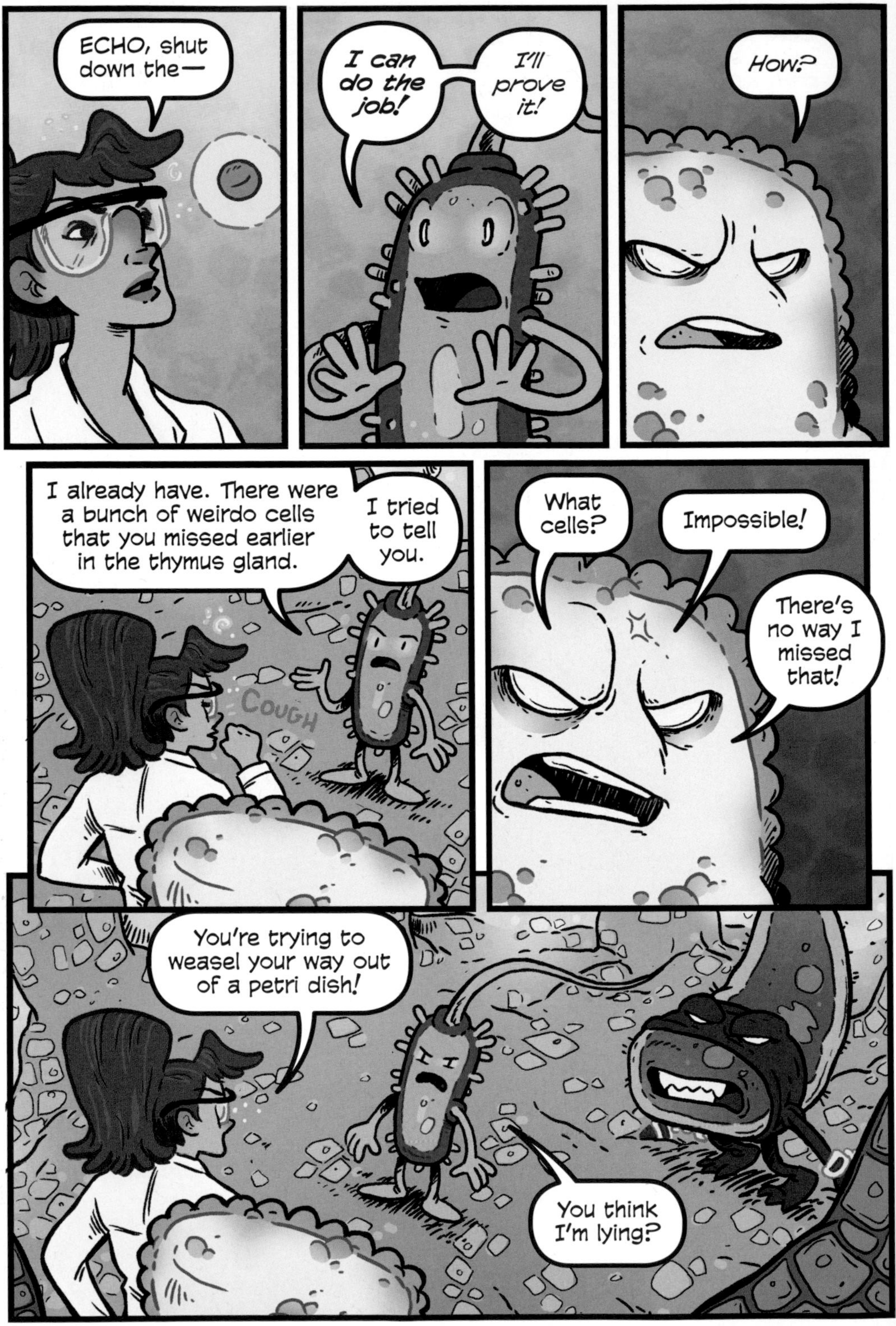
ECHO, shut down the—
I can do the job!
I'll prove it!
How?
I already have. There were a bunch of weirdo cells that you missed earlier in the thymus gland.
I tried to tell you.
COUGH
What cells?
Impossible!
There's no way I missed that!
You're trying to weasel your way out of a petri dish!
You think I'm lying?

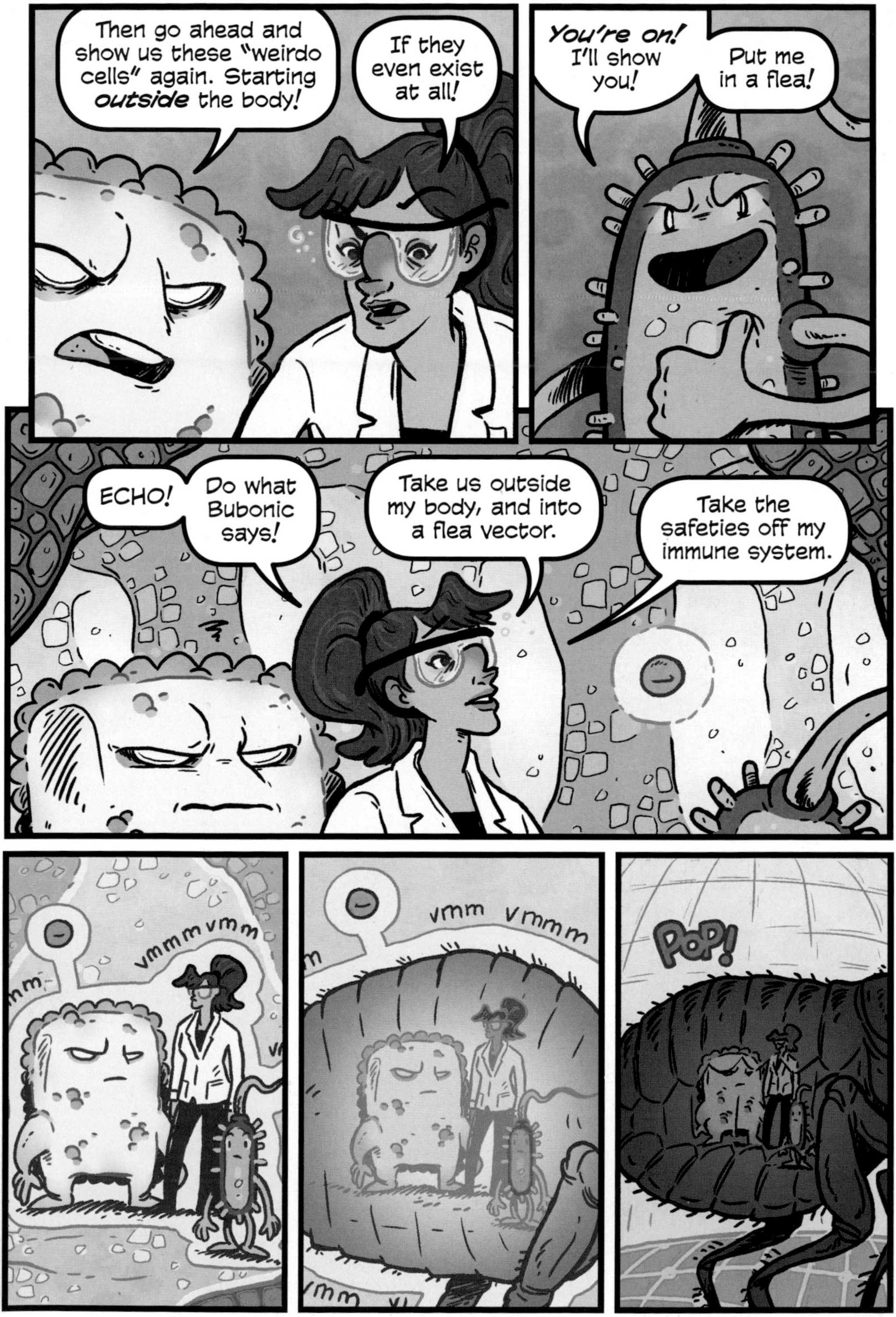
Then go ahead and show us these "weirdo cells" again. Starting *outside* the body!
If they even exist at all!
You're on! I'll show you!
Put me in a flea!
ECHO!
Do what Bubonic says!
Take us outside my body, and into a flea vector.
Take the safeties off my immune system.
vmmmvmm
vmm vmmm
POP!

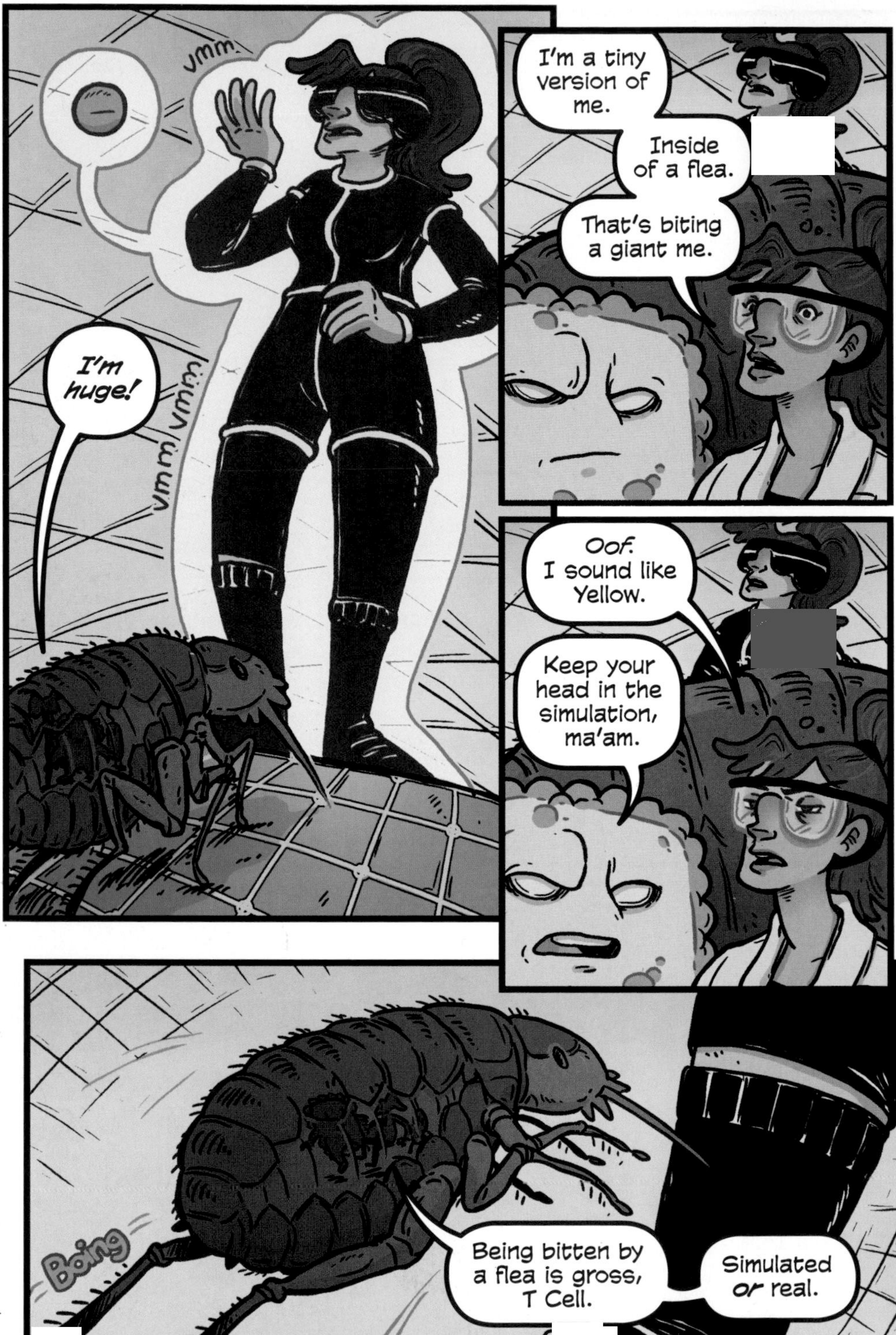
umm.
I'm huge!
umm umm
I'm a tiny version of me.
Inside of a flea.
That's biting a giant me.
Oof. I sound like Yellow.
Keep your head in the simulation, ma'am.
Boing
Being bitten by a flea is gross, T Cell.
Simulated *or* real.

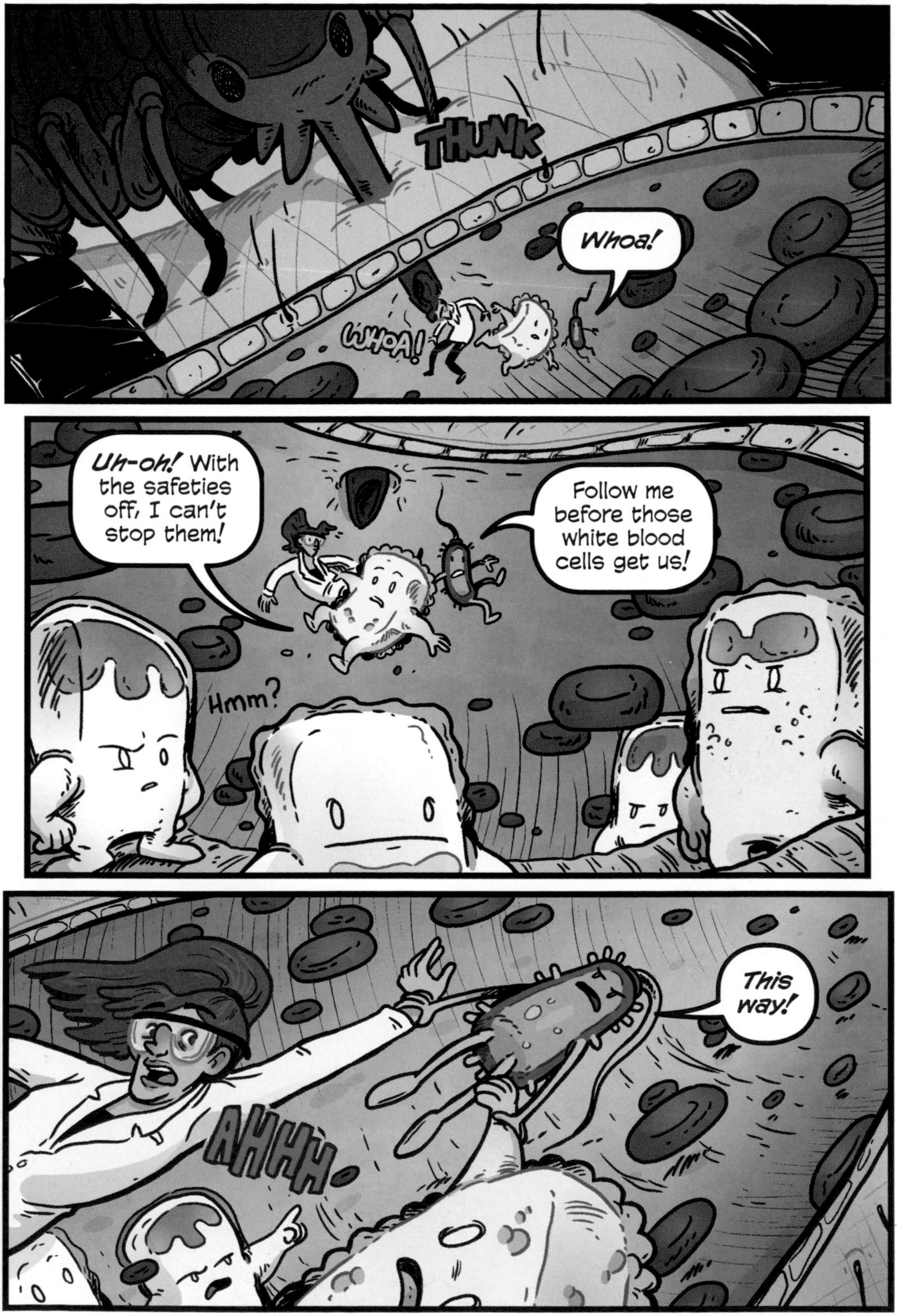
THUNK
WHOA!
Whoa!
Uh-oh! With the safeties off, I can't stop them!
Follow me before those white blood cells get us!
Hmm?
This way!
AHHH

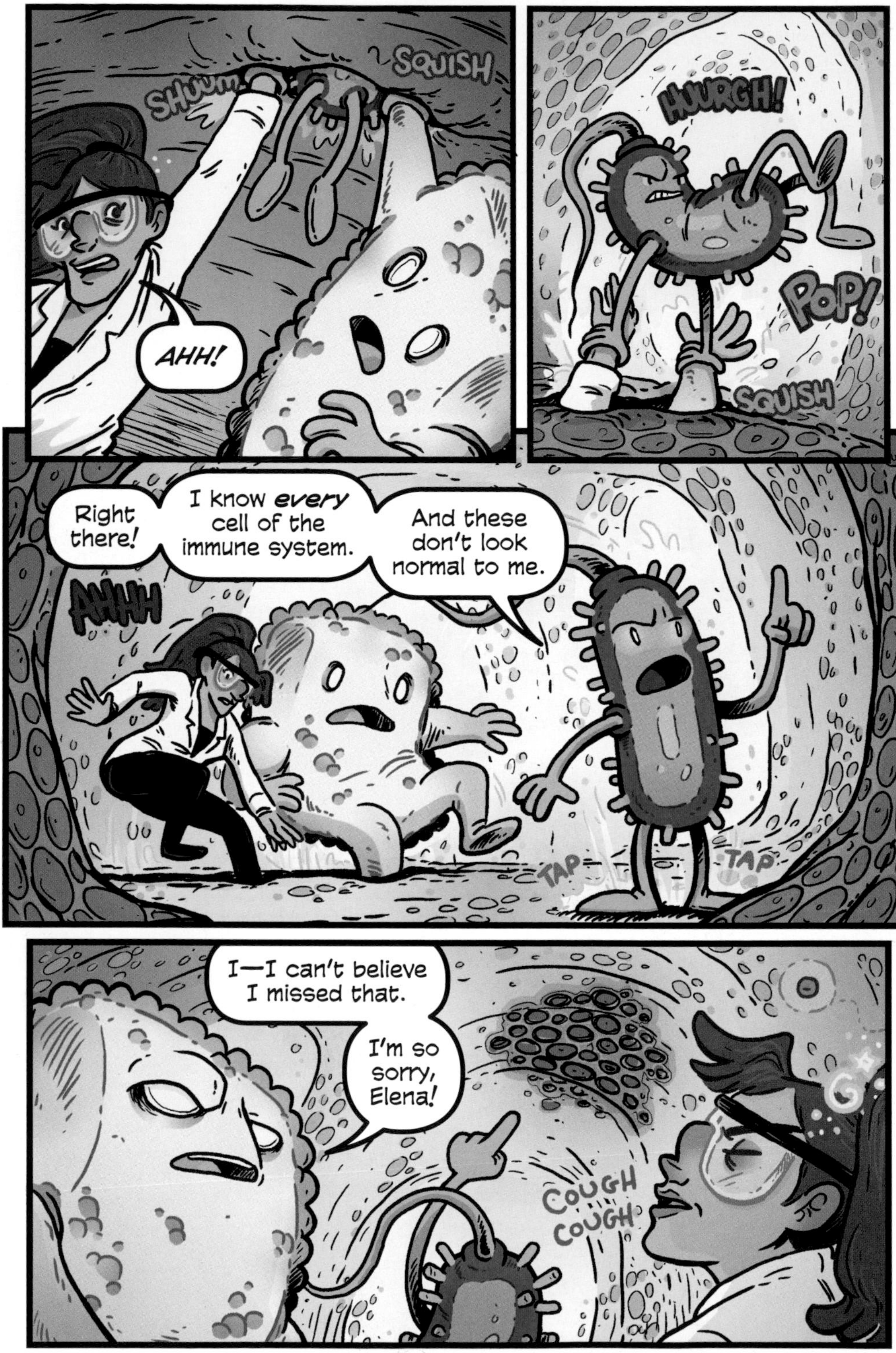
SHUUM
SQUISH
AHH!
HUURGH!
POP!
SQUISH
Right there!
I know *every* cell of the immune system.
And these don't look normal to me.
AHHH
TAP
TAP
I—I can't believe I missed that.
I'm so sorry, Elena!
COUGH
COUGH

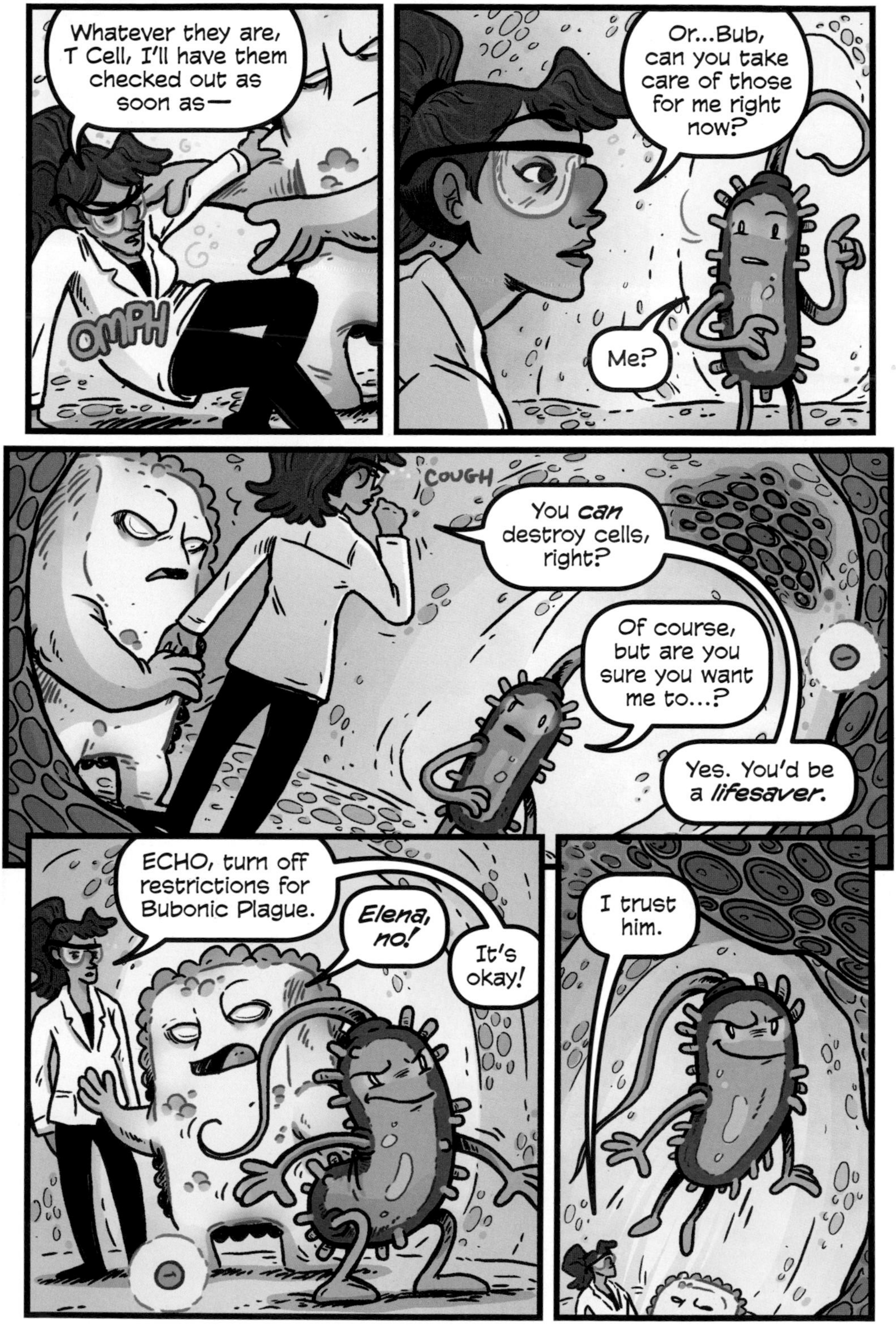
Whatever they are, T Cell, I'll have them checked out as soon as—
OMPH
Or...Bub, can you take care of those for me right now?
Me?
COUGH
You *can* destroy cells, right?
Of course, but are you sure you want me to...?
Yes. You'd be a *lifesaver.*
ECHO, turn off restrictions for Bubonic Plague.
Elena, no!
It's okay!
I trust him.

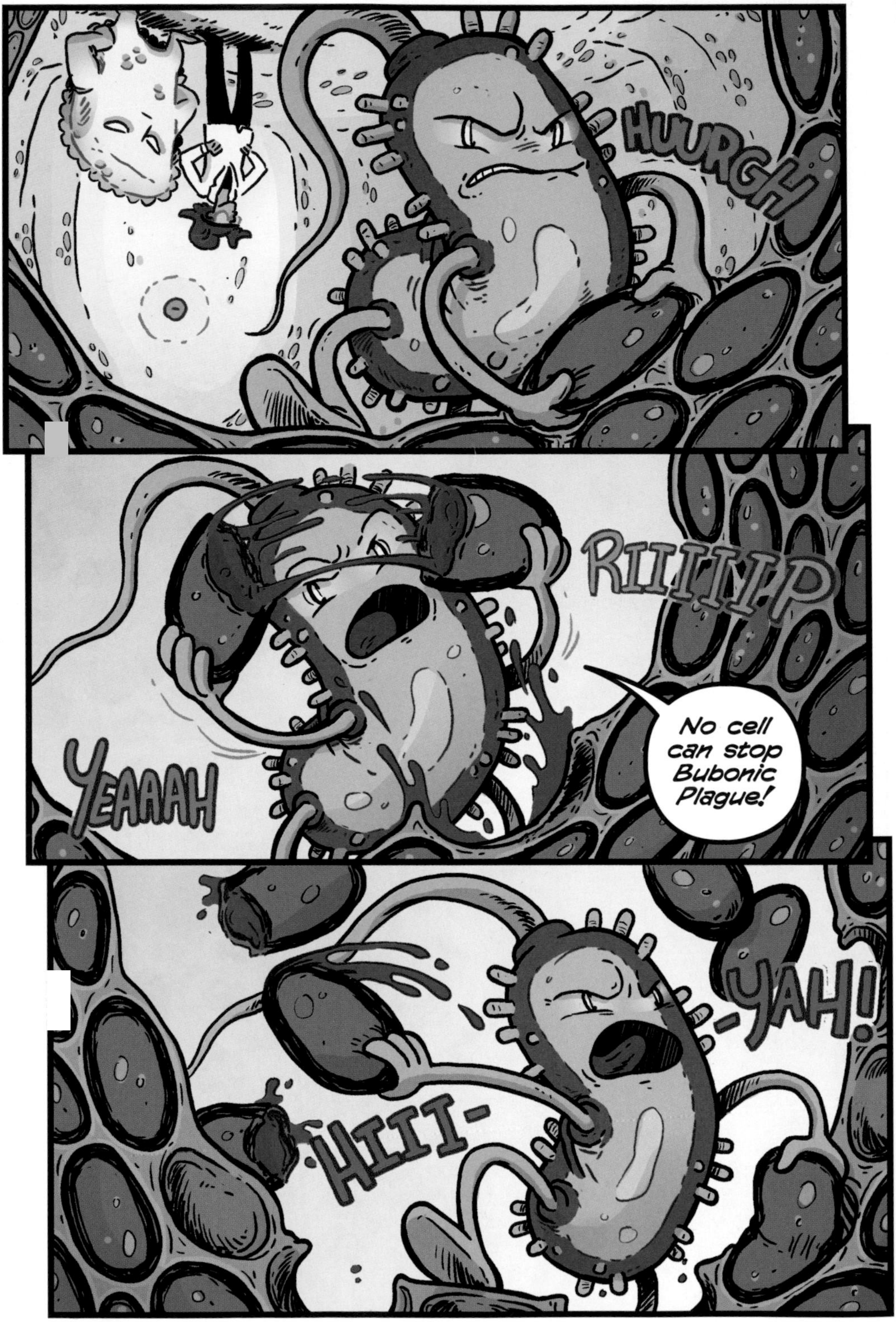
HUURGH
RIIIIIP
YEAAAH
No cell can stop Bubonic Plague!
HIII-
-YAH!

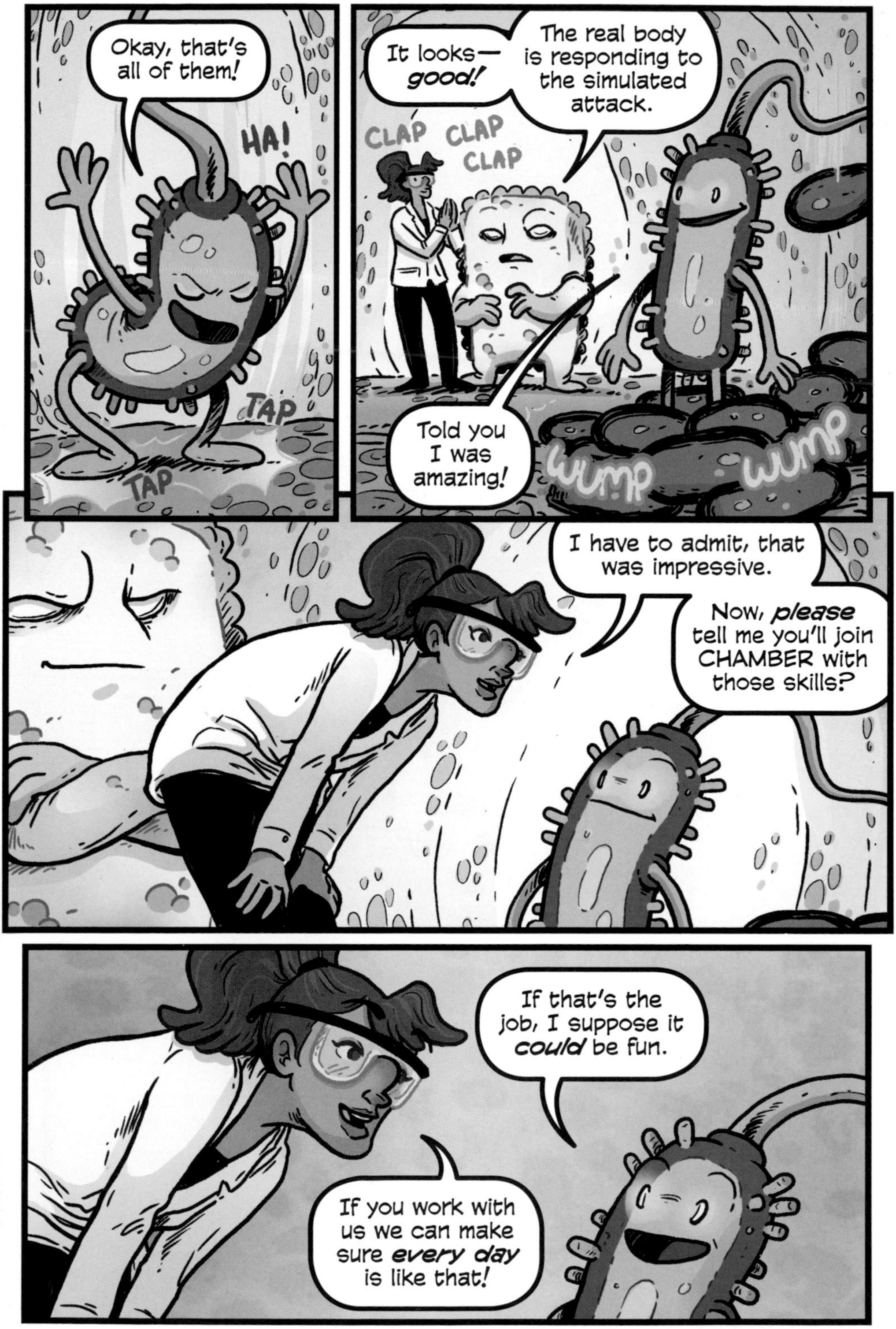
Okay, that's all of them!
HA!
TAP
TAP
It looks—good!
The real body is responding to the simulated attack.
CLAP CLAP CLAP
Told you I was amazing!
WUMP WUMP
I have to admit, that was impressive.
Now, please tell me you'll join CHAMBER with those skills?
If that's the job, I suppose it could be fun.
If you work with us we can make sure every day is like that!

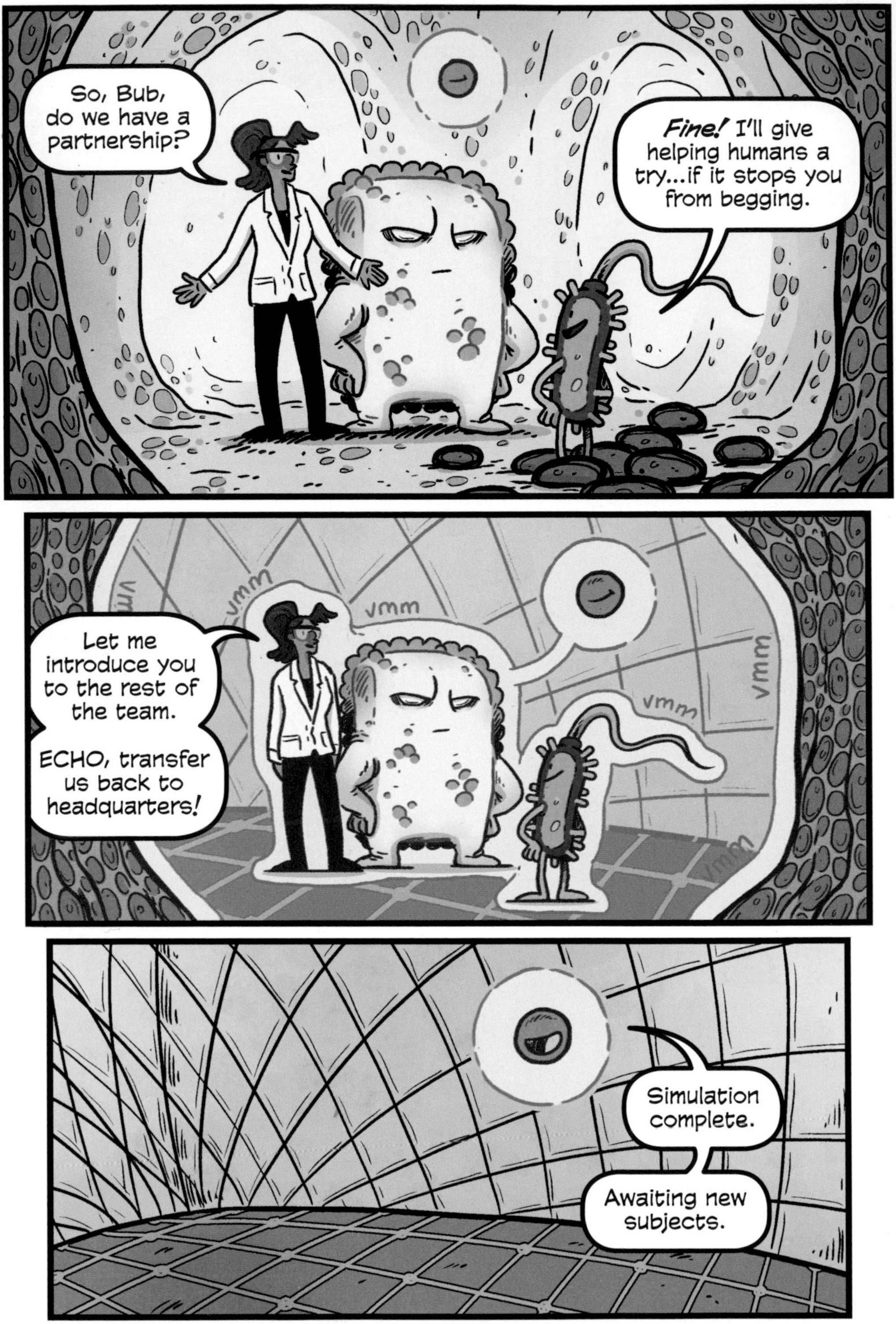
So, Bub, do we have a partnership?
Fine! I'll give helping humans a try...if it stops you from begging.
vmm
vmm
vmm
Let me introduce you to the rest of the team.
ECHO, transfer us back to headquarters!
vmm
vmm
vmm
Simulation complete.
Awaiting new subjects.

GLOSSARY

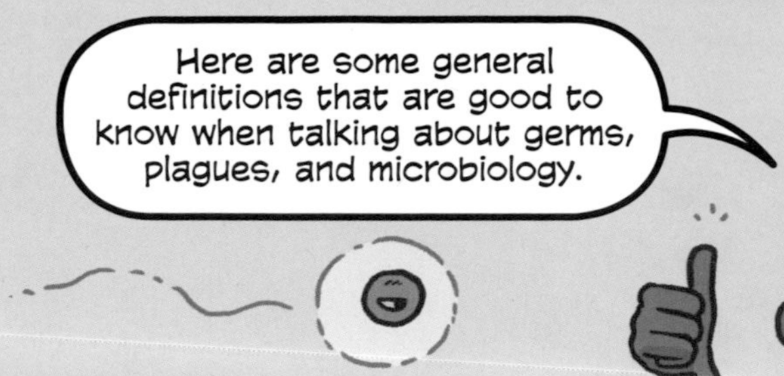
Here are some general definitions that are good to know when talking about germs, plagues, and microbiology.

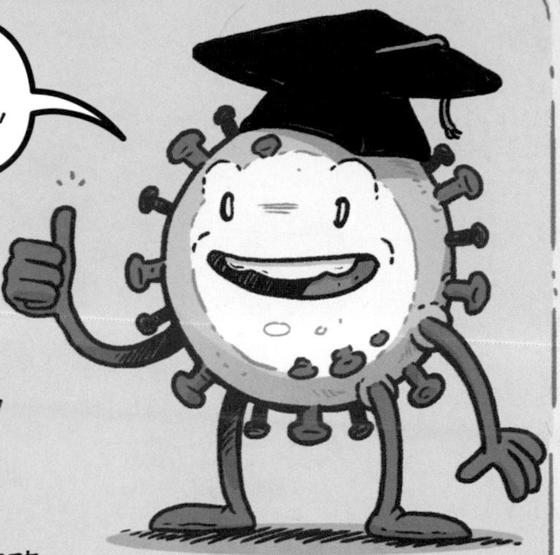

Antibody
Protein produced to counteract a specific antigen. Combines chemically with viruses or substances that the body recognizes as harmful.

Antigen
A toxin or other foreign substance that induces an immune response in the body and the production of antibodies.

Endemic
A disease or condition regularly found among people in a certain area.

Epidemic
A widespread disease in a community during a particular time.

Germ
A microorganism that causes disease.

Immunity
Natural or acquired resistance to a disease using the ability of a white blood cell to react in the presence of an antigen.

Inoculation
Introducing a serum, vaccine, or antigenic substance into the body, to stimulate the production of antibodies or to boost immunity to a specific bacteria, virus, or disease.

Microbe
A microorganism, normally single-celled.

Microorganism
An organism only seen with a microscope and typically only a single cell. Includes bacteria, virus, protozoa, and certain fungi and parasitic worms.

Pandemic
A disease that is spreading in more than one continent at the same time.

Pathogen
An organism causing disease, often a microorganism but also any parasite.

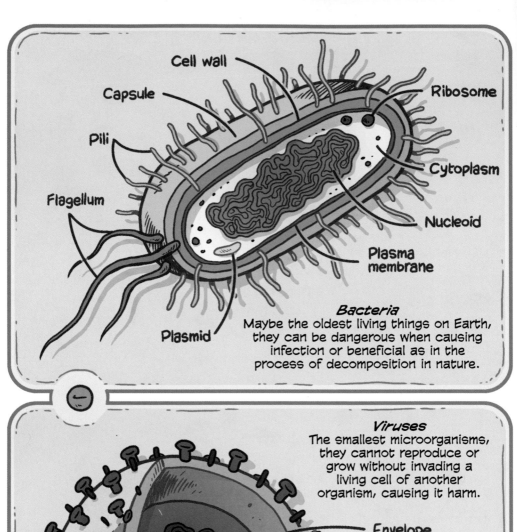

Cell wall

Capsule

Pili

Flagellum

Plasmid

Ribosome

Cytoplasm

Nucleoid

Plasma
membrane

Bacteria
Maybe the oldest living things on Earth,
they can be dangerous when causing
infection or beneficial as in the
process of decomposition in nature.

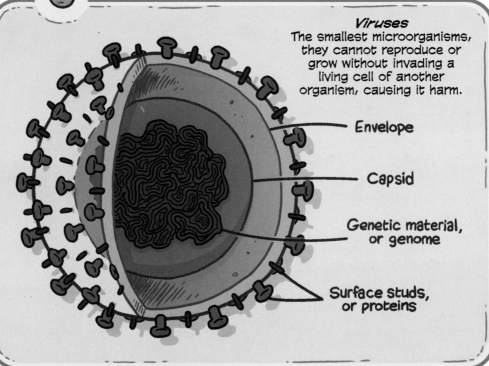

Viruses
The smallest microorganisms,
they cannot reproduce or
grow without invading a
living cell of another
organism, causing it harm.

Envelope

Capsid

Genetic material,
or genome

Surface studs,
or proteins

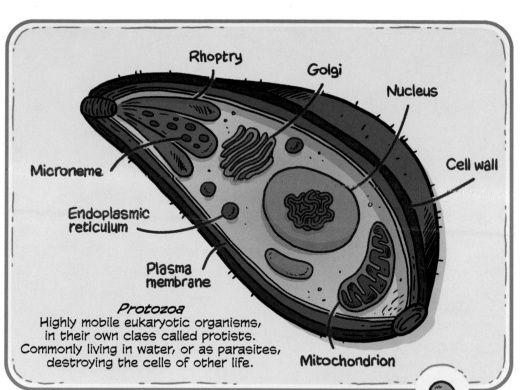

Rhoptry

Golgi

Nucleus

Microneme

Cell wall

Endoplasmic
reticulum

Plasma
membrane

Protozoa
Highly mobile eukaryotic organisms,
in their own class called protists.
Commonly living in water, or as parasites,
destroying the cells of other life.

Mitochondrion

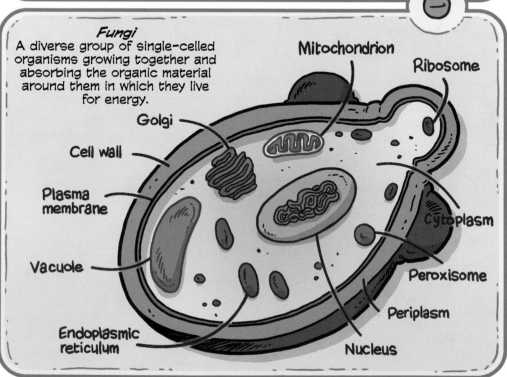

Fungi
A diverse group of single-celled
organisms growing together and
absorbing the organic material
around them in which they live
for energy.

Mitochondrion

Ribosome

Golgi

Cell wall

Plasma
membrane

Cytoplasm

Vacuole

Peroxisome

Periplasm

Endoplasmic
reticulum

Nucleus

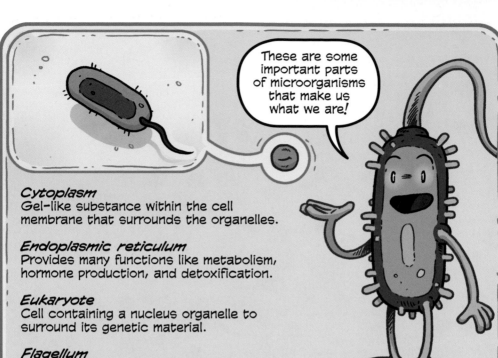

These are some important parts of microorganisms that make us what we are!

Cytoplasm
Gel-like substance within the cell membrane that surrounds the organelles.

Endoplasmic reticulum
Provides many functions like metabolism, hormone production, and detoxification.

Eukaryote
Cell containing a nucleus organelle to surround its genetic material.

Flagellum
Whiplike appendage that protrudes from the body of certain cells. Primarily used for movement but also acts as a sensory organelle.

Golgi apparatus
An organelle collecting and dispatching proteins received from the endoplasmic reticulum.

Mitochondrion
The power of the cell, this organelle generates most of the cell's energy.

Nucleoid
An irregularly shaped region within a prokaryotic cell that contains genetic material. It is not surrounded by a membrane.

Nucleus
An organelle in eukaryotic cells that contains genetic material and controls metabolism, growth, and reproduction.

Organelle
Any structure within a eukaryotic cell with its own purpose.

Pili
Hairlike appendage found on the surface of many bacteria that can help exchange genetic material or adhere to other cells.

Prokaryotic
Unicellular microorganism that lacks a nucleus containing genetic material.

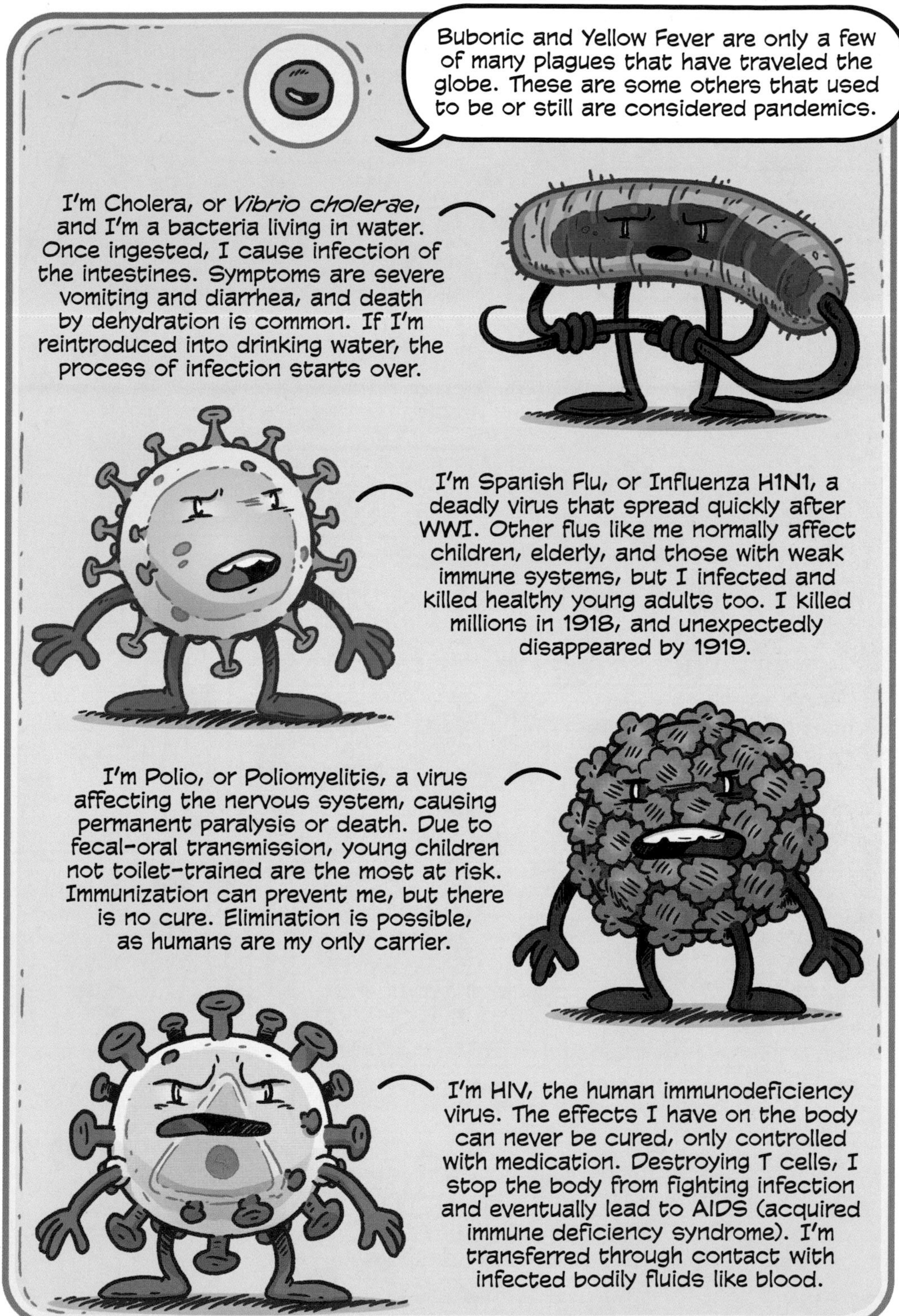
Bubonic and Yellow Fever are only a few of many plagues that have traveled the globe. These are some others that used to be or still are considered pandemics.
I'm Cholera, or *Vibrio cholerae*, and I'm a bacteria living in water. Once ingested, I cause infection of the intestines. Symptoms are severe vomiting and diarrhea, and death by dehydration is common. If I'm reintroduced into drinking water, the process of infection starts over.
I'm Spanish Flu, or Influenza H1N1, a deadly virus that spread quickly after WWI. Other flus like me normally affect children, elderly, and those with weak immune systems, but I infected and killed healthy young adults too. I killed millions in 1918, and unexpectedly disappeared by 1919.
I'm Polio, or Poliomyelitis, a virus affecting the nervous system, causing permanent paralysis or death. Due to fecal-oral transmission, young children not toilet-trained are the most at risk. Immunization can prevent me, but there is no cure. Elimination is possible, as humans are my only carrier.
I'm HIV, the human immunodeficiency virus. The effects I have on the body can never be cured, only controlled with medication. Destroying T cells, I stop the body from fighting infection and eventually lead to AIDS (acquired immune deficiency syndrome). I'm transferred through contact with infected bodily fluids like blood.

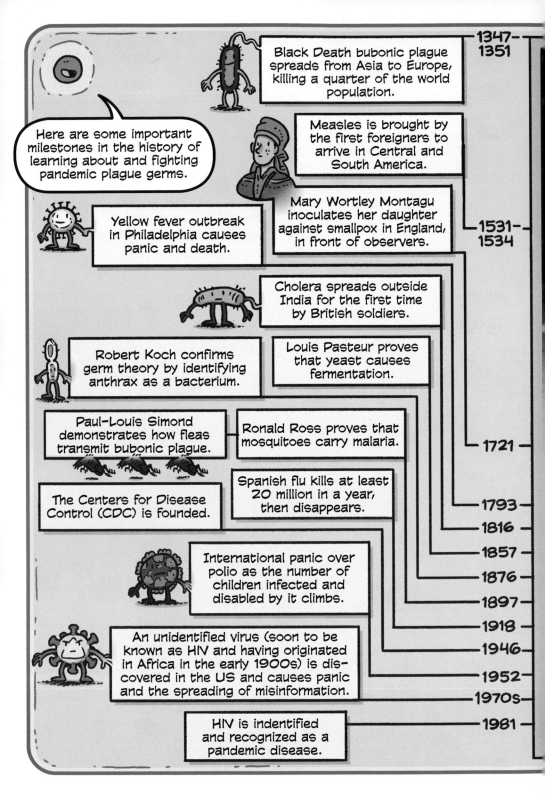

Here are some important milestones in the history of learning about and fighting pandemic plague germs.

Black Death bubonic plague spreads from Asia to Europe, killing a quarter of the world population.

Measles is brought by the first foreigners to arrive in Central and South America.

Mary Wortley Montagu inoculates her daughter against smallpox in England, in front of observers.

Yellow fever outbreak in Philadelphia causes panic and death.

Cholera spreads outside India for the first time by British soldiers.

Robert Koch confirms germ theory by identifying anthrax as a bacterium.

Louis Pasteur proves that yeast causes fermentation.

Paul-Louis Simond demonstrates how fleas transmit bubonic plague.

Ronald Ross proves that mosquitoes carry malaria.

The Centers for Disease Control (CDC) is founded.

Spanish flu kills at least 20 million in a year, then disappears.

International panic over polio as the number of children infected and disabled by it climbs.

An unidentified virus (soon to be known as HIV and having originated in Africa in the early 1900s) is discovered in the US and causes panic and the spreading of misinformation.

HIV is indentified and recognized as a pandemic disease.

1347–1351

1531–1534

1721

1793

1816

1857

1876

1897

1918

1946

1952

1970s

1981

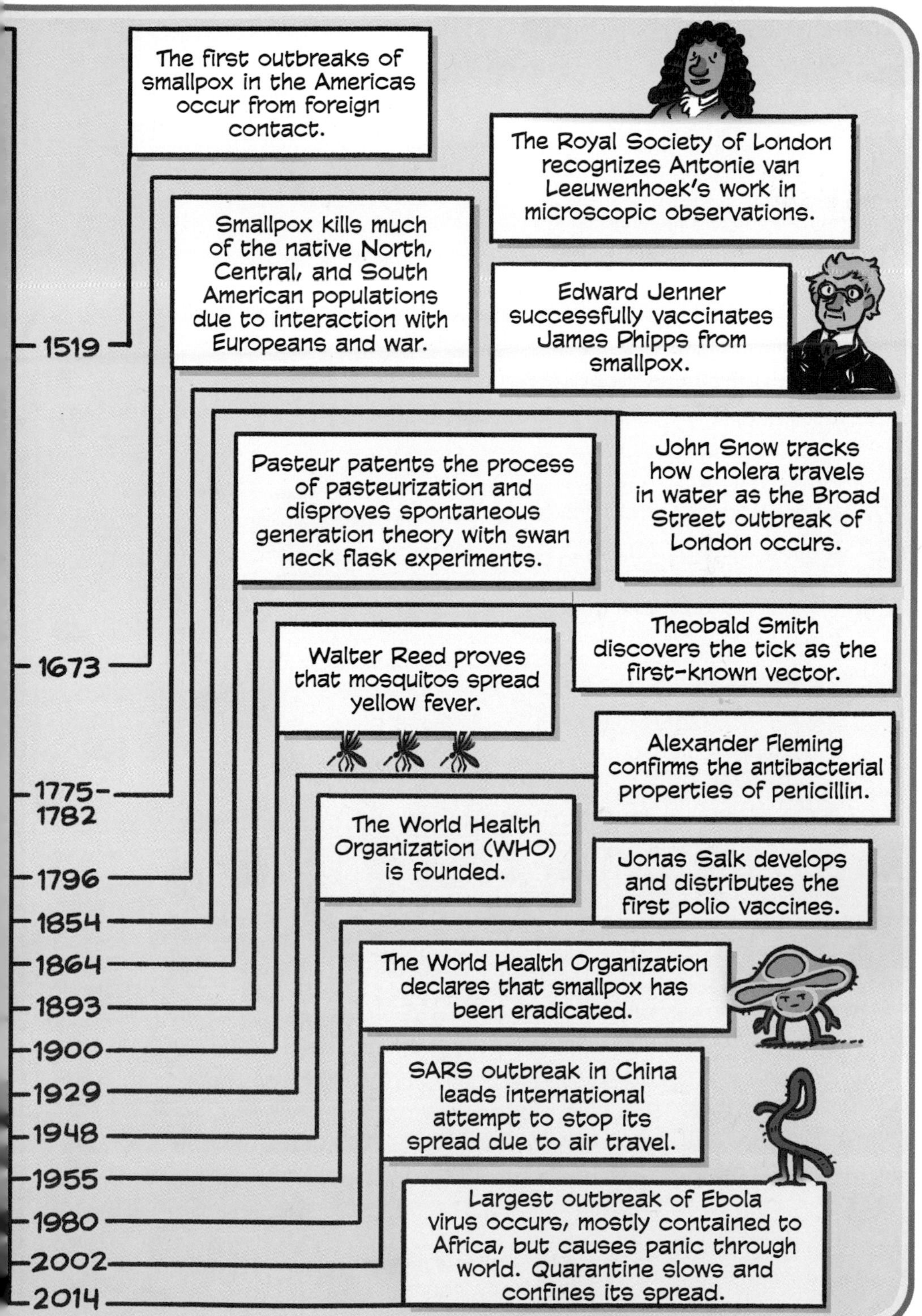
The first outbreaks of smallpox in the Americas occur from foreign contact.
The Royal Society of London recognizes Antonie van Leeuwenhoek's work in microscopic observations.
Smallpox kills much of the native North, Central, and South American populations due to interaction with Europeans and war.
Edward Jenner successfully vaccinates James Phipps from smallpox.
John Snow tracks how cholera travels in water as the Broad Street outbreak of London occurs.
Pasteur patents the process of pasteurization and disproves spontaneous generation theory with swan neck flask experiments.
Theobald Smith discovers the tick as the first-known vector.
Walter Reed proves that mosquitos spread yellow fever.
Alexander Fleming confirms the antibacterial properties of penicillin.
The World Health Organization (WHO) is founded.
Jonas Salk develops and distributes the first polio vaccines.
The World Health Organization declares that smallpox has been eradicated.
SARS outbreak in China leads international attempt to stop its spread due to air travel.
Largest outbreak of Ebola virus occurs, mostly contained to Africa, but causes panic through world. Quarantine slows and confines its spread.
1519
1673
1775-1782
1796
1854
1864
1893
1900
1929
1948
1955
1980
2002
2014

—NOTES—

Page 37, panel 4

We've been trying to classify living thing into categories since at least the ancient Greeks. The six-kingdom system is the classification system proposed by Simpson and Roger. It is only one of several classification systems. Woese has a three-kingdom sytem, and Simpson and Roger updated their system in 2015 to a seven-kingdom system.

Page 42, panel 2

The second plague pandemic actually ended in the 19th century. It was at its most virulent 1347–51, but reoccured in the centuries thereafter, including the London plagues of 1360–63, the Great Plague of Seville (1647–52), the Great Plague of London (1665–66), the Great Plague of Vienna (1679), the Great Plague of Marseille (1720–22), the Great Plague of 1738, and the Russian plague of 1770–72. It remained a problem in North Africa and the Middle East into the early 1900s.

> These are some books that both young and adult readers can enjoy to continue learning about germs, plagues, and their influence on human history as well as individual lives.

—FURTHER READING—

Barnard, Bryn. *Outbreak: Plagues That Changed History*. Dragonfly Books, 2015.

Crawford, Dorothy H. *Deadly Companions: How Microbes Shaped Our History*. Oxford University Press, 2009.

Sachs, Jessica Snyder. *Good Germs, Bad Germs: Health and Survival in a Bacterial World*. Hill and Wang, 2008.

Marrin, Albert. *Dr. Jenner and the Speckled Monster: The Search for the Smallpox Vaccine*. Dutton Juvenile, 2002.

Henderson, D. A. *Smallpox: Death of a Disease*. Prometheus Books, 2009.